TEACHER'S MANUAL

INTELLECTUAL PROPERTY IN THE NEW TECHNOLOGICAL AGE

Third Edition

Teacher's Manual

Robert P. Merges
Professor of Law
University of California at Berkeley School of Law

Peter S. Menell
Professor of Law
University of California at Berkeley School of Law

Mark A. Lemley
Professor of Law
University of California at Berkeley School of Law

ASPEN
PUBLISHERS

1185 Avenue of the Americas, New York, NY 10036
www.aspenpublishers.com

ISBN 0-7355-3653-8

Copies of this manual are available on computer diskette. Teachers who have adopted the casebook may obtain a copy of the diskette, free of charge, by calling the Aspen Publishers sales assistant at 1 – 800 – 950 – 5259.

Permissions
Aspen Publishers
1185 Avenue of the Americas
New York, NY 10036

1 2 3 4 5

Table of Contents

I. Introduction

The purpose of this Manual is (1) to help orient you in the underlying themes that unite the mass of material that constitutes the substance of this book; (2) to suggest ways to link up disparate sections of the book in the context of a typical law school course; and (3) to provide outlines of topics and answers to the Problems that are sprinkled throughout the book.

A. Approach of the Book

As its title indicates, this book is designed to present the law of intellectual property in a way highly relevant to contemporary industries and concerns. The "New Technological Age" referred to in the title is the age of ubiquitous computers, pioneering biotechnology, electronic networks, and massive research and development (R&D) spending in many disparate fields. While it would be a mistake to separate any subject from its historical origins, the emphasis here is on presenting the law in a way that makes it easy for students to see how it applies in industries central to current economic growth.

In addition to this very practical payoff, we also believe that focusing on new technologies enhances study of the field at the conceptual level. New technologies reveal fundamental truths and tensions buried inside accepted practices and rules. Thus developments on the pioneering periphery lead to insights about the core of the field. In patent law, biotechnology poses difficult questions concerning the rules of patentable subject matter, nonobviousness and infringement -- questions that influence our thinking about patent law in general.. The same is true of copyright and trademark: pervasive electronic networks and massive, easily accessible databases -- both driven by powerful software engines -- have forced new thinking about issues such as the originality standard, proper copyrightable subject matter, and trademark "use in commerce."

1) Using the Problems

The Problems included in the casebook are analyzed in the next section of this Teacher's Manual. The Problems can be used in several ways. These Problems include each major issue within the general topic areas of the book. You can therefore use them as the focal point for class discussion. Many have found this to be an interesting alternative to the usual "march through the cases" approach. Of course, the Problems are constructed so that students must draw from the cases to discuss them intelligently and propose strategies and solutions based on them.

Some professors prefer to use the Problems as the focal points only occasionally, in areas where the cases are confusing or split or otherwise difficult to use as the foundation of teaching. The analysis and sample discussions in this Teacher's Manual will help orient you to this perhaps unfamiliar approach.

For others, the Problems will not form the basis of frequent class discussion. They may be referred to occasionally; but their primary use under this approach is as a review and overview for students. The sample analyses and discussions in this Teacher's Manual may nevertheless be useful in answering student questions stemming from the Problems, or in gaining an overview yourself -- e.g., in preparation for writing the exam.

2) Background Reading on New Technologies

Many professors are interested in the new technologies featured in this book, yet would like some background sources for reference purposes. While reading such as this is ***absolutely not required*** for one to make profitable use of this casebook, we provide a few suggestions below.

In the computer area, a very good source is the straightforward book, **How Software Works**, written by Ron White in 1993. The publisher is Ziff-Davis, which can be reached at 11 Davis Drive, Belmont, California, 94002; phone (800) 601-2000; Fax (510) 601-2155; home page http://www.ziff.com.

For biotechnology, we recommend **Understanding DNA and Gene Cloning: A Guide for the Curious (3d ed. 1997)**, written by Karl Drlica and published by John Wiley & Sons, Inc. Wiley can be reached at 605 Third Ave, New York, NY 10158; phone (800) JWILEY NET; Fax (212) 850-6118; e-mail science@wiley.com; home page http://wiley.com.

3) Powerpoint Slides and Handouts to Accompany the Course

The material in this course lends itself particularly well to the use of Powerpoint slides. Professor Menell has prepared a comprehensive, graphically illustrated set of slides and handouts to present the cases, concepts, doctrines, and problems in this book. If you are interested in these using these materials, please contact Professor Menell at Menellp@law.berkeley.edu.

B. Sample Syllabi

Our theory in putting together this book was to be inclusive, rather than overly selective. We applied this approach both across areas -- witness the extensive treatment of trade secrets and patents in their own chapters -- but also *within* each area. The trademark chapter, for example, goes into a fair amount of detail for an "introductory" book.

Of course, the downside of this inclusive approach is that, in designing your introductory course, you will have to pick and choose from the book's generous offerings. Unless you choose to teach a yearlong course, you will not be able to cover all the material. While your course will naturally be shaped primarily by your individual approach and interests, in addition perhaps to a desire to focus on whichever areas are "red hot" that semester, some suggestions might make sense. In talking to Intellectual Property professors around the country as we were writing this book, it became clear that there are many ways to teach this course. Without too much violence to individual approaches, however, the courses taught around the U.S. seem to break down roughly into three models or approaches. These are described below; sample syllabi tailored to each approach are included.

A Word in Defense of the Traditional Overview Course

Many who teach an introductory course on intellectual property struggle to give it in-depth coverage of at least some issues. Several of the course models described below take this approach, which have the appeal of making the introductory course highly substantive. But it should be noted that the traditional overview course has some advantages as well. For one thing, it allows the specialized, upper-division courses to begin from a common footing, and to progress more quickly into advanced topics. Likewise, the "division of labor" between the introductory and upper-level courses -- a common concern -- can be managed by (1) requiring the introductory course as a prerequisite, and (2) minimizing the amount of duplicated material in the two courses by integrating the syllabi into a single coherent curriculum. Although this may involve persuading colleagues to adopt a different view of their course's goals, it is most rewarding from the point of view of the student and ought to be encouraged.

The relation of the introductory intellectual property course to the advanced courses is roughly akin to that between Corporations and its follow-on upper level courses, Corporate Finance, Securities Regulation, Partnerships, Corporate Tax, etc. The depth and complexity of the follow-on courses provide the rationale for the continuation of the general Corporations course. The same is true of intellectual property.

Model 1: The General Overview

Probably the most pervasive approach to the subject is the general overview. This emphasizes the three major federal IP systems (patent, copyright, trademark), but includes smatterings of trade secrets, various state forms of protection, and antitrust-related issues such as patent and copyright misuse. This is the broadest-brush type of course; it tries to give students an overview of the vast expanse of the IP field, while preparing them in a general way for more specialized courses in IP subject, such as the Copyright course or a course in Patent Law.

The sequence of the chapters in our book is laid out specifically with this course approach in mind. Thus we begin with theory (Chapter 1) and trade secrets (Chapter 2), then progress through the major federal rights systems (Chapters 3-5). State protection and antitrust-related issues are next (Chapters 6 and 8).

Many find it desirable to achieve a fair degree of depth in all the major areas of intellectual property. This approach would emphasize fairly detailed coverage of chapters 1-5. Since Chapter 6 contains additional material on state law forms of protection (such as idea submission cases and the right of publicity), it should be considered part of a course of this nature as well. The state preemption material, also in Chapter 6, would also make sense at the end of such a course.

Chapter 7, on computer-related issues, represents a novel ingredient in the standard sequence. It might make sense to draw from this material, even in a course not specifically focused on new technologies, for two reasons. First, given the importance of computer hardware and software in the IPR-intensive industries, it is reasonable to add some material from this chapter as an additional topic after the major federal rights have been encountered. Second, Chapter 7 is designed in such a way that those who wish to teach computer-related issues as special topics within the major federal rights can simply draw on the relevant portions of Chapter 7 as interludes in the march through Chapters 3, 4 and 5. Suggestions to this effect are reflected in the Syllabus, below. Note that for those who wish to delve deeper into these issues, a companion casebook, ***Software and Internet Law*** (Lemley, Menell, Merges & Samuelson) is available from Aspen.

Syllabus: Comprehensive Survey (4 credit hours)

Week	Material	Pages
1	Chapter 1: Introduction Chapter 2: Trade Secret: Introduction, Subject Matter, Misappropriation	1-26 27-59
2	Chapter 2: Trade Secret: Misappropriation continued, Agreements to Keep Secrets, Remedies Chapter 3: Patent: Introduction, Subject Matter	59-104 105-35
3	Chapter 3: Patent: Utility, Novelty, Nonobviousness, Written Description	136-215
4	Chapter 3: Patent: Infringement, Defenses	215-291
5	Chapter 3: Patent: International, Remedies, Design and Plant Patents Chapter 4: Copyright: Introduction, Requirements, Subject Matter	291-318 319-378
6	Chapter 4: Copyright: Ownership and Duration, Rights (Infringement)	378-450
7	Chapter 4: Copyright: Defenses, Digital Copyright Law, International, Remedies	450-528
8	Chapter 5: Trademark: Introduction, Types, Establishment of Rights,	529-614
9	Chapter 5: Trademark: Infringement	614-75
10	Chapter 5: Trademark: Defenses, International, Remedies	675-738
11	Chapter 6: State Intellectual Property: Misappropriation, Contract, Idea Submissions, Right of Publicity, State Moral Rights	739-820
12	Chapter 6: State Intellectual Property: Trespass to Chattels, Preemption Chapter 7: Economics of Computer Markets, Trade Secret, Copyright	820-854 855-890
13	Chapter 7: Copyright continued, Patent, Trademark, Sui Generis	890-988
14	Chapter 8: Antitrust	989-1084

Syllabus: Comprehensive Survey with Integrated Treatment of Computer Software (4 credit hours)

Week	Material	Pages
1	Chapter 1: Introduction Chapter 2: Trade Secret: Introduction, Subject Matter, Misappropriation	1-26 27-59
2	Chapter 2: Trade Secret: Misappropriation continued, Agreements to Keep Secrets, Remedies Chapter 3: Patent: Introduction, Subject Matter	59-104 105-35
3	Chapters 3 and 7: Patent: Subject Matter (Software and Business Methods), Utility, Novelty, Nonobviousness	932-49, 136-96
4	Chapters 3 and 7: Novelty and Nonobviousness (Computer Software and Business Methods), Written Description	949-61, 196-214, 962-64
5	Chapters 3 and 7: Patent: Infringement, Defenses	215-69, 964-73, 269-91
6	Chapter 3: Patent: International, Remedies, Design and Plant Patents Chapter 4: Copyright: Introduction, Requirements, Subject Matter	291-318 319-378
7	Chapter 4: Copyright: Ownership and Duration, Rights (Infringement)	378-450
8	Chapter 7: Copyright Protection for Computer Software	855-62, 869-932
9	Chapter 4: Copyright: Defenses, Digital Copyright Law, International, Remedies	450-528
10	Chapter 5: Trademark: Introduction, Types, Establishment of Rights,	529-614
11	Chapter 5: Trademark: Infringement	614-75
12	Chapter 5: Trademark: Defenses, International, Remedies	675-738
13	Chapter 6: State Intellectual Property: Misappropriation, Contract, Idea Submissions, Right of Publicity, State Moral Rights, Trespass to Chattels, Preemption	739-854
14	Chapter 8: Antitrust	989-1084

Syllabus: General IP Survey (3 credit hours)

Week	Material	Pages
1	Chapter 1: Introduction Chapter 2: Trade Secret: Introduction, Subject Matter	1-26 27-54
2	Chapter 2: Trade Secret: Misappropriation, Agreements to Keep Secrets, Remedies	54-104
3	Chapters 3 and 7: Patent: Introduction, Subject Matter, Utility	105-35, 932-49, 136-47
4	Chapter 3: Novelty and Nonobviousness	147-96
5	Chapter 3: Patent: Written Description, Infringement	196-251
6	Chapter 3: Patent: Defenses, Remedies Chapter 4: Copyright: Introduction, Requirements	274-91, 297-307 319-344
7	Chapter 4: Copyright: Subject Matter, Ownership and Duration	344-402
8	Chapter 4: Rights (Infringement) Copyright Protection for Computer Software	402-50, 872-88
9	Chapter 4: Copyright: Defenses, Digital Copyright Law	450-517
10	Chapter 4: Copyright: Remedies Chapter 5: Trademark: Introduction, Types	521-28 529-46
11	Chapter 5: Trademark: Establishment of Rights	546-614
12	Chapter 5: Trademark: Infringement	614-75
13	Chapter 5: Trademark: Defenses, Remedies Chapter 6: State Intellectual Property: Misappropriation	675-721, 726-38 739-52
14	Chapter 6: State Intellectual Property: Contract, Idea Submissions, Right of Publicity, Preemption	752-95, 831-52

Model 2: The Copyright and Trademark Emphasis

Many IP professors emphasize copyright and trademark as the central federal rights systems in the introductory course, preferring to leave patent law primarily for a specialized course. This frees up time to discuss trade secrets in some depth; state law issues; and antitrust-related topics. A syllabus for this type of introductory course is set forth below.

The casebook can be used in a course with this emphasis quite easily. The heart of such a course would be Chapters 1-2, and 4-6. Note that the state law and preemption material in Chapter 6 would appear to be a natural fit under this approach. In addition, the non-patent parts of Chapter 7 could be used as a supplement. Drawing on Chapter 7 in this manner would bring in some new technology issues, while still leaving patent issues for a separate course.

One note: while in the past, patent law was a relatively specialized field, distinct both conceptually and professionally from other areas of IP law, that has changed a good deal in recent years. General practice firms that once shunned patent law now litigate high-stakes patent cases routinely. General business lawyers, those whose practice concentrates on traditional transactional issues, now increasingly must have some familiarity with patent law principles. And finally, it is clear that at the conceptual level patent law has many points of close contact with the other areas of intellectual property. For all these reasons, one might consider adding at least a bit of patent law to a traditional copyright and trademark-centered course. See "An Alternative Model: The New Technology Emphasis" below.

Model 3: The One-Topic Emphasis: "Copyright Plus" or "Trademark Plus" Courses

At a few schools, an increase in the number of intellectual property courses has brought with it a rethinking of the place of the introductory course. Some professors have concluded that a general overview is no longer necessary, or that it fits poorly in a curriculum featuring specialized courses in each area of intellectual property. One response is to concentrate in the introductory course on one area of intellectual property, while still leaving time for a "whirlwind tour" through the other areas. The idea is that the introductory course serves both as the primary course in a particular subject matter area and also as a brief introduction to other areas.

Copyright and trademark are the most common subjects to be treated in depth in such a course. It begins by assigning the entire chapter on Copyright or Trademark, and then selects other topics in the book to comprise a whirlwind overview.

One variant on this approach emphasizes intellectual property as one element in the larger topic of business regulation. A course with this emphasis has traditionally been referred to as "business torts." The emphasis here would be on Chapters 2,5,6 and 8; an overview of patents might also be helpful, necessitating some assignments from the basic cases in Chapter 3. Chapter 8, on Antitrust, would serve as an especially important component in such a course.

Syllabus Suggestions

The syllabus for this course should be centered around the chapter that covers the main topic of the course. For a "Copyright-plus" course, this would include also the Copyright sections in Chapter 7, Protection of Computer Software. In addition, Chapter 6 should be covered in its entirety. It is an important source of additional material on state-based substitutes for trademark and copyright, and also covers preemption. The limited time remaining could be split evenly between a very quick introduction to patent law and a similarly brief overview of trade secrets. Chapter 1 can still be assigned at the outset for background.

An Alternative Model: The New Technology Emphasis

As is clear from the title of the book, we believe that the new technologies that have emerged since the 1960s are reshaping the basic fabric of intellectual property law. For those who share this view, and who want to explore in depth legal issues pertaining to these new technologies, this casebook should prove ideal. The approach we have used when teaching a course of this nature is to cover essentially all of Chapters 1, 2, 3, 7 and 8. In addition, to cover the patent issues relating to biotechnology in careful detail, you may find it useful to assign the biotechnology primer included in the statutory supplement.

The Problems included later in this Teacher's Manual can very successfully be employed in this type of course. Many of them emphasize real-world situations confronting innovators and startup companies. While they are designed to call forth discussion of all relevant intellectual property rules and their policy underpinnings, they may help students interested in new technologies understand how legal issues fit in the process of bringing those technologies to market.

Syllabus Suggestions

The following cases and notes are particularly well-suited to a course of this nature:

Chapter 3: Brenner v. Manson; Note and Problem Note on Analog Claims in Chemical and Biotechnology Patents; *Larami Corp v. Amron*; *Genentech v. Wellcome Fdn.*; *Warner-Jenkinson v. Hilton-Davis Chem. Co.*; Notes and Problem; Note on Analog Claims in Chemical and Biotechnology Patents; Note on Equivalents in Means-Plus-Function Claims; *Kingsdown Medical Consultants v. Hollister.*

Chapter 4: *Baker v. Selden* and related notes; *Brandir* and related notes; Digital Copyright Law

Chapter 5: Note on Extension of Trademark by Contract; Note on Expanding Frontiers of Trademark Law; Note on Priority and Trademark Theory (contains material on Internet domain names).

Chapter 6: Contract and Trespass to Chattels

Chapter 7: The entire chapter

Chapter 8: The entire chapter

C. Changes in the Third Edition

1. Introduction

   No case changes

2. Trade Secret Protection

   No case changes

3. Patent Law

   Graver Tank v. Linde Air Products omitted; *In re Dembiczak, Festo Corp. v. Shoketsu Kinzoku Kogyo Kabushiki Co.,* and *Johnson & Johnson Associates Inc. v. R.E. Service Co.* added.

4. Copyright Law

Midway Mfg. Co. v. Arctic International, Quality King Distributors, Inc. v. L'anza Research International, Inc.; *Aalmuhammad v. Lee, Anderson v. Stallone, Fonovisa v. Cherry Auction,* and *A&M Records, Inc. v. Napster, Inc.* added.

5. Trademarks and Trade Dress

Knitwaves, Inc. v. Lollytogs, Ltd,. Brookfield Communications v. West Coast Entertainment Corp., Stormy Clime Ltd. v. Progroup Inc., The New Kids on the Block v. News America Publishing, Inc., and *L. L. Bean, Inc. v. Drake Publishers, Inc., Wal-Mart Stores, Inc. v. Samara Brothers, Inc., Shields v. Zuccarini , People for the Ethical Treatment of Animals v. Doughney, TrafFix Devices, Inc. v. Marketing Displays, Inc.,* and *Mattel, Inc. v. MCA Records* added.

6. State Intellectual Property Law & Federal Preemption

ProCD Inc. v. Zeidenberg and *Specht v. Netscape Communications Corp.* added in new section on Protection by Contract; *Downey v. General Foods Corporation* replaced by *Nadel v. Play-by-Play Toys & Novelties, Inc.*; *Goldstein v. California* and *National Car Rental System, Inc. v. Computer Associates International, Inc.* replaced by *ProCD, Inc. v. Zeidenberg*; *Estate of Hemingway v. Random House, Inc.* and *Sears, Roebuck & Co. v. Stiffel Co.* omitted; *Comedy III Productions, Inc. v. Gary Saderup, Inc.* (Right of Publicity) and *eBay, Inc. v. Bidder's Edge, Inc.* (Theory of Trespass to Chattels) added.

7. Protection of Computer Software

Pennwalt Corp. v. Durand-Wayland, Inc. replaced by *British Telecommunications Plc. v. Prodigy Communications Corp.*; *Whelan Associates v. Jaslow Dental Laboratory, Apple Computer, Inc. v. Microsoft Corp., Micro Star v. Formgen Inc., In re Alappat, Pennwalt Corp. v. Durand-Wayland, Inc., Creative Labs, Inc. v. Cyrix Corp.,* and *Panavision International L.P. v. Toeppen* omitted. *Amazon.com, Inc. v. barnesandnoble.com, inc. and British Telecommunications v. Prodigy Communications Corp.* added.

8. Intellectual Property and Competition Policy

United States v. General Electric Company and United States v. Line Material Co. omitted; In re Cardizem CD Antitrust Litigation added

II. Selected Case Summaries and Notes

Chapter 1 Introduction

A. Philosophical Perspectives

The introductory material is designed to give students a grounding in several of the major theories that have been employed to explain the emergence and content of intellectual property rights.

It might seem anomalous that a book emphasizing new technology begins with ideas drawn from some decidedly old and untechnological thinkers -- Locke and Hegel. A word in defense of the approach is therefore in order.

In a time of rapid change, we believe that underlying theory is more important than it might be otherwise. New technologies and new industries churn out radically new legal questions, which cannot be answered (effectively anyway) with the standard tools of analysis -- the usual rules and doctrines that emerge to govern the ordinary disputes of a settled regime. The only tools left are fundamental principles, basic conceptions -- in short, theory. Thus the anomaly: it is precisely because new technology is pushing at the accepted categories and definitions underlying the field that we need to resort to foundational principles. The introductory readings provide the rudiments of those principles.

The main point to emphasize to skeptical students is that the abstract issues raised by these readings have some very real and immediate applications in the chapters that lie ahead. For example:

- Expanding boundaries of **patentable subject matter** can be fruitfully discussed and understood in terms of any of the primary theories discussed in chapter 1, Lockean, personhood, or utilitarian.
- Extensions of copyright term and other proposals to enhance copyright are often based on personhood theories emphasizing the importance of continuing authorial control of copyrighted works.
- Lockean labor theory has crept into trademark discussions in recent years, especially as regards extension of trade dress principles (*see e.g., Two Pesos*, in Chapter 5). Utilitarian arguments have contributed to the re-shaping of this area of law as well; see the trademark priority discussion in the *Zazu Hair Design v. L'Oreal* case and associated notes.

PROBLEM 1-1

You are a botanist exploring a remote region of a small tropical country. You stumble across a field of strange flowers that you have never encountered before. The tribespeople tell you that they use the flower to heal various ailments by rubbing its petals on the skin and chanting a healing prayer. You pluck one of the flowers and when you return to your campsite that night, you show it to a fellow explorer who is an expert in biochemistry. The biochemist smells the flower and says that it is vaguely reminiscent of substance P. Substance P is a medicine widely used to treat a variety of serious diseases. She tells you that substance P is easy to detect: It turns bright yellow when exposed to intense heat. That evening, you put the flower over the campfire and, sure enough, it turns bright yellow. When you return home, you work for months to isolate the active ingredient in the flower. It is not substance P, but a close structural analog. In chemical experiments, the extract shows great promise for fighting many of the diseases that Substance P can treat without Substance P's dreaded side effects.

1. What rights, if any, should you have in this discovery and research? Should those rights prevent anyone else from going back to the tropical country, finding the flower, and isolating the chemical you have discovered?

2. You make a profit selling your medicine throughout the world, including to the native tribespeople of the tropical country. John, a chemist in your company, is angered by this policy. Your formula is a carefully guarded secret, but John publishes it in the New England Journal of Medicine. A nonprofit organization begins producing the medicine and selling your product to the native tribespeople at a discount. The organization advertises that it is selling your medicine for pennies a year. Should you be able to stop them from selling your medicine? Should you be able to stop them from using the name of your medicine in their ads?

3. You have named your medicine "Tropicurial." To advertise the product, one of the employees in your advertising department writes a song based on the very distinctive sounds of the wind in the inland coves of the country mixed with the native birds' calls. The tribespeople of the tropical country have a song that sounds remarkably similar to your advertising tune. The song is important to their tribal identity, and they argue that it is inappropriate to use their tribal identity song to commercialize your product. They ask you to stop using it. Should they be able to stop you from using the name or song?

4. When you refuse to stop using the Tropicurial song to advertise your product, the tribespeople write a new version of their song entitled "Tropicursical" with angry lyrics claiming that your product destroys culture. Should you be able to stop them from singing the song? National Geographic records the tribespeople singing "Tropicursical." The recording plays as part of the news report on their television show. It is also available for download on National Geographic's website. Individuals download copies of the song and e-mail it to their friends. It spreads like wildfire over the Internet and eventually popular radio stations begin playing it over the air. Should you be able to stop these copies and performances?

Analysis

Problem 1-1: Robert Nozick has a very interesting treatment of a similar problem in his book **Anarchy, State and Utopia**.

This problem is designed to point up some of the problems with applying theories of real property in general, and Locke's theory in particular, to intellectual property. The basis of Locke's theory is that mixing your own labor with pre-existing tangible goods in their natural state gives you a property right over those goods. Applying this theory to intellectual property requires a further leap -- that intellectual labor confers a right not just over the goods you have worked, but a right to exclude others from using those ideas on other goods. Indeed, if it is to justify patent protection, the labor-desert theory must extend so far as to exclude bona fide independent inventors -- those who also put their own labor into working natural goods, while ignorant of the patent owner's similar efforts. It is not at all clear that Locke would go this far.

Another point worth noting is Locke's reliance on labor as the justification for property. It is hard to find a similar appreciation for the "sweat of the brow" in U.S. intellectual property law. First, a series of cases suggest that labor alone is not enough to confer protection, unless the product worked exhibits the necessary novelty or originality to qualify under particular intellectual property rights. [We discuss the *Feist* case in Chapter 4]. Second, the absence of effort does not preclude intellectual property protection: "accidental" inventions on the order of 3M's Post-It notes or (more fancifully) the Reese's Peanut Butter Cup are still entitled to intellectual property protection. [Indeed, section 103 of the patent act is quite explicit that the manner in which an invention was made cannot adversely affect its patentability].

A final issue raised by this problem is the "Lockean proviso." Locke's writings assume a world without scarcity, at least of land and its products, a view which looks rather naive from a modern perspective. Further, Locke's injunction against "engrossment" does not account for modern capital markets, where a single individual can "make use of" a virtually infinite supply of any product by marketing it. It is not clear how Locke would respond to a "public interest" argument in the drug context. If he would be unwilling to grant patent rights over a drug because of fear that others would be unable to get access to it at a "reasonable" price, that fact casts a certain amount of doubt on his support for intellectual property rights in general.

This problem can also be used as a vehicle to introduce different types of intellectual property protection. Consider the possible legal rules we might create to protect Substance P:

Since it is information, you have a public goods problem in trying to protect it. In particular, suppose that I want to get in on this racket. Rather than develop my own medicine, I would like to use yours. What can I do to get it?

Suppose I sneak into your house while you're on vacation, and steal your formula and research notes. Then I set up a competing business, and advertise that I have your medicine for 1/2 price. Is that OK? It strikes most people as unfair. What can we do to prevent such an incursion? First, society can prevent invasions of physical property allowing access to information. This is not really IP at all, because the focus is the physical intrusion. Alternatively, you might prevent me from advertising that I have "your" medicine. But should we, if I am truthfully advertising that I have Joe's numbers?

Trademark and Unfair Competition.

Suppose instead that I stand on the public street near your office and, with a set of binoculars, read the formula from your desk. Now I have not violated any property rights. Can we prevent this? A legal rule might be established creating an affirmative right to protect secrets against "unreasonable" efforts to discover them, even if those efforts would otherwise be legal.

Trade Secrets

If I can't do that, suppose instead I approach one of your customers and offer to pay her if she will tell me the formula for the medicine [Or that I buy the medicine from her, and subject it to a relatively simple reverse engineering process to determine its contents]. Not an extraordinary measure, but one that takes advantage of the public goods nature of information. Can we prevent this? You might attempt to avoid this via **Contract** -- for example, an agreement saying "I will give you this information, but only on the condition that you will not disclose it to others." The problem is that it is tough to contract for the continued secrecy of mass-produced goods. Such a contract might be specific to the information at issue, or it could be a part of an underlying employment relationship; whatever his feelings on the commercial use of Tropicurial, John might be violating an express or implied confidentiality arrangement by disseminating this information. Moreover, the New England Journal of Medicine might also face liability issues if it willfully makes use of information it knows to have been wrongfully obtained. My ability to enforce this kind of contract depends greatly on jurisdiction; it is worth remembering that the extent of Trade Secret protection is largely a matter of state, not federal, law.

Alternatively, we might give you a stronger right in the information -- you can disclose it to others for a price, and they are free to *use* that information (i.e. take the pill), but not to *disclose* it to others themselves. This approximates **Copyright** -- can't make a "copy" of the formula, even if it is publicly disclosed. Such a right will allow the public dissemination of Substance P, while still allowing you to control it.

Copyright doctrine may also be brought to bear upon the problem regarding the advertising tune. A sound recording based on sounds found in nature (wind, songbirds) might not meet the originality threshold of copyright law. While the issues of access, probative similarity, and substantive similarity may become focal points of discussion, I would also point to another fundamental issue regarding copyright infringement: independent creation. Copyright protection only enjoins conscious or unconscious copying, whereas **Patent** protection has the power to enjoin exploitation even of independently created work. This chapter will not yet have introduced your students to such distinctions, but the issue may be raised by students with experience in biochemistry or computer software, where industry practice often involves "clean room" processes.

Additionally, discussion of the tribespeoples' "Tropicursical" tune will bring to issue the tension between the owner's rights to the value of his or her work and the expressive rights of others. The doctrine of Fair Use and the subtopic of parody will probably arise, and the focal point of the introductory discussion should probably note both what is protected, and why. The mechanics of the doctrines are considerable, and while it may take considerable time to discuss them, their reason for being should not be ignored.

Finally, suppose that I hire the "highly skilled chemist" referred to in the problem, and she develops the formula herself. Is there any way for you to prevent this? The strongest form of protection would prevent *any* use of your formula, even if I developed it independently. This is **Patent** protection. Note the differences between allowing others to appropriate the value of your work, and giving you all the value of the product you made, regardless of how produced.

All of the above are *market-based* types of protection, in the sense that we are helping Joe appropriate part or all of the value of his idea, and the reward to him is based on the marketability of the idea. Alternatively, we could give direct government subsidies to research. We do this now in a variety of contexts-- NIH, NASA, state universities. Could replace IP with research grants to private companies. The advantage of this approach is that those giving the grants can reward ideas for their potential social value, even if it doesn't equal market value. Potential problems include almost inevitable bureaucratization and lock-in of world-views among grantors. We may trust the government less than we trust the market.

PROBLEM 1-2

Building on your lifelong interest in music and computers, you have just spent ten years creating a computer-based Encyclopedia of Music. The encyclopedia, based on a CD-ROM, includes text, snippets of recorded music (no longer than seven seconds each), pictures, and other graphics, all of which can be called up by the user. It is thus an instance of the new generation of "multimedia" computer products.

Like many other multimedia products, your encyclopedia allows the user to select a topic of interest and see (or hear) more about it. For example, from the opening menu a user can select classical composers; then select Mozart; and then choose from a biographical sketch (with text, pictures, and samples of sheet music) or musical samples that actually play on the computer's speakers.

To make it easier for computer users to access all the information in your encyclopedia, you have used an "access interface" similar to the widely-used "MediaMate" interface written and made popular by multigazillionaire computer impresario Gil Bates. (Bates adapted the "MediaMate" interface from a publicly available interface designed by the U.S. Army to teach electronics and other technical subjects to new recruits.) Although MediaMate has now become the standard interface program, Bates, because of his awesome programming talent, wrote the program in his spare time over several weeks while watching soap operas. According to his autobiography, he "never broke a sweat" while writing it; "in fact, it was a breeze."

Since Bates' company, MacroLoft, also owns many of the legal rights needed to play music from such musicians as Jimi Hendrix and Aretha Franklin, you have decided it is time to negotiate directly with Bates prior to placing your encyclopedia on the market. Note that although Bates has received valid licenses in the relevant copyrights for these songs, it is widely known that some of the musicians who created the songs are not pleased with the use of short snippets on inadequate computer sound systems, some of which sound "tinny."

You are aware that negotiating with Bates is far different from standard business practice. He is known to do all negotiating standing up in an unheated room in a mountain cabin, with no lawyers or assistants of any kind. Most unusually, he is not interested at all in formal legal rights. Reflecting his training as a serious student of philosophy, he insists on negotiating from what he calls "first principles." This usually involves long discussions of who should have which rights in which situations, and why.

You would like to convince Bates to let you market your encyclopedia without paying any royalties to him for songs, the access interface, or anything else. Failing this, you would like to keep these royalties to a minimum. Draw up a negotiating strategy that will convince him.

Analysis

Problem 1-2: This problem is designed to introduce the balancing of competing interests that is central to intellectual property protection. A number of different parties have contributed value to the multimedia product: you (who compiled the data), the original songwriters, the artists who recorded the songs, and Bates (who contributed the computer interface).

In order to convince Bates that you should not have to pay him any money, you will need first to determine what theoretical basis Bates has for believing in intellectual property protection. [If you can convince him that intellectual property protection is altogether unjustified, then of course you won't have to pay royalties]. Some of the arguments below might prove persuasive:

1. the moral rights to songs and interface belong to others (those who created the works), or are in the public domain.
2. Bates isn't selling in this market, so he isn't "losing" anything.
3. Bates didn't invest any effort in developing either one, so he has no claim to compensation for the labor he spent.
4. there is social value in including the music in the encyclopedia, which Bates does not deserve to capture. This is intrinsically an economic argument, based on the transformative value of your new contribution.
5. 7-second excerpts from songs do not compete with the songs themselves, which is what Bates owns. This is an "unfair competition" argument, and is related to argument # 2.
6. Bates has already received ample reward for the interface from other sales. This is an application of Locke's injunction against engrossment.
7. Bates *gains* value from our use of his interface, because of positive network externalities. This is also an instrumental/economic argument, but of a somewhat different nature.

PROBLEM 1-3

MEMORANDUM

To: Associate
From: Senior Partner
Re: HEALTHWARE Inc.

Janet Peterson called me yesterday about a new venture that she plans to try to get off the ground. As you may know, Janet is a computer programmer and a registered nurse. She has an interesting idea for a new venture and would like our advice on how she might structure the business so as have the best potential for success.

The proposed venture will be called Healthware. Janet believes that she can tap into the current diet/health/environmental/personal computer craze by developing a user-friendly computer program that would monitor the user's diet and fitness activity. The user would input information on his or her health (e.g., age, weight, medical history, dietary restrictions). Each day, the user would input information on diet and physical exercise. The program would have simple "pull down" menus for making this quick and easy; nutritional information on all foods would be stored in the program. The computer would periodically provide an analysis of the user's health, as well as suggestions for achieving the user's goals, whether weight reduction, better fitness, or general health. In addition, the program would compile a record of the user's activities which could be brought to annual physicals. Other sub-routines would be available for pregnant and lactating women, children, the elderly, diabetics, vegetarians, triathletes, etc.

Janet thinks that she could put together the diverse people necessary to pull this project off: programmers, a nutritionist, a physician, a fitness consultant. She is concerned, however, that any one of these people could, after they are familiar with the product, develop a competing program.

What are the options for structuring Healthware? What problems do you foresee in structuring this venture? Assuming that the product is popular, what are the major risks to Healthware's success? How can we structure Healthware so as to overcome these problems?

Analysis

Problem 1-3:

It is important to recognize that the competencies needed to analyze this problem fully go beyond what students beginning the course will typically command. On the other hand, the varied background of students in the class (including some students with "real world" work experience, and some who have studied organizational behavior, business, economics, computer programming, health sciences) can produce an interesting assessment of this problem. From our standpoint, the most valuable aspect of the problem is in getting students to see how the ownership structure of an enterprise, like the structure of a law firm, is critical to its financial success (and other non-financial objectives, such as creating an enjoyable and stable working environment). The problem also brings out some larger themes:

- the limitations of formal property rights in protecting intangible resources;
- the ways in which formal intellectual property rights, formal systems of enterprise ownership (profit-sharing, partnership, etc.), and informal systems of governance are substitutes and complements;
- some of the relationships among the fields of property law, intellectual property law, business associations law, and securities/business finance law;
- the roles that lawyers can and do play in structuring business plans to achieve particular objectives; and
- the challenges of practicing law in the growing high technology practice area.

The resource in this problem is an idea — a software product that would monitor the user's health, diet, and exercise regimen and provide advice about how to achieve the user's health goals. Ideas are easily appropriated by others. A general business idea, like Janet Peterson's, is particularly difficult to protect. From a business standpoint, Janet faces three sets of problems: (1) developing a superior product that consumers will want to buy; (2) ensuring that others won't free-ride on her investment, enabling them to undercut her price and take over the market for this type of product; and (3) earning a profit on her investment of capital and effort.

As noted in the problem, Janet cannot develop the product by herself. She will need to assemble a complementary team of programmers and health professionals. In addition, she will undoubtedly need to have capable management, sales, and marketing professionals as part of her business plan. While critical to the success of her venture, these members of her "team" pose a risk to her profit stream. They will know intimately how her product and business operate, and therefore could be in a position to develop a competing venture. In addition, once the product is out on the market, other businesses will be able to examine the product and develop competing products. Even if she is able to succeed in the marketplace, Janet faces other risks to profiting from her venture. Depending upon how her company is financed, much of the profit stream could be diverted to outside investors. In addition, if the product is defective, Janet's company could face liability problems.

The chart below summarizes the principal risks to Janet's business and various legal and business means for minimizing these risks.

Potential Appropriator	Appropriation Risk	Ways to Protect the "Idea", Minimize Appropriation Risk, and Earn a Profit
1. Competitors	Introduce competing product without having to make as large an investment in developing the idea.	Intellectual Property: patent protection for aspects of the computer program; copyright protection for aspects of the computer program; trademark protection for the business name and product(s); trade secret protection by distributing product in object code form (machine-readable code can be expensive and time-consuming to reverse engineer). Contract: HEALTHWARE could seek to limit competition by licensing rather than selling its products in the marketplace. It could include provisions prohibiting the "reverse engineering" of its products. The enforceability of such provisions is open to question. See generally Zeidenberg v. ProCD, 86 F,3d 1447 (7th Cir. 1996); Lemley, Intellectual Property and Shrink-Wrap Licenses, 68 S. Cal. L. Rev. 1239 (1996). Lead-time: HEALTHWARE can stay ahead of potential competitors by getting to market quickly and constantly upgrading its products. Partnership (with most viable competition): HEALTHWARE could partner with other companies. Such companies may bring a lot to the table (such as established marketing channels, technical expertise, complementary products). Licensing of Idea: Janet could try to market the idea in exchange for an up-front payment or ongoing royalties. She would face the same problems as Captain Downey in *Downey v. General Foods Corp*. Without an established reputation, few companies would be willing to pay Janet very much. She may be better off showing that the idea has commercial potential before approaching potential buyers.

Potential Appropriator	Appropriation Risk	Ways to Protect the "Idea", Minimize Appropriation Risk, and Earn a Profit
2. Employees	Leaving HEALTHWARE to develop their own product; taking advantage of the knowledge that they gained from working on the HEALTHWARE development team. *Classic example*: Mitch Kapor, an employee at Visicorp. (maker of the first microcomputer spreadsheet (Visicalc) for the Apple II platform), left to develop a version of the program to run on the IBM/MS-DOS platform.	HEALTHWARE needs to motivate its employees to create while protecting its proprietary information. There are two general approaches to this dual-edged problem: (1) the stick — protecting the information through intellectual property and contractual restrictions; and (2) the carrot — encouraging employee loyalty (and productivity) by giving them a share of the profits. These approaches are not mutually exclusive and it is common to see both approaches used in tandem. Intellectual Property: By protecting its information through trade secrecy, patent, copyright, and/or trademark means, HEALTHWARE has some ability to limit employees' ability to take the information elsewhere. Intellectual property created by HEALTHWARE employees would be treated as "work for hire" and would be owned by HEALTHWARE. Contract: HEALTHWARE can require employees to enter into non-disclosure and non-competition agreements to prevent the "leakage" of valuable information. Technical "know how" and general skills developed by employees cannot be perfectly protected through these means. Some states (including California) do not enforce non-competition clauses. In addition, courts are reluctant to limit employee mobility. Business Structure: The company could be structured so that few employees have access to all of the proprietary information needed to develop a competing venture. The stick approach cannot, however, ensure that all valuable proprietary information is secure. Perhaps more significantly, an overly restrictive work environment will make it more difficult to recruit the best employees and discourages the sharing of information that is critical to team creativity. Hence, rather than focusing on the protection of the technology, HEALTHWARE may wish to use property rights to the stream of profits as an important part of its business plan. Stock options, profit sharing, and performance-based bonuses stock promote employee loyalty and productivity. This approach could also save Janet some money during the early stages of development. A partnership/profit-sharing model allows HEALTHWARE to pay lower wages up-front, since the partners will be motivated by future profit-sharing. This model encourages synergy and the creation of "firm-specific" capital (as described by Gilson and Mnookin).

Potential Appropriator	**Appropriation Risk**	**Ways to Protect the "Idea", Minimize Appropriation Risk, and Earn a Profit**
3. Consultants	HEALTHWARE could "out source" some of the development work for its products through contractual relationships. For example, it could hire a computer software consulting firm to develop the code for its products. Such consultants, however, could develop competing products.	Intellectual Property: Intellectual property protection for HEALTHWARE's products would provide some protection against such competition. Contract: HEALTHWARE could require the consultants to do all of their work as "work for hire," thereby assigning all intellectual property rights in work product to HEALTHWARE. In addition, since this contractual agreement would be directly negotiated (unlike shrinkwrap licenses with consumers), their enforceability would be reasonably guaranteed. Business Structure: HEALTHWARE could limit consultants' access to information.
4. Consumers	Consumers could distribute copies of the program to others. They could also reverse engineer the product for the purpose of developing competing products.	Intellectual Property: Intellectual property protection could be used to prevent piracy of software products. Small scale copying, however, is often difficult to police. Contract: HEALTHWARE can license rather sell their products. They could use "shrinkwrap", "break the seal", or "clickwrap" licenses prohibiting reverse engineering and other practices. The enforceability of such provisions is open to question. See above. Technical Protections: Copyright protection technologies can be used to prevent copying of software, although this method may limit the users' ability to customize the product. Pricing and Upgrade Strategy: HEALTHWARE can charge a lower price and offer periodic upgrades as means of discouraging piracy.
5. Investors	In order to develop and market the product effectively, HEALTHWARE will need to raise capital. The terms of this financing, however, could affect the viability of the company and Janet's ability to share in the profits.	Financial Structure: Janet can raise money through a variety of means including venture capital investment, partnership, public offering, and debt-financing. These methods vary in terms of the extent to which they share the risks of the venture, affect Janet's control over the company, and impose regulatory costs. Venture capital financing, for example, would likely require Janet to risk her control and share of the company in exchange for lower cost capital. If the company fails to meet milestones established in the venture capital agreement, she could lose the company entirely. Debt-financing allows Janet to control the company, but may saddle it with costly interest burdens.

Potential Appropriator	Appropriation Risk	Ways to Protect the "Idea", Minimize Appropriation Risk, and Earn a Profit
6. Tort Victims	Defects in the product could cause harm to consumers and possibly third parties. Tort suits could injure HEALTHWARE's reputation and result in costly litigation and court-awarded damages.	Quality Control: By putting greater effort into testing the product, HEALTHWARE can minimize the actual risk of defects. Disclaimer: HEALTHWARE could attempt to disclaim product defects in its product licenses. Insurance: HEALTHWARE could obtain insurance against defect risks. Incorporation: By incorporating the company, Janet could limit her liability to her equity interest in HEALTHWARE.

Overall, it is unlikely that Janet will be able to get much in the way of intellectual property protection for her raw business idea. Cf. *Downey v. General Foods Corp.*. It is questionable whether the business model is patentable, although a recent case opens the way for a wider range of business method patents. See *State Street Bank & Trust Co. v. Signature Financial Group Inc.*, 146 F.3d 1368 (Fed. Cir. 1998); 'Boom' in Business Method Patent Filings Has Followed 'State Street' Ruling, PTO Says, 57 BNA Patent, Trademark & Copyright J. 115 (Dec. 10, 1998). She might be able to get patent protection for some features of her computer program, but there is nothing in the problem to suggest that she met the exacting standards of patent law (novelty, utility, and non-obviousness). A computer program using pull-down menus is not novel. She might, however, develop some methods for implementing her idea that are patentable. If so, she would be able to prevent others from using these inventions (for the statutory period of patent protection). Other companies, however, could develop competing products so long as they did not copy expressive features of the program. Trademark protection could prove valuable in this marketplace, and HEALTHWARE would do well by getting the endorsement of established health care organizations.

Before any of this can happen, however, HEALTHWARE must produce a strong product. Janet may wish to provide equity interests to the key employees so as to motivate them to do their best work and to reduce the risk that they would work for a competitor. As with law firms, the ways in which Janet structures ownership, profit sharing, and decisionmaking within the company will likely be critical to its success.

Chapter 2 Trade Secret Protection

A. Introduction

B. Subject Matter

Rockwell Graphic Systems, Inc. v. DEV Industries, Inc., page 42, is an example of a trade secret case in which absolute secrecy is not required for a trade secret to exist. The plaintiff made printing presses and enjoyed a monopoly over replacement parts. Rockwell Graphics took reasonable precautions to protect the piece part drawings (the trade secret) in a vault. However, the plaintiff also gave piece drawings to vendors. DEV hired ex-Rockwell Graphic employees, one of whom was caught stealing the drawings. The court said that the fact that vendors and failed bidders possessed "piece-part" drawings did not forfeit trade secret protection. The court reasoned that it was necessary for Rockwell to give these drawings to the sub-contractors who made the components and that a duty of confidentiality was imposed on these vendors. You might ask why the internal security measures were being discussed when there were so many piece part drawings floating around with vendors and failed bidders. The answer, of course, is that reasonable precautions may serve as evidence that Rockwell considered the drawings were a trade secret. It is worth pressing this point, by asking whether this amounts to a "notice" function, and if so, whether there is a better (i.e., cheaper) way to serve notice that a firm believes its technology is a trade secret. This may lead naturally to a discussion of whether precautions against disclosure are necessarily wasteful. You might also point out that the assembly drawings and the presses themselves might allow a competitor to reverse engineer Rockwell's trade secret. Why no discussion in the cases about access restrictions over the machines themselves? How practical would it have been to license the presses on condition that they never be reverse engineered vs. selling the presses?

Smith v. Dravo Corp., noted below, also serves as food for thought on the fundamental nature of trade secrets. Dravo Corp. could have easily ascertained the specifications and dimensions of the cargo containers through purchase and inspection. Merely treating information as a secret does not render it such. This also illustrates one of the basic tradeoffs of Trade Secret protection; potentially infinite duration, for protection weaker than Patent. Though *Smith v. Dravo Corp* is properly concerned with misappropriation, the issue of ascertainability may have relevance as an argument for the defense.

C. Misappropriation of Trade Secrets

In *E. I. du Pont de Nemours v. Rolfe Christopher*, page 55, photographers flew over DuPont's construction site to take pictures of the internal configuration of the plant (the trade secret). The case serves as the traditional point of departure for discussion of what types of acts constitute misappropriation; there was no "independent wrong" [i.e., non-trade secret legal violation] committed by the photographers. What they did was perfectly legal; there was no trespass or physical taking. However, the court found that they violated the "commercial morality" at the time by flying over the site. It may have been reasonable to prevent someone standing on higher ground from viewing the plant, but presumably du Pont could not protect against someone flying over the plant without spending a huge amount of money. You might ask your students what level of security would have been optimal in this case. Is it clear that other precautions (e.g., building a tent over the construction site) would have been prohibitively expensive? Without a trade secret cause of action, there would be no cost-effective way to protect trade secrets. This case is also distinctive because there was no pre-existing relationship between the parties, as is so often found in trade secret cases. Pointing this out is a way to emphasize the "independent wrong" point, and also serves as a reminder that the "wrong" in many (if not most) trade secret cases arises from a relationship, either express or implied. Looking at it this way, *DuPont* may be seen as the trade secret analogue to a class of "implied in law" contracts cases often studied in the first-year contracts course, such as *Cotnam v. Wisdom*, 104 S.W. 164 (1907) and *Mills v. Wyman,* 20 Mass. 207 (1825). If this analogy seems fruitful, you might consult any of a number of articles by Professor Wendy Gordon of Boston University; for example *On Owning Information: Intellectual Property And The Restitutionary Impluse*, ,78 Va. L. Rev. 149 (1992).

Smith v. Dravo Corp., page 59, represents a more conventional trade secret misappropriation case in which the focus in on whether there was a confidential relationship between the parties. Smith designed a modular shipping container and disclosed information to Dravo, a potential purchaser of the business. This is a situation where legal instinct and business relationships conflict. The business person wants to sell the whole containerization business and to avoid trotting the lawyers out too early with the non-disclosure agreements. However, this case points out what can happen when these agreements are not signed. The court describes the trade secrets disclosed during the transaction between Smith and Dravo: patent applications (truly a trade secret), blueprints (like *Rockwell Graphics),* letters from possible users, and further correspondence with potential users. The latter two are typical business trade secrets—customer lists, occupancy rates, pricing, etc. You might ask why it is valuable to have early access to a patent application. Here are two reasons: (1) to discover the technology, as some manufacturing details may not be disclosed in the patent application; and (2) to gain information about what the patent will cover so that you can build something that will not infringe. These items raise interesting issues of damages. One measure of the harm was how much more rapidly Dravo was able to create a rival container as compared to how long it would take if he had no information. This is a standard way to calibrate damages—based on the notion of a "head start." Dravo was able to put out 500 containers within 18 months of the failed negotiations. The shipping container business is an example (though perhaps not an obvious one) of a "standards market." The company that owned the design for the standard for interchangeable containers would be in an enviable competitive position; it could license all comers for use of the standard, and control the development of the technology – perhaps in ways that favored its own container designs. You might highlight what's at stake by analogizing Smith to Betamax and Dravo to VHS.

Chicago Lock Co. v. Fanberg, page 67, is a reverse engineering case. Unlike the complex printing presses in *Rockwell*, a skilled locksmith can reverse engineer the correct key for a particular tubular lock. The Fanbergs compiled the codes and published them in a book. The court concluded that the trade secret was not obtained through improper means. While the customers owe a duty to Chicago Lock to keep the information confidential, the duty does not carry over to a third party locksmith. You might ask what Chicago Lock could have done to prevent what the Fanbergs did from becoming widespread practice. (i.e., what reasonable precautions could they have taken?) Chicago Lock could have voided the warranty if a certified service person was not used. They also could have tried to patent the tubular lock technology (encouraging others to infringe the patent would make Fanbergs liable under contributory infringement). Is this case an example of the way IP law "channels" firms and technologies into using particular modes of legal protection? You might argue, for example, that if the lock design is really valuable, then it should be patented for 20 years instead of trying to maintain perpetual protection under trade secrets

Wexler v. Greenberg, page 74, presents the facts of a garden variety employee departure case. The facts, and the court's highlighting of the policy issues involved, make it a fine teaching case. A word of caution is necessary at the outset, however. As the Notes point out, the case is somewhat unusual in some respects. It is important to note these peculiarities, lest the students take the wrong conclusions from the case: (1) there is no employee nondisclosure/assignment provision, which may have been more common in 1960 than in our trade secret- (and IP-) conscious commercial world; and (2) Greenberg worked alone in developing the formulas, and did not in the process apparently draw from his employer's preexisting stock of knowledge and information. It is important to bring these factors out during the discussion, lest the students get the idea that the court's cogent elaboration of the policy in favor of employee mobility always carries the day in "departing employee" trade secret cases. Judicious reference to the cases in the Notes (e.g., *Lippancy,* on point (2) above), and subsequent cases in this Chapter, should be enough to dispel this misconception.

Wexler is a sure-fire jumping off point for a discussion of two sets of issues: the "Silicon Valley" model of rapid employee mobility and resulting "informal" inter-firm technology sharing – on which see the Annalee Saxenian book cited in the text, still the best discussion of these issues; and the "fairness" of enforcing "pro-employer" assignment/nondisclosure agreements widely demanded of new employees today. For some indications of countervailing "pro-employee" aspects of employee mobility law, see Merges, "The Law and Economics of Employee Inventions," 13 Harv. J. L. & Tech. 1 (2000).

D. Agreements to Keep Secrets

Warner-Lambert Pharmaceutical Co. v. Reynolds, Inc., page 92, is infamous for the "Listerine clause." At one point the ingredients for Listerine were a trade secret and probably difficult to reverse engineer. There was no clause in the licensing agreement that would terminate the royalty payments if the trade secret ever became known (which it did). The court enforced the agreement. Why would contracting parties agree on continuing payments even after the trade secret has been made public? Maybe the payments are an installment payment plan? This has been suggested as the rationale for certain licensing agreements calling for royalty payments beyond the expiration of a statutory IP right, e.g., a patent. Does it make sense to honor the payment plan structure for a trade secret but not for patented technology?

PROBLEM 2-1

Company X possesses a valuable piece of information about the process for making its product. That information is not known at all outside company X. Suppose X discloses the information to two companies, A and B. A receives the information in confidence, and subject to a written agreement that it will not use or disclose the information outside the bounds of the relationship. B receives the information without any restrictions whatever on its use. Does X have a protectible trade secret that it can assert against A? Against B? Against C, an individual who steals the information from X's computer network?

Does your answer change if X, A, B, and C are the only companies in the industry?

PROBLEM 2-2

StartUp, Inc. is the only participant in a new market. The market is based on a product for which StartUp has a nonexclusive license from the inventor; that is, StartUp cannot prevent others from obtaining a similar license. Nonetheless, StartUp has exhaustively researched the demand for the product, has concluded that a market exists, and has worked to stimulate demand. As a result, it has both "made" a market for the product and developed a comprehensive list of customers.

Thaddeus, a sales representative for StartUp, leaves to found his own company. He gets a license to make the product from its inventor. He takes with him from StartUp the customer list he worked with as an employee, his personal knowledge of and contacts with specific customers, and StartUp's knowledge of the market. StartUp sues Thaddeus for misappropriation of trade secrets. What result?

PROBLEM 2-3

Research Co. is a major pharmaceutical company working on a cure for certain types of cancer. Derek is a molecular biologist employed by Research. After several years on the job, Derek leaves Research for Conglomerate, Inc., another pharmaceutical company which has decided to work on the same cancer cure. At the time Derek leaves, Research has not been successful in finding a cancer cure. However, as a result of his work at Research, Derek is able to help Conglomerate avoid several unproductive avenues of research. Aided in part by this knowledge, Conglomerate (using scientists other than Derek) develops a cancer cure before Research. Research sues Conglomerate, alleging misappropriation of trade secrets. Does Research have a case?

PROBLEM 2-4

The Church of True Belief is a religious group founded around a set of closely guarded scriptural materials supposedly handed down to Church's elders from Church's deity. After a bitter theological dispute, a group of adherents leave the church to form the House of Absolute Belief. They take with them a copy of Church's confidential scriptures, which they rely on in gaining adherents and founding the new House. Church sues House for misappropriation of trade secrets.

At trial, the issue is whether the scriptures qualify as a trade secret. The evidence indicates that the scriptures had never before been removed from the confines of Church, that both Church and House are tax-exempt nonprofit organizations that rely on donations for their funding, and that Church (but not House) rations access to the scriptures in proportion to the size of an adherent's donation.

Can the scriptures qualify as a trade secret? Does your answer depend on whether the governing law is the UTSA, the Restatement of Torts, or the Restatement (Third) of Unfair Competition?

Analysis

Problem 2-1: A trade secrets claim is a tort law claim, and operates between private parties. There is no central governmental authority "issuing" trade secrets. This raises the possibility that a particular piece of information may be a trade secret as to some competitors but not others. This is certainly a realistic possibility as a practical matter. Courts applying one of the vague definitions found in the text could well come to different conclusions as to the validity of a trade secret.[1] Whether such a result is consistent with the principles behind trade secret law is a tougher question. On the one hand, several of the factors used in the Restatement of Torts in defining trade secrets (such as value to the recipient and the relationship between the parties) are likely to differ on a case-by-case basis, suggesting that different outcomes are possible.

On the other hand, it seems doubtful that something can be a secret under the objective definition of the Uniform Act as to some defendants but not others. Most courts would conclude that the disclosure of the information to B without any form of protection defeats a trade secret claim, at least if that disclosure makes the information "generally available" in the industry. Restatement of Torts § 757, comment b takes this position; *but see Metallurgical*, which suggests that some non-confidential disclosures are allowable. Obviously, B is not liable for misappropriation even if the information remains secret, because there is no element of *misappropriation* in B's conduct. Whether A and C are liable depends on whether the disclosure to B destroyed the secrecy of the information. As a practical matter, therefore, the full effect of the disclosure to B may depend on such things as what B does with the information, and how many companies there are in the industry who might use the information. For example, if X, A, B, and C are the only companies in the industry, it would seem odd to hold C liable for acquiring a secret that (literally) everyone else knew.

The problem brings out two important points: (1) the existence of a trade secret is a prerequisite to recovery for misappropriation. X cannot sue A or C on a theory of misappropriation of trade secrets unless X actually has a trade secret.[2] (2) trade secrecy is fragile protection, because lawful (or even unlawful) public disclosure by one person can destroy the trade secret owner's protection vis-a-vis *all* users of the information.

Problem 2-2: Business information represents an often-overlooked and under-analyzed segment of trade secrets law. Because the definition of a trade secret is so broad, business as well as technical

---

1 Nonmutual collateral estoppel is likely to bar a secret holder from claiming trade secret protection in a second suit if it has lost in the first suit. Collateral estoppel does not work the other way, however. See Parklane Hosiery Co. v. Shore, 439 U.S. 322 (1979). This means that someone seeking to enforce a trade secret will have to prove the secret's validity in each successive suit. This imbalance may weaken trade secret protection as a practical matter.

2 Note that X may have other remedies against both A and C -- against A for breach of contract, if A misuses the information or discloses it to a third party, and against C for conversion. We discuss the possibility of continuing contractual liability in section D of this Chapter.

information clearly seems to fall within the scope of trade secrecy. What is less clear is how to protect that information. Customer lists are a good example. Most courts have held that customer lists constitute protectable trade secrets. See, e.g., *Allen v. Johar, Inc.*, 823 S.W.2d 824 (Ark. 1992); *ABBA Rubber Co. v. Seaquist*, 286 Cal. Rptr. 518 (Ct. App. 1991).[3] This is not a universally accepted rule, however. For example, in *Zoecon Indus. v. American Stockman Tag Co.*, 713 F.2d 1174, 1179 (5th Cir. 1983), the court held that customer lists were not protectible trade secrets. The lists in that case constituted publicly available information that could be compiled with minimal effort, however. *Zoecon* suggested in dictum that lists which were the product of a great deal of effort and which were not publicly available could be protectable. From a practical standpoint, one lesson from these cases is that taking physical things or documents is far more likely to be considered actionable than taking information in your head.

There are two other trade secret issues in this problem as well. First, StartUp has clearly obtained a business advantage by compiling and using information on the market demand for its product. The result is that StartUp entered the market and no one else did, giving StartUp a temporary monopoly. StartUp would like to protect that market information -- and the conclusions that it drew from that information -- as a trade secret. While the information itself may fall within the definition of a trade secret, StartUp is unlikely to be successful, because it has already put that information out in the public by entering the market itself.[4]

Second, this problem introduces the tension between the rights of an employee and those of the corporation which is at the heart of much of trade secrets law. T has information in his head which he has learned as a result of his job. Much of that information overlaps with or supplements StartUp's protectible customer list. However, because it is personal knowledge that T has gained in the course of his job, it is hard to see how he can "unlearn" it. In the words of one California court, the law "does not require a frontal lobotomy." In the case of personal knowledge, most courts will be unwilling to order T not to use this information, or (even more problematic) not to enter the market as a competitor. But see *Allen*, 823 S.W.2d at 827 (upholding injunction preventing the use of *memorized* customer lists for solicitation).

Problem 2-3: Traditionally, so-called "blind alleys" were not protectable under the Restatement of Torts, because the information was not thought to be "used in one's business." Today, blind alleys are generally considered protectible information. They fall within the definitions of a trade secret in the UTSA and the Restatement of Unfair Competition (which protects "any information that can be used in a business or other enterprise"), assuming their existence is not generally known. The value of a blind alley in a competitive market is likely to stem precisely from the fact that it is not generally known, satisfying the UTSA requirement. Protecting knowledge of blind alleys also makes economic sense, as economists are unlikely to distinguish between "positive" and "negative" information.

As demonstrated in this problem, knowledge of blind alleys may be tremendously valuable to a competitor. The value of such "negative information" -- as well as the value of much positive information -- is often measured by the "lead time" gained by the defendant. That is, if a company would take 24 months to enter a market without a piece of information, but improperly acquires information which allows it to cut that time to 14 months, the value of the trade secret is the value of the 10 months it has saved in getting to market. In the case of pharmaceutical and medical device companies which face and FDA approval process, that value can be enormous.

---

3 Consider whether California's rule is influenced by the fact that a trade secret may be protectable even though it is "readily ascertainable," under California's modification to the Uniform Trade Secrets Act.

4 Of course, particular market strategies or projections may be based on confidential information. That information and those strategies, if not yet implemented, may be protectable.

This problem also raises the thorny problem of personal knowledge again. D has worked for years in this industry; can she really be expected to look the other way for two years while her employer pursues an avenue she knows to be fruitless? If she were required to do so, would she be marketable? There are no clear answers to these questions, and courts seem to take them on a case-by-case basis.

Problem 2-4: This problem is based on an actual case involving the Church of Scientology. *See Religious Technology Center v. Wollersheim*, 796 F.2d 1076 (9th Cir. 1986). The Ninth Circuit held in *Wollersheim* that scriptures were not protectible trade secrets because their value was spiritual rather than commercial. This holding is certainly open to dispute. After all, if possession of the materials helps one side or the other gain converts, it may have a direct economic impact. This problem is useful for introducing discussion about the economic value required to constitute a trade secret.

The real question is, what is the requirement for commercial value? UTSA says economic value. If the Scriptures helped in starting the church, in gaining converts, and in gaining donations, arguably they meet this test. Second, does the value result from not being generally known? Perhaps, if limited access to the materials is part of religious advancement. Compare -- Restatement of Torts says "information which is used in one's business" -- depends on how you define business, but doesn't seem likely to apply to a church. Rest of Unfair Comp says "any information that can be used in the operation of a business or other enterprise" -- clearly satisfied -- so long as it can "afford an actual or potential economic advantage over others". Here, the question is whether the value is "economic," which in turn will depend on how broadly that term is defined.

Note that the Church of Scientology has been actively attempting to protect its trade secrets on the Internet, resulting in a series of recent decisions. In one of those decisions, *Religious Technology Center v. Lerma*, 908 F. Supp. 1362, 1368-69 (E.D. Va. 1995), the court apparently assumed that the Scientology scriptures constituted the sort of information that *could* qualify as a trade secret, though it held that they had lost their secrecy through disclosure.

PROBLEM 2-5

Smith, a bar owner in rural Alabama, develops by accident one night the relatively simple formula for a new alcoholic beverage. The drink is simply a mixture of three common ingredients. Smith begins selling the drink, which he calls "Mobile Mud," in his bar. However, he instructs his bartenders not to reveal the formula to anyone and has them premix "Mud" in the back of the bar, out of sight of customers. Smith is outraged when he learns that Jimmy Dean, an international distributor of alcoholic beverages, has copied his formula and is marketing it under a different name. At trial, Dean employees and independent experts unanimously testify that it is possible for someone with experience in the beverage industry to determine the formula for Mud by looking at, smelling and tasting the drink.

Has Smith taken reasonable precautions? What more could he have done to protect the "secret formula" of Mobile Mud? Is the secret so obvious to consumers that selling the product on the open market destroys protection? Does your opinion of the case change if you learn that Dean's representative went to Smith's bar and bribed a bartender to disclose the formula?

PROBLEM 2-5a

MidContinent is a small manufacturer of signs and decals. It has only five employees, two of whom are father and son and two more of whom are family friends. The company describes itself as having a "relaxed, congenial" working atmosphere. In order to avoid what the president considers excessive formality, the employees have never been required to sign confidentiality agreements, and documents kept within the company aren't stamped confidential. The company has never conducted "exit interviews" or instructed its employees about trade secrecy. According to the company president, "we trust our employees, and that trust have never been misplaced." On the other hand, the company does take certain steps to keep outsiders from accessing its customer lists and its adhesive manufacturing process. And there is little history of economic espionage in the decal-manufacturing business.

Has MidContinent taken reasonable efforts to protect its secrets? Should it matter whether the party accused of stealing those secrets is an employee or an outsider?

Analysis

Problem 2-5: This problem is based on an actual case from the Alabama Court of Appeals involving the formula for "Lynchburg Lemonade." *Mason v. Jack Daniels Distillery*, 518 So.2d 130 (Ala. Ct. App. 1987). ["Mobile Mud" = Lynchburg Lemonade, "Smith" = Mason, and "Jimmy Dean" = Jack Daniels] The fundamental lesson of this problem (though not necessarily of the case) is that in some cases selling a product is simply inconsistent with taking "reasonable efforts" to protect the secret embodied in the product. Here, Smith restricts disclosure of the trade secret by "fencing" -- mixing the drink in the back room -- and by restricting knowledge and constraining employees. There is not too much more Smith *could* have done to keep the drink secret, at least within reason. (In theory, he could presumably have had customers sign confidentiality agreements when they ordered a drink, but that seems impractical).

The evidence in the problem is that experienced drinkers could tell the ingredients just by smelling and tasting the drink. So it is in "plain view" to customers in a certain sense. Smith has taken "reasonable precautions" in the sense that there isn't much more that he reasonably could have done -- but under trade secret law, that fact alone may not protect him. Note that this means certain secrets are inherently unprotectable, at least after sales begin. Issues of disclosure of secrets and reverse engineering are also bound up in this problem -- even if it is (or was) a secret, it does not necessarily follow that the use JD made of that secret was illegal.

In the actual case, the court held that JD's ability to reverse engineer the product is only one factor weighing against a finding of secrecy, and on balance (applying the Restatement of Torts) the court concluded that the drink remained a secret. This holding is questionable; it may be that the court disbelieved JD's evidence that its agents obtained the formula by reverse engineering.

Problem 2-5a: This problem, whatever its outcome, may be useful in pointing out that there are many informal mechanisms for enforcement that lie outside the legal system. In practice, where the company is small and the relationships quite personal, the damage to the relationship may serve as the primary deterrent. And in the entertainment industry, even a successful defense against misappropriation of a trade secret may harm the defendant's credibility to the point that he may "never do lunch in this town again."

PROBLEM 2-6

Suppose that, at trial in the *duPont* case, the Christophers proved that they could have discovered the secrets contained in the layout of the duPont plant from another source (such as a copy of the blueprints on file with the Environmental Protection Agency and available under the Freedom of Information Act) that placed no restrictions on their use of the information. Are the Christophers then relieved from liability for misappropriation of trade secrets? Would your answer change if they had obtained the photos by sneaking onto duPont property on the ground?

Analysis

Problem 2-6: The key to this problem is not the use of improper means at all, but the secrecy of the information. It is important to remind students that "misappropriation" of a trade secret cannot occur unless there is actually a secret. In this case, it may be that the publicly available documents make the "secret" readily ascertainable; though whether that is in fact the case will depend on how hard it is to obtain this information. It is also worth noting that under *Ruckelshaus v. Monsanto Co.*, 467 U.S. 986, 1001-04 (1987), a government agency that makes a private company's secrets available to the public may have a Fifth Amendment obligation to compensate the private party.

This problem presents once again the battle between those courts that seem to take the position that "bad acts" alone are enough for misappropriation (*e.g. Franke v. Wiltschek*, cited in the text) and those courts which properly distinguish two separate requirements (*e.g. Van Prod. Co. v. General Welding & Fabricating Co.*, 213 A.2d 769 (Pa. 1965).

PROBLEM 2-7

Solomon, a regular customer of ToolCo's products, comes up with an idea for a new tool. He sends the idea to ToolCo, suggesting that they manufacture it. ToolCo does in fact produce and sell the new tool. Is Solomon entitled to compensation for ToolCo's use of his idea? Does it make any difference if (1) ToolCo actively solicited the idea from Solomon? (2) Solomon sent the suggestion to ToolCo along with a letter saying he wanted to open negotiations over a possible licensing arrangement to use the idea? (3) ToolCo has in the past had an informal, unwritten policy of compensating inventors who submit good ideas?

PROBLEM 2-8

VenCo, a venture capitalist in the business of financing start-up companies, investigates TechCo in an effort to decide whether or not to finance it. To aid in its investigation, VenCo asks for and receives confidential information about TechCo's products and market position. VenCo eventually decides not to finance TechCo because of concerns about its management, but it does finance a start-up competitor of TechCo in the same field. Are VenCo or the start-up liable to TechCo? What obligations, if any, does VenCo undertake as a result of its exposure to TechCo's secrets?

Analysis

Problem 2-7: This problem is based on *Smith v. Snap-On Tools*, 833 F.2d 578 (5th Cir. 1987). This case is relatively straightforward -- unsolicited unilateral disclosure of an idea does not create a confidential relationship giving rise to trade secret protection. (Indeed, such disclosure may well destroy the secrecy required for protection in other contexts). Variations on this problem, however, can raise tougher issues. What if S had requested compensation? In that case, the unilateral request alone is unlikely to create a confidential relationship. There is no reason for the recipient to know that the information is conferred in confidence. However, it is possible for S to establish the circumstances for a confidential relationship. For example, if he had attached to an envelope containing the idea a confidentiality statement, demanding that the envelope not be opened and the idea not be used or disclosed unless the recipient agrees to the terms of the statement, courts might be willing to find a confidential relationship. In that case, the recipient has both notice of confidentiality and an opportunity to reject the information. In practice, large companies routinely reject unsolicited ideas without reviewing them unless the person submitting the idea signs a form waiving all rights to it.

Solicitation of ideas and a policy of paying for them will not alone obligate a recipient to pay for a valuable idea, but both may be evidence from which a court might imply a confidential relationship. In *Joyce v. Halsey*, 551 N.E.2d 172 (Ohio 1990), the Supreme Court of Ohio held that a company policy of compensating employees for valuable suggestions did not create a property or contractual right to such compensation. Justice Holmes filed a vigorous dissent, citing a number of cases in which employee suggestion plans were held to create binding relationships.

Creation of a confidential relationship from conduct also has bearing on an important class of cases in the software industry -- those involving the enforcement of shrinkwrap licenses. Vendors who mass-market their software often attempt to unilaterally bind purchasers to a confidential relationship by means of a printed license inserted within the box of software. Most courts have held such licenses unenforceable; *e.g., Step-Saver Data Systems v. Wyse Technology*, 939 F.2d 91 (3d Cir. 1991); *Vault v. Quaid*, 847 F.2d 255 (5th Cir. 1988). *Contra ProCD v. Zeidenberg*, 86 F.3d 1447 (7th Cir. 1996). *See generally* Mark A. Lemley, *Intellectual Property and Shrinkwrap Licenses*, 68 **S. Cal. L. Rev.** 1239 (1995).

Problem 2-8: This problem presents what is known in the venture capital industry as the "make or buy" decision. Venture capitalists often approach an industry considering a number of options, including investment in an existing company and starting their own company. Venture capitalists as a matter of policy will not sign confidentiality agreements before looking at secret information. The law is not clear on whether they are nonetheless liable for subsequently using that information. TechCo can argue that they gave their most confidential information to VenCo with an expectation that it would be used for their benefit, not to their detriment. Depending on the information, it may be impossible for VenCo to hold it separate in funding the new venture. *Smith v. Dravo* certainly suggests that the absence of an agreement will not be sufficient to protect venture capitalists. On the other hand, VenCo can argue that they have to evaluate multiple companies in order to decide whether to invest, and that implying a confidential relationship will unfairly restrict capital investment by binding venture capitalists to the first company they happen to investigate. Further, VenCo's refusal to sign a confidentiality agreement arguably puts TechCo on notice that VenCo will not be bound to a confidential relationship.

In practice, the answer will probably depend on the circumstances -- general information is not likely to be considered misused, while the taking of schematics would probably be viewed differently. Further, if the proposed "purchase" was in fact a sham designed to obtain information, defendants will be liable. *Phillips v. Frey*, 20 F.3d 623 (1994).

This problem also raises the point that parties who receive and use trade secrets from a third party, knowing that the secrets were improperly taken or disclosed (VenCo's new start-up, in this case), are also liable for misappropriation.

PROBLEM 2-9

MegaGene (MG) is a genomics company: a company whose business is to isolate and identify individual human genes. Founded in 1996, MG was originally conceived as a company that would accumulate patents on various genes and partial gene sequences. The idea was that as researchers – either within MG or outside of it – figured out what particular proteins were produced ("coded for") by individual genes, some of those genes would be very valuable. Some might code for important proteins that some humans needed as disease therapies; others might contain errors that caused diseases, and thereby be useful in diagnosing or treating the diseases.

MG's original strategy was to obtain patents on as many genes and partial gene sequences as it could. Today it has over 100 such patents, almost exclusively on full gene sequences. Those patents were acquired because MG was able to establish the actual function of each of the genes. Legal changes – most notably a tighter interpretation of patentable "utility" (see Chapter 3) – precluded MG from acquiring any patents on partial gene sequences, however.

Although some of the full-gene patents may someday be valuable, none are as yet. So to try to generate cash in the short term, MG has been pursuing another approach to the genomics business: it charges users for access to its database of gene sequences and related information. The database has been painstakingly assembled not only from information in MG's own 100 patents, but also from various public domain sources. It includes a great deal of information from the publicly funded Human Genome Project.

For example, it includes information on many "markers" which help researchers determine which individual chromosome certain sequences come from. It also contains a great deal of information about individual genes: when they are expressed or repressed, and what they code for in various tissue samples and patient populations. This information helps researchers identify which genetic sequences are part of genes that may be important – because they are associated with a disease, for example.

IceGene is a company based in Iceland that has designed a highly promising approach to genomics. IceGene has combined a vast genetic database with detailed information on disease incidence in specific people. This is made possible by the fact that for many years detailed genealogical records have been kept for the highly homogenous Icelandic population. Now, IceGene has compiled a large database of tissue samples from individual Icelanders. Its business goal is to identify, from genealogical records, specific individuals whose family histories show they may be at risk for certain diseases and other conditions. Then, with access to the genetic code of the individual in question, IceGene can locate specific genetic variations and mutations that might be associated with the disease or condition. Once a correlation of association is established, specific genes and genetic problems can be identified for future research. (Much of this information is derived with reference to public data, including the Human Genome Project data.) IceGene plans to pursue some of these research opportunities itself, but there will be too many for the firm to research all of them. So it too plans to establish a database of genes and individual genetic variations that will be accessible (for a fee) to other companies doing genomics research.

Both MG and IceGene have established web-based access to their databases. The web pages are accessible only by subscribers of the firms' respective services, but customers can subscribe online using an interactive signup menu. The signup procedure requires users to agree to a "Database and Trade Secrecy Access Agreement," which includes these two provisions:

[1] Customer, upon accepting this Access Agreement, agrees that the Genetic Data accessible hereon is and will be a Trade Secret of Company, and further agrees not to disclose, publish, or otherwise disseminate said Genetic Data to any other company, person, or institution. Customer also agrees that payment under the Payment provision herein will continue as provided for in this Agreement, notwithstanding the subsequent disclosure, publication or other dissemination of any portion of said Genetic Data by a third party not subject to this Agreement. . . . [2] Customer agrees to pay to the Company a royalty of 5 per cent of the gross selling price of any diagnostic kit, therapeutic drug, or other commercial product developed as a result of Customer's access to or use of the Genetic Data contained herein.

MG becomes the dominant genomics database firm, with over 8,000 subscribers. It is widely known in the industry that virtually every serious researcher uses MG data in his or her genomics research. Meanwhile, IceGene has become an accepted source for information about the relationship between certain gene mutations and actual human diseases. Gene O'Mick, a researcher based in Europe, is a subscriber to both the MG and IceGene databases. In the course of his research, Gene discovers a gene, called "Cobb1," that he believes is linked to a rare genetic disorder called Ty Cobb syndrome. (Sufferers are mentally unstable and often kleptomaniacs) Although Gene is an MG subscriber, he contends that he did not use the database in locating the Cobb1 gene; his published research on the subject reveals that he used the publicly available Human Genome Project database to first hone in on the gene's location and then sequence it. Gene now wants to confirm the link between the Cobb1 gene and Ty Cobb syndrome, by running an analysis using the IceGene database. He balks, however, when he comes to clause [2] above in the IceGene Access Agreement. Gene believes that the rarity of Ty Cobb's disease will make it very difficult to interest pharmaceutical firms in developing a therapy to deal with it. (This could for example take the form of a chemical compound that inhibits expression of the Cob1 gene, effectively suppressing the disorder.) Because of this, Gene wants to keep the cost of any Cobb1 therapy as low as possible. So he objects to the "reach through" or "pass through" royalty called for in Clause [2].

Gene has asked you to argue his position with MG and IceGene. What arguments would you marshal on his behalf?

PROBLEM 2-10

Atech and Alpha both manufacture complex medical devices used in diagnosing a variety of ailments. These devices are sold almost exclusively to hospitals, since they cost in excess of $100,000 each. There are several hundred Atech devices currently in use in hospitals throughout the country. Atech, which claims a trade secret in the internal workings of its device, carefully monitors the purchasers of its device. Alpha pays a third party to buy a device from Atech without disclosing that it will be given to Alpha. Once it has obtained the device, Alpha disassembles it and studies it in order to compare it to Alpha's own device. In the course of opening it up, Alpha's engineers pick two internal padlocks on the Atech device. When Atech discovers that Alpha has obtained the device, it demands the unit's return, offering to refund the purchase price. Alpha refuses, and Atech sues for misappropriation of trade secrets.

1) Assume that Atech's trade secrets were worth $5 million. Assume further that the padlocks cost $5 each, and that it costs $100 per lock to pick these padlocks. Has Atech taken reasonable precautions to preserve its secrets? What other security measures must Atech take -- and at what cost -- both to deter Alpha (and others) from reverse engineering and to preserve its secrecy? Does Atech's sale of the products on the open market automatically preclude a finding of secrecy?

2) Assume Atech has presented the buyer of the machine with a contract that licenses (rather than sells) the machine, subject to the following restrictions: (a) the buyer is prohibited from disclosing anything it learns during the course of using the machine; (b) the buyer is prohibited from reselling the machine; and (c) the buyer is liable for Atech's damages in the event that any third party learns of Atech's secrets from the buyer or the buyer's machine. Is such an agreement enforceable? Would you advise a client thinking of licensing an Atech machine to sign the contract? How would you redraft the agreement to protect the buyer?

3) Assume that, after Alpha's engineers picked the padlocks, they gained access to the inner workings of the machine. Assume further that they discovered numerous flaws in the imaging mechanism that caused potentially serious defects in the images (and hence the diagnoses) stemming from the Atech machine. Finally, assume that Alpha's engineers not only fixed these problems but significantly improved on Atech's design and hence the reliability of the machine. Should these facts affect Alpha's liability? Atech's remedy?

PROBLEM 2-11

Bonnie Bluenote, a world-famous blues guitarist, is noted for her distinctive sound, which she gets by tuning her guitar specially every time before she plays. Although the guitar itself is a standard professional model, Bonnie's adjustments of settings on the guitar, amplifier, and sound system combine to produce a distinctive sound. Because the sound is so important to her image, Bonnie guards it carefully. While she is tuning her guitar, only band members and close associates are allowed in the room. When she records in a new studio, she has the sound engineers sign nondisclosure agreements.

One day Freddie Fender-Rhodes, a big fan of Bonnie's and a budding bluesman himself, is hanging around outside the studio where Bonnie is recording her newest album. He happens to see an ID tag, worn by all guests in the studio, in the wastebasket. He fills in his name and walks into the studio. The band members and recording engineers, seeing the tag, let Freddie stay. He observes how Bonnie tunes her guitar, sees the sound board settings, and makes extensive mental notes.

Five months later, Bonnie is shocked to see in a record store a CD by Freddie titled "The Bonnie Bluenote Sound." Upon investigation, she discovers that Freddie is planning to publish an article in Blues Guitar magazine revealing the secrets to Bonnie's sound. Does she have any recourse against Freddie?

Analysis

Problem 2-9:

MG Arguments

Gene could begin by arguing that any gene sequence that was published in the public human genome database *before* inclusion in the MG database precludes trade secret status for those sequences. There would be very little competitive advantage in sequencing a gene that is already available for free on the world wide web. The difficulty of proving priority in this setting may prove problematic for both Gene and MG, however.

For sequences that were first available in the MG database, Gene's argument becomes more difficult. Recall clause [1] of the MG Agreement that Gene signed:

> [1] Customer, upon accepting this Access Agreement, agrees that the Genetic Data accessible hereon is and will be a Trade Secret of Company, and further agrees not to disclose, publish, or otherwise disseminate said Genetic Data to any other company, person, or institution. Customer also agrees that payment under the Payment provision herein will continue as provided for in this Agreement, notwithstanding the subsequent disclosure, publication, or other dissemination of any portion of said Genetic Data by a third party not subject to this Agreement.

The issue here is partly contractual: does the phrase "Genetic Data accessible hereon" refer to data specifically derived from access to the database, or to all data identical to that contained on the database, however derived?

The issue presents some interesting problems of proof; these might conceivably bear on the substantive resolution of the issues involved. MG may well argue that Gene was led to a particular sequence by first consulting the database. The "independent discovery" of a sequence in this scenario would be merely an after-the-fact cover for use of the database. Indeed, the attractiveness of this course of action might influence a court's interpretation of the contract. "Genetic Data accessible hereon" could be interpreted to mean data identical to the database data, whether actually derived from the database or not.

On the other hand, such an interpretation would arguably be at odds with the policy judgment underlying the "competitive advantage" standard for trade secrets. Permitting trade secret status for widely-known information imposes costs with no offsetting benefit.

What if Gene had in fact derived the sequence from the MG database, but it later became freely publicly available in the Human Genome Database? Under the classic *Warner-Lambert* case, Gene is out of luck: the agreement provides for continuing royalties, and the fact that the information subsequently became publicly available is irrelevant. The only argument Gene might muster here is speculative: because the *Warner-Lambert* case was truly a bilateral trade secret license, it may have been fair to permit the contractual undertaking to trump trade secret policy, which (as noted earlier) disfavors trade secret status for widely available information. Gene could argue that the online form license ought not to be treated as seriously as the more conventional bilateral contract in *Warner-Lambert*.

IceGene Arguments

The key issue with respect to IceGene will be the "reach through" license provision, which reads:

> [2] Customer agrees to pay to the Company a royalty of 5 per cent of the gross selling price of any diagnostic kit, therapeutic drug, or other commercial product developed as a result of Customer's access to or use of the Genetic Data contained herein.

Gene will try to argue that this "reach-through" agreement violates antitrust law or equitable principles underlying trade secret law. This may prove difficult in the trade secret context. While some cases hint at the possibility of a trade secret "misuse" doctrine, discussion of the doctrine has for the most part been limited to situations involving formal property rights – patents and copyrights in particular. *See.* Bayer AG v. Housey Pharmaceutical, 228 F.Supp.2d 467 (D.Del. 2002) (patent misuse alleged in reach-through royalty arrangement in biotechnology industry; misuse defense rejected after careful analysis of licensing practices). The "take it or leave it" nature of online contracting may figure into this argument, but it is not clear whether that will be an important factor. Traditional misuse cases often involve situations where a licensor "imposed" terms on an unwilling licensee, but the usual proof of this is that the licensee proposed, and the licensor rejected, less oppressive terms. Negotiation and dickering of this sort are of course not possible in the online contracting environment.

Problem 2-10: This case is loosely based on the facts of *Acuson Corp. v. Aloka Co.*, 257 Cal. Rptr. 368 (Ct. App. 1989). The California Court of Appeal held that "Alpha" was immune from liability, on the theory that once a product was released in commerce, it was liable to reverse engineering, regardless of how Alpha obtained it. The California Supreme Court "depublished" *Acuson* -- removing it from the official reporters, a procedure which generally indicates dissatisfaction with a result but does not leave California with any affirmative law on the subject. Other courts have reached a similar conclusion to the Court of Appeal in *Acuson*. *See Roboserve, Ltd. v. Tom's Foods, Inc.*, 940 F.2d 1441 (11th Cir. 1991). On the other hand, other courts have condemned more extreme forms of espionage even though the subject products were in the public domain. *See, e.g., Rockwell Graphic Systems v. DEV Industries*, 925 F.2d 174 (7th Cir. 1991); *Integrated Cash Management Services v. Digital Transactions, Inc.*, 920 F.2d 171 (2nd Cir. 1990).

This problem serves once again to remind students to look to the definition of a trade secret, rather than merely to the means used to get a hold of one. The law in this area is not completely satisfying, however. Should the result in a case involving products in the "public domain" depend on the methods used to get those products? Suppose that Alpha had physically broken into Atech's offices and stolen a machine. This constitutes larceny, certainly, but misappropriation of trade secrets? Why is the machine more of a secret than a VCR stolen out of a private home?

The problem also raises the important issue of whether Atech could change this result by contract. The key is whether the license to users would be enforced; if it is, this would make Alpha's acquisition wrongful. The Fifth Circuit in *Vault v. Quaid* [cited in the text] held that you couldn't prevent reverse engineering by shrinkwrap license in the *copyright* context, but it is not clear that the same result would obtain for trade secrets law. Indeed, some courts [cited in the text] have come to the opposite conclusion in the case of bargained contracts involving trade secrets. The Supreme Court's decision in *Kewanee Oil Co. v. Bicron* strongly suggests that reverse engineering is a necessary part of trade secret law, mandated by federal patent preemption. It is reasonable to conclude from this that states can't abolish the reverse engineering limitation; perhaps for similar reasons private parties can't either. This issue is important and unresolved; we discuss it in more detail in Chapter VI.

The other facts in the problem -- the ease of reverse engineering and the value added by Alpha -- are really side issues. While providing only minimal protections within a product might be evidence that a trade secret owner has not taken reasonable precautions to protect the secret, in this case the limited sales and close supervision Atech engaged in suggest that it has done enough to satisfy this requirement. The improvements Alpha makes to Atech's secrets are not legally relevant to the misappropriation case, though one could make the argument that they should be.

Problem 2-11: The problem assumes that this is a protectable secret, though it is possible that the information would not qualify as secret if anyone at a concert with binoculars and a tape recorder were able to discover the settings. The real issue in this problem is: did Freddie get access to the information by "fair and honest means", as the comment to UTSA § 1 requires? The answer seems fairly clearly to be no -- Bonnie took at least some measures to prevent him from accessing the studio. However, it is interesting to note that other visitors were allowed, and they could lawfully have reverse-engineered the sound. The problem may be used to get students discussing the policy merits of reverse engineering, and in particular the idea that some people but not others may be permitted to use the resulting information.

PROBLEM 2-12

Helen, an employee of CarTech, is assigned to work on solving a particular problem in car design. She works for two years on that problem for CarTech, without success. Two months after Helen leaves CarTech to start her own company, she puts out a product that incorporates a solution to the same problem. CarTech sues Helen for misappropriation of trade secrets. At trial, CarTech proves that Helen came up with her system while at CarTech, and that she decided to start her own company to exploit her invention rather than disclose it to CarTech. As a result, CarTech had no knowledge of the idea until Helen came out with her product. Should CarTech prevail in its trade secrets suit, assuming that there was no employment or invention contract between the parties?

Analysis

Problem 2-12: Interestingly, courts say no. The theory is that information in H's possession which was never revealed to CarTech can not be CarTech's trade secret. Since CarTech has no trade secret, H cannot be liable for misappropriation. *SI Handling Systems v. Heisley*, 753 F.2d 1244, 1259 (3rd Cir. 1985). Of course, H should be liable for other torts, such as a breach of duty of loyalty or breach of confidence. H may be liable for breach of contract as well.

Whether this is a valid reading of the trade secrecy requirement probably depends on the jurisdiction in which it is applied. Under the Restatement of Torts, a trade secret is defined as "information . . . used in one's business," suggesting (as the court found) that information not used by the employer does not belong to that employer. Both the UTSA and the Restatement (Third) of Unfair Competition, by contrast, are silent regarding the required knowledge of the putative trade secret owner, speaking instead only in terms directed to the secret itself (ie. that it must derive economic value from not being generally known). It is doubtful whether the same result would obtain in a jurisdiction that followed either rule.

This problem also provides a useful introduction to the next section of the reading, regarding assignment and trailer clauses. Employers use such contractual provisions in large part to avoid problems like that faced in *SI Handling*. Such clauses make it clear that the employee has the *duty to assign* to employer inventions made during employment, or for a certain time thereafter. Failure to assign such inventions, or a former employee's use of them after assignment, may provide an independent basis for liability.

PROBLEM 2-13

You have been offered a position with a high-technology start-up company. They ask you to sign the following agreement. Do you sign it? Is it enforceable?

EMPLOYMENT, CONFIDENTIAL INFORMATION, AND INVENTION ASSIGNMENT AGREEMENT

As a condition of my employment with Science Company, its subsidiaries, affiliates, successors, or assigns (together the "Company"), and in consideration of my employment with the Company and my receipt of the compensation now and hereafter paid to me by the Company, I agree to the following:

1. ***Confidential Information***

(a) ***Company Information.*** I agree at all times during the term of my employment and thereafter, to hold in strictest confidence, and not to use, except for the benefit of the Company, or to disclose to any person, firm or corporation without written authorization of the Board of Directors of the Company, any Confidential Information of the Company. I understand that **"Confidential Information"** means any Company proprietary information, technical data, trade secrets or know-how, including, but not limited to, research, product plans, products, services, customer lists and customers (including, but not limited to, customers of the Company on whom I called or with whom I became acquainted during the term of my employment), markets, software, developments, inventions, processes, formulas, technology, designs, drawings, engineering, hardware configuration information, marketing, finances, or other business information disclosed to me by the Company either directly or indirectly in writing, orally, or by drawings or observation of parts or equipment. I further understand that Confidential Information does not include any of the foregoing items which has become publicly known and made generally available through no wrongful act of mine or of others who were under confidentiality obligations as to the item or items involved.

(b) ***Third Party Information.*** I recognize that the Company has received and in the future will receive from third parties their confidential or proprietary information subject to a duty on the Company's part to maintain the confidentiality of such information and to use it only for certain limited purposes. I agree to hold all such confidential or proprietary information in the strictest confidence and not to disclose it to any person, firm, or corporation or to use it except as necessary in carrying out my work for the Company consistent with the Company's agreement with such third party.

2. ***Inventions***

I agree that I will promptly make full written disclosure to the Company, will hold in trust for the sole right and benefit of the Company, and hereby assign to the Company, or its designee, all my right, title, and interest in and to any and all inventions, original works of authorship, developments, concepts, improvements or trade secrets, whether or not patentable or registrable under copyright or similar laws, which I may solely or jointly conceive or develop or reduce to practice, or cause to be conceived or developed or reduced to practice (collectively referred to as "Inventions"), during the period of time I am in the employ of the Company and for three months thereafter, except as provided below. I further acknowledge that all original works of authorship which are made by me (solely or jointly with others) within the scope of and during the period of my employment with the Company and which are protectable by copyright are "works made for hire," as that term is defined in the United States Copyright Act.

3. ***Conflicting Employment***

I agree that, during the term of my employment with the Company and for a period of one year thereafter, I will not engage in any other employment, occupation, consulting, or other business activity in competition with or directly related to the business in which the Company is now involved or becomes involved during the term of my employment, nor will I engage in any other activities that conflict with my obligations to the Company.

4. ***Returning Company Documents***

I agree that at the time of leaving the employ of the Company, I will deliver to the Company (and will not keep in my possession, recreate or deliver to anyone else) any and all devices, records, data, notes, reports, proposals, lists, correspondence, specifications, drawings, blueprints, sketches, materials, equipment, other documents or property, or reproductions of any aforementioned items developed by me pursuant to my employment with the Company or otherwise belonging to the Company, its successors or assigns.

5. ***Notification to New Employer***

In the event that I leave the employ of the Company, I hereby grant consent to notification by the Company to my new employer about my rights and obligations under this Agreement.

6. ***Solicitation of Employees***

I agree that for a period of twelve (12) months immediately following the termination of my relationship with the Company for any reason, whether with or without cause, I shall not either directly or indirectly solicit, induce, recruit or encourage any of the Company's employees to leave their employment, or take away such employees, or attempt to solicit, induce, recruit, encourage, or take away employees of the Company, either for myself or for any other person or entity.

Analysis

Problem 2-13: This problem should allow students to recap all of the rules learned in this section. A number of state statutes which govern contractual restrictions on employees, and in particular covenants not to compete, may be relevant in deciding whether the contract is enforceable in a particular jurisdiction. Examples of such statutes include:

Cal. Labor Code § 2870, which provides that an employer may demand that an employee assign his or her rights in all inventions developed while at the company, except that inventions which do not relate to an employer's business and were developed wholly on an employee's spare time need not be assigned.

Cal. Bus. & Prof. Code § 16600, which broadly provides that "every contract" restraining someone from engaging in a business or profession is void. California courts have interpreted the language of this section narrowly, to allow "reasonable" restraints on competition only in certain limited circumstances, such as when the restrictions are ancillary to the sale of a business. Even those restraints must be narrow and strictly defined.

Texas Bus. & Com. Code Ann. § 15.50, which provides that covenants not to compete are lawful only if they are ancillary to an enforceable agreement and contain reasonable limitations on the time, scope and area of restraint.

On the basis of the common law, and most state statutes, most of the provisions set forth in the problem are enforceable to some extent. Some present problems, or at least issues, however.

First, there is no obvious geographic limitation to the work prohibition. This is not necessarily fatal, *see Comprehensive Technologies* [cited in the text], but it is suggestive of overbreadth and is likely to be closely scrutinized. Courts often apply a "least restrictive means" sort of analysis to such provisions, seeking to determine whether the employer could have protected itself with a narrower provision. In such cases, it is an open question whether the court should rewrite the restriction itself or declare the entire agreement unenforceable. *See Texlon Corp. v. Hoffman*, 720 F. Supp. 657, 663-66 (N.D. Ill. 1989) (Illinois no longer maintained per se rule against worldwide restraints; worldwide restraint was unnecessary in this case; court would therefore refuse to enforce agreement at all). The one year provision seems reasonable, but the restriction is not directly limited to competition with the former employer. If drafted more narrowly, it would have a greater chance of survival. Note, though, that some cases appear to demonstrate unremitting hostility to noncompetition agreements. *See Puritan-Bennett Corp. v. Richter*, 679 P.2d 206, 210-12 (Kan.

1984) (non-competition agreement was enforceable only to the extent necessary to prevent disclosure of trade secrets).

A second questionable provision concerns the assignment of inventions clause, which extends beyond the term of the employment contract. Whether this particular provision is overbroad will depend on the jurisdiction in which it is being enforced. Most courts have been willing to enforce such holdover provisions in some cases, but they scrutinize them strictly. *See Ingersoll-Rand Co. v. Ciavatta*, 542 A.2d 879 (N.J. 1988). In California, the provision is likely to be doomed under Cal. Labor Code § 2870 because it does not include an exemption for inventions made outside the scope of employment.

The definition of confidential information covered in the contract, while broad, is probably generally acceptable. The only problem may be presented by the inclusion of an employee's personal customer contacts in the definition of a trade secret. Courts may define such information as within the general knowledge of an employee, particularly since such personal relationships are virtually impossible to restrict in a reasonable way.

Chapter 3 Patent Law

A. Introduction

B. Elements of Patentability

1. Patentable Subject Matter

Diamond v. Chakrabarty, page 120, expanded the already broad categories of patentable subject matter to include (in the famous dictum) "anything under the sun that is" human-made. Chakrabarty, a microbiologist, filed a patent application for genetically engineered bacterium that could break down crude oil. The PTO wanted these kinds of inventions to be patentable but found themselves limited by the Plant Patent Act and the Plant Variety Protection Act which stated that living things were generally not patentable; this was in essence a ginned-up "test case" where both parties favored the same outcome. (Would better advocacy have changed the result, or did the PTO make all the obvious arguments here?) You might point out that when the Plant Patent Act was enacted (1930) nothing that scientists were doing was in any way "threatening" (e.g., grafting was not patentable because people were worried that they would not be able to adequately describe inventions under patent law's disclosure/enablement requirement.) Contrast this with the current fear (paranoia?) over "frankenfoods" that are genetically engineered. The formalist dissent in *Chakrabarty* stated that it was Congress' role to broaden or narrow the reach of the patent laws.

In *Parke-Davis v. Mulford,* page 128, the court held that human intervention rendered a process for isolating purified adrenaline patentable. Judge Learned Hand distinguished the process and product at issue from *Latimer*, an earlier case in which fiber taken from the needles of a pine tree was deemed not patentable. Learned Hand determined that the purified substance was "a *new* thing commercially and therapeutically" (emphasis added). This eminently pragmatic result was crucial to the later development of the biotechnology industry. It is also a fine example of judicial resistance, or at least response, to the sorts of metaphysical distinctions and analyses that IP law all too often presents. The case may also be used to introduce (or, in a pinch, even cover) the topic of "novelty" in patent law; "nature's library" serves as a good example of the "prior art" against which patentability is measured.

You may also want to discuss the current status of patenting business concepts here and the effect that it has had on software patents. After *State Street Bank* [Chapter 7], methods of business are patentable. A concept or way to carry out business no longer needs to be tied to a specific program or hardware. You may ask your students whether patenting something like Federal Express would be a good or bad idea. The key point is that we (society) received the benefit of Federal Express in the mid-1970s without granting a patent on it; indeed, competition in this area was rapid and robust, with the expected (downward) effect on price.

PROBLEM 3-1

Inventor A discovers a technique for purifying Hormone Z from human tissue and applies for a patent on the purified form of the hormone. Inventor B discovers the gene coding for the hormone, clones it, and obtains expression in a mammalian cell culture environment. Are these inventions/discoveries patentable?

Analysis

Problem 3-1: In fact, both types of inventions are patentable. The *Parke-Davis* and *Merck* cases discussed in the text clearly suggest that purifications of natural products are patentable subject matter, at least to the extent that the purification is sufficient to create a new utility for the product. [*Brenner v. Manson*, discussed in the next section, suggests at least some potential limits on purification patents].

Is there a difference between purification of a hormone from human or animal tissue and production of the hormone through genetic manipulation in bacteria that ought to affect patentability? While genetic manipulation tends to raise more moral hackles than purification from animal tissue, perhaps simply because the technology is so new, the courts and the Patent Office clearly permit such patents. [The **Nature** article cited in the text suggests that many such patents already exist]. The most problematic of such patents from a patentable subject matter standpoint are the patents issued for human genes or gene fragments simply because they have been identified and isolated. These gene fragments are clearly "products of nature," though one could argue that they have been "purified" by analogy to *Parke-Davis*, and that they have therefore been given a new utility.

The final question raised by this problem concerns the form such patents should take. Courts tend to find process patents uncontroversial, but patentees tend to prefer product patents because their potential scope is much broader. *Chakrabarty* and *Parke-Davis* both suggest product patents are available for purification, isolation, or recombination. But perhaps the product-by-process claim in *Merck* represents a reasonable middle ground in terms of scope.

PROBLEM 3-2

In 1986, an American scientist by the name of John Anderson perfected a process that yielded a new man-made chemical element. The element, named Litigacium (Li), was assigned atomic number 116. Anderson's method of synthesizing the element involves using a neutronic reactor at relatively high power (about 200 kilowatts) for approximately 100 days. Anderson's patent application noted that a suitable reactor for producing Litigacium is described in a 1984 patent of Dr. Enrago Firmi.

Although Anderson's process claim met with no resistance from the Patent and Trademark Office, the claim relating to the product Litigacium raised more difficult issues. An examiner notified Anderson that his claimed element was not patentable because it preexists in nature, in some form, since a chemical element can not truly be "man-made."

Dr. Anderson has asked you to represent him in his appeal to the Federal Circuit. The appeal presents the following issues:

a) The Patent Office admits that the level of Litigacium produced under natural circumstances -- e.g., in the intense heat and pressure that accompanies the collapse of certain large stars -- would be minuscule. For example, the examiner states that using well-known theoretical calculations star collapse would result in an infinitesimally small amount of the element spread throughout an enormous amount of other matter under tremendous heat and pressure. How can the mere possibility that a star would create an undetectable amount of Litigacium permit rejection of your client's patent application?

b) The examiner concedes that it would not be practical given current technology to "harvest" Litigacium from natural sources such as stars. Should this have a bearing on the outcome of the case? Is it the function of section 101's patentable subject matter requirement to find patentable anything that is cheaper (i.e., more efficient) for humans to make than to harvest in raw form from nature? Or is section 101 an expression of a deeply felt aversion to permitting humans to claim "authorship" over products given to us by nature's bounty? Is there a viable distinction between things we "find" in nature and things we ourselves "invent"? Does the language in the patent clause of the Constitution -- i.e., that patents shall be conferred to inventors for their "discoveries" -- shed any light on these matters?

PROBLEM 3-3

You are a newly elected United States Senator. As part of your duties on the legislative committee assigned to introduce intellectual property legislation, you have been asked to co-sponsor a bill that seeks to re-write section 101 of the patent code. According to the sponsor of the bill, the "archaic" language of the current section 101 was drafted during the era of "quill pens and buggy whips." She claims that it is therefore "out of step in an era of computers and space shuttles."

Several lobbyists have seized on the occasion to introduce their pet revisions into section 101. Environmentalists have asked that "newly discovered natural products" be added to the categories of patentable subject matter; they believe this addition will create an incentive to identify and preserve rare species of potential benefit, e.g., as ingredients in medicines or as sources of raw materials. In addition, academic scientists have testified that they feel "slighted" by the exclusion of natural laws and scientific principles from the coverage of the current patent act. They have stated that they fail to see why the patent system should discriminate against basic research, especially in an era when federal funding of science is shrinking. Even the social scientists have gotten into the act. A famous economist who pioneered a revolutionary technique for measuring the volume of money in circulation testified in hearings on the bill that he would have continued thinking up pioneering ideas like this but "the current system gave me no incentive to do so, at least after I made tenure." And some sports stars have sent letters to your committee, claiming that they wish they had received some form of protection for what everyone refers to as their "patented" backhand or putting style or hurdling technique.

How can you evaluate these claims? Is there any justification in refusing to change the current language -- e.g., because it has shown enough flexibility to adapt to computer technology and biotechnology and the like? Is there anything special about traditional technology -- machines, manufactures, etc. -- that makes it more valuable, or more in need of protection, than other "innovations" such as newly discovered natural products, new "pure" science results, new academic theories, or new techniques for doing business (such as the leveraged buyout, or the multidivisional corporate structure)? Why not grant property rights over all sorts of new things, and let the market figure out which ones are truly worthwhile?

Analysis

Problem 3-2: This problem is based on *In re Seaborg*, 328 F.2d 996 (C.C.P.A. 1964), in which Glenn Seaborg claimed "Element 95." The court's opinion deals primarily with the "inherency" doctrine, which is treated in the section on novelty. A refined version of the problem is presented there. However, the case also presents interesting issues regarding the "product of nature" limitation on patentability. The case is somewhat more problematic than most recombinant DNA cases, since those cases present heterologous bacteria which would never exist in nature. By contrast, the product of an element merely replicates in a laboratory physical processes which can and do occur in nature, albeit in an inaccessible location.

Should that natural existence bar patentability of "man-made" Litigacium? *Parke-Davis* would seem to say no. But how much difficulty is required? Is it patentable if the natural one can be found only in Antarctica? If it costs 10 times as much? 50% more? 5%? In practice, courts seem to draw the line of patentability at "practical utility" -- only improvements significant enough *to affect the market* for the stuff are patentable. It is worth considering whether this test is workable, and what problems it might produce if applied to ordinary process or apparatus patents.

Another interesting question is raised by the fact that Anderson does not get a "product by process" patent, but instead claims "Element 116." Presumably, this includes natural residue too. Should he be forced to limit himself to a product-by-process claim?

Problem 3-3: Should we limit patentable subject matter at all? In particular, why not allow the patenting of formulae? Of natural products? Of sports moves? [One example of the last is U.S. Patent No. 5,498,162, issued for a method of demonstrating a weightlifting technique].

One problem may be practical -- everyone would require licenses for some laws of nature (e.g. gravity), and for thinking certain thoughts. But this is not necessarily a debilitating objection to most patents, and indeed there are certain industries where doing virtually anything requires the doer to traverse a minefield of patents. Further, the limited duration of patents arguably alleviates this problem to some extent: Einstein might be able to patent $E = mc^2$, but only for a limited time.

There may also be moral objections to certain of these patents, but hardly more than the objections to patenting life.

A more practical question may be to ask whether such patents will really encourage more basic research and invention in a variety of fields. Since basic research by definition is not immediately applicable to products, a market-based reward (rather than, say, government or private subsidies) seems entirely the wrong way to go about encouraging it.

At the business end of the spectrum, the problem may be the opposite -- patents are *too* effective in rewarding their owners. Business methods might be judged self-rewarding; companies like Federal Express have sufficient incentive to innovate because of first-mover advantages and the like, and awarding them a patent would simply reduce the healthy competition expected from other businesses. On the other hand, excluding such patents at the subject matter level sweeps awfully broadly, and it is not clear that there is any empirical reason to believe that business methods are less deserving of reward than any particular area of technology.

Finally, in some cases the restrictions are necessary to "channel" certain types of innovation into protection by one form of intellectual property rather than another. The printed matter exception, for example, rejects patents on new books primarily because such books are separately protected by copyright law. These channeling mechanisms are imperfect, however, as we will see when we consider computer software in Chapter 7.

2. Utility

Brenner v. Manson, page 136, shows the Supreme Court measuring the purpose of a patent by asking when in the inventive process a valid patent application may first be filed. The Court stated that promising results did not meet the utility requirement. The Court rejected J. Story's definition of utility which would allow any invention that did not positively harm society to be patented. The Court worried that an early granted patent would block off research and not provide society with any tangible benefit. An inventor after *Brenner* now has to wait longer to file a patent application with any confidence that a patent will be issued. However, the lack of patent protection may make it difficult for an inventor or small company to obtain capital to fund more research and development.

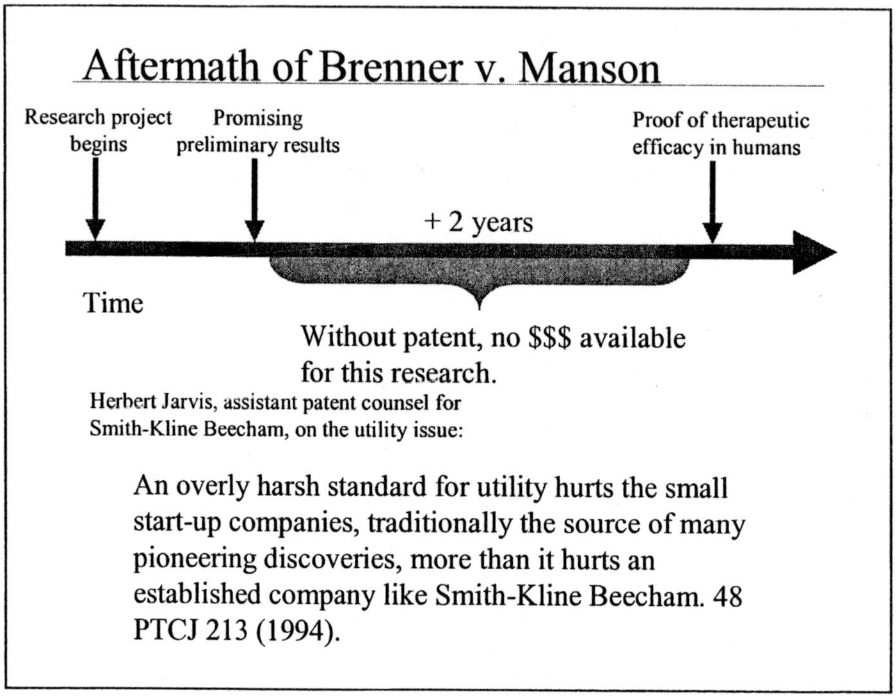

This figure can be used to illustrate one of the implications of *Brenner*.

PROBLEM 3-4

Acid Look, Inc. (ALI) is a fabric design company that specializes in designing jeans for the high-end fashion market. ALI develops a process for producing a "random faded effect" on the fabric of new jeans, catering to the market for new jeans that appear to be pre-worn. ALI seeks a patent not only on the process of treating the jeans to produce a random faded effect, but on jeans treated by this process. The patent examiner rejects the claim to pre-faded jeans on the ground that they lack utility. Is this rejection proper? What test of utility is being applied here?

PROBLEM 3-5

Craig Venter, a scientist at the National Institutes of Health, began a project in 1991 to obtain the genetic sequences for many of the natural chemical compounds or proteins that work in the human brain. His plan was to take advantage of the fact that of the many DNA sequences in human genetic material, only those that "code" for operational proteins are found in a certain form -- the "cDNA" form. (The "c" in cDNA stands for complementary.) A complementary DNA sequence is one that is constructed at the site of the gene and is transported to the protein-creating site in the cell -- the ribosome. (The cDNA sequence forms as chemicals called bases "match up" with the base pairs comprising the DNA sequence on the gene; the "matching up" occurs because the DNA's double helix structure allows it to split apart temporarily like a zipper unzipping.) Scientists believe that only 3 percent of the DNA in the body actually "codes" for some useful protein -- the other 97 percent is a mystery.

Venter's project was to get a listing of the sequence of base pairs in the active, protein-encoding DNA sequences in a human brain. Getting all the "raw" sequences together was easy; he used widely available "libraries" of all the active DNA sequences found in various bodily tissues. (These are made by working backward from the cDNA "complementary copies" of the sequences that can be found in the relevant cells.) His contribution was to partially "sequence" the DNA -- to obtain a base pair by base pair "listing" for as many cDNAs as he could. Before his work, there were libraries of DNA fragments, but no one had obtained detailed base pair sequences for each fragment.

In practice, he only had to sequence a portion of the DNA segments, and from that portion the entire sequence could be identified. (He called the partial sequences "expressed sequence tags," or ESTs.) This is one part of the larger project to sequence the entire human genome.

In a patent application, Venter claims each of the ESTs he has produced. He also claims fragments of the ESTs, complementary versions of each, and other variants.

Venter claims there is utility in his invention. Specifically, he asserts that the ESTs can be used to (1) map chromosomes, i.e., help give a general idea of the location of the genes on a chromosome; (2) identify tissue types (specifically, tell whether a given sample of tissue comes from the brain or not); and (3) identify gene regions associated with a disease, by drawing cDNA from patients, matching it with its associated EST, and seeing if the EST identifies a particular gene region unique to those with the disease.

Has Venter in fact recited utility? Are the suggested applications "too remote" from known, practical applications? If in fact each application Venter recites is no more than an invitation to further research -- e.g., assistance in mapping chromosomes is helpful only when the mapped chromosome is later used to identify and treat a genetic problem -- how do you distinguish this case from *Brenner*?

Analysis

Problem 3-4: This problem is based on the facts of a 1995 case from the Southern District of New York involving a patent for "stone-washed jeans." *See Levi Strauss & Co. v. Golden Trade*, No. 92 Civ. 1667 (RPP), 1995 U.S. Dist. LEXIS 4899 (S.D.N.Y. Nov. 30, 1995). The court in that opinion rejected the patent on utility grounds, reasoning that "there was no *useful* difference between the jeans made with the applicant's process which displayed a random faded effect and those made with prior art processes which displayed uniform effect." The case presents the interesting question of utility for "frivolous" inventions. Acid-washed jeans don't *do* anything except look fashionable, but that is generally sufficient. Entertainment is sufficient utility to satisfy the patent laws. Indeed, there are any number of patents that issue for simply bizarre inventions (such as U.S. Patent NO. 4,998,724, for a "ThumbWrestling Game Apparatus With Stabilizing Handle." An entertaining collection can be found in Rick Feinberg, **Peculiar Patents** (Citadel Press 1994)). Further, it is reasonable to object to the court's opinion on the grounds that the patented products were marketable because of the invention -- that is, for whatever reason, they commanded a higher price than jeans not treated with the process. Surely an increase in market value suggests utility.

How does the existence of "useful" patents for frivolous (or at least nonproductive) inventions interact with *Brenner*? The chemical there is arguably at least as "useful to society" as faded jeans or thumb-wrestling rings. The difference seems to be not that the chemical doesn't *have* any utility, but that the chemists in *Brenner hadn't discovered* that utility. In the words of the court: "such a patent may confer power to block off whole areas of scientific development, without compensating benefit to the public." If there is a good argument for the result in *Brenner*, it is that the chemists there were engaged in "preemptive patenting" -- locking up inventions without discovering what use they might have.

Brenner has not been treated well by subsequent courts. The recent Federal Circuit decisions on biotechnology, *In re Brana* in particular, seem flatly at odds with the decision. Further, Justice Harlan's dissent seems the better view, at least in cases where the "intermediate product" is itself marketable to scientists for research purposes.

Problem 3-5: Much has been written on Craig Venter and the cDNA patent applications. *See, e.g.,* Rebecca S. Eisenberg & Robert P. Merges, *Opinion Letter as to the Patentability of Certain Inventions*

Associated With the Identification of Partial cDNA Sequences, 23 **AIPLA Q.J.** 1 (1995). Venter abandoned the patent application under public pressure after a non-final rejection by the Patent Office. For examples of actually issued "gene fragment" patents, see US Pats. 5,817,479 and 5,654,173.

The Craig Venter problem presents two different utility issues. First, it is an extreme test of *Brenner*. The basic point of the first stage of the human genome project is to produce a general map of the base pairs. That map doesn't do anything. Further, it doesn't tell you anything of practical utility about the genes in the sequence. But it does allow future efforts to locate the genes that cause specific functions or diseases, and possibly future efforts to repair or replace defective genes. If you don't give Venter a patent, arguably there will be no incentive to produce this needed map. [In fact, however, federal and university funding of much of the genome project may cast serious doubt on this argument.] If you do give him a patent, Venter can control subsequent work with immense practical consequences. If most of the value of the project is resident in stages of the work that have yet to be done, granting broad patent rights on early stages may discourage competitors from doing socially productive work using the ESTs. For a stimulating account of why this might be so, see Michael Heller and Rebecca Eisenberg, *Can Patents Deter Innovation? The Anticommons in Biomedical Research*, **280 Science 698 (1998)** (arguing that mistakes in biomedical patent policy may create too many fragmented rights and result in too few life-saving innovations).

Second, the question of patenting parts of the human genome raises issues of moral utility. Most people have a negative reaction to the idea of "patenting life," even though the concept is well-established by now in patent law. ESTs aren't "life", of course, in the sense that the transgenic mouse [*see* U.S. Patent No. 4,736,866] is life. On the other hand, they are a part of the human body, and patenting them conjures up cyberpunk-style fears of patent ownership of living human beings. Thus, the Venter problem is one way to introduce the issue of moral limits on patentability.

3. Novelty and Statutory Bars

A trio of cases demonstrates the rigid, mechanical nature of the novelty standard in patent law. A useful way to organize discussion is to start by asking what purposes such a rule might serve. It might be pointed out that multiple requirements for patentability serve as successive screens or "filters" for weeding out meritorious inventions from unpatentable ones; thus an argument can be made for a simple, mechanical, relatively uncontroversial (and therefore cheap) screen at the initial stage, followed by more fine-grained but nuanced filters later in the process. Of course, mechanical rules can produce unfair results; and even "bright line" rules can lead to controversy – witness the difficulty in determining just how "public" a reference must be to be within the prior art.

Rosaire v. National Lead Co., page 149, reveals a patent for oil prospecting invalidated because another inventor used the same method more than one year prior. Here the novelty requirement was not met even though the information was not published. Novelty is an absolute standard; it does not matter what the inventor subjectively knew at the time of the invention. It might be worth asking why the patent examiner who worked on the patent application that led to the patent in the case did not turn up this particular prior art "reference" (i.e., prior public use); this is a good entre to a discussion of judicial review of patents, the presumption of validity under 35 USC § 282 (should it stay in force where a court confronts prior art not before the examiner), and similar issues of patent system "design." Some treatment here of the (relative) rigors of the examination system will lay the foundation for a comparative inquiry into the minimalist copyright system and the less-rigorous but nontrivial trademark registration process.

PROBLEM 3-6

As described in an earlier problem, physicist John Anderson has isolated and produced a new element in the laboratory -- Litigacium, element 116. Although Anderson is the first person to have produced Litigacium in any appreciable amount, and the first to have isolated it, mathematical calculations based on prior experiments show that Dr. Firmi's nuclear reactor inherently produces 3/1,000,000,000 of one gram of Litigacium every year that it operates. Further, this minute amount of Litigacium is spread among 40 tons of highly radioactive uranium fuel, making it impossible to recover or isolate. Nonetheless, Dr. Firmi and his coworkers were aware at the time they ran the reactor that it was producing trace quantities of Litigacium. Dr. Anderson claims "element 116" in a patent application. Is this claim anticipated by Firmi's prior work?

Analysis

Problem 3-6: This was the issue in the *Seaborg* case (*In re Seaborg*, 328 F.2d 996 (C.C.P.A. 1964)). Anderson produces Litigacium and isolates it by a new method. The Patent Office rejects his claim on the grounds that Firmi's reactor *inherently* produces identical material in undetectable trace amounts. Further, Firmi knew of the existence of Litigacium in his reactor, though he had no desire and no way to get access to it. Is the patent anticipated?

The problem presents an oblique take on the problem of "secret prior art." If an open process is all that is required, Anderson could not obtain a patent, especially since Firmi knew of the existence of the trace elements. But since Fermi couldn't isolate the stuff, perhaps it is more reasonable to say that the product was not "known or used" in any meaningful sense by Firmi, even though he "made" it. Certainly Firmi has not given the public the "benefit" of the new element, while Anderson has.

There is also a *Brenner* issue here, since it is not clear what use element 116 is to anyone other than theoretical physical chemists.

In re Hall, page 154, concerns a patent barred by publication of a graduate thesis that was in the prior art more than one prior to the application. Although the dissertation was in a foreign library, there was sufficient public access to the work. Here is the "bright line" approach at work: it is unlikely the thesis would meet the requirements of a more fact-intensive or open-ended novelty standard such as "reasonably accessible to the public." But again, this has its virtues: there is little controversy in most applications of the test. In some areas of patent law, evidently, hard cases have not in fact made bad law. Instead, the law says "tough luck" – in the interest of greater certainty.

PROBLEM 3-7

In late 1967 the Navy encountered a problem with its new fighter plane. The Navy's aircraft - stationed on aircraft carriers - were more likely to suffer structural damage than Air Force planes of the same type that were positioned on land. Navy scientists concluded that the widespread problem of fuselage cracking, known as "stress corrosion," was attributable to the harsh marine environment. The Navy presented its problem to the aluminum industry and Algol Corp. was awarded a research contract to develop a new alloy that would be more resistant to the phenomenon.

Pursuant to the terms of the defense contract, Algol would periodically report on its research results in "progress letters." The Navy drew up a distribution list of 33 designees to receive Algol's progress letters, and each letter bore the following "export control" notice: "This Document is Subject to Special Export Controls and Each Transmittal to Foreign Governments or Foreign Nationals May Be Made Only With Prior Approval of the Naval Air Systems Command."

The designees included aluminum producers (including Algol's competitors), aircraft manufacturers, government agencies, branches of the military, and academic researchers. Several progress letters were mailed, the last on April 5, 1969. As of the last progress letter, Algol had succeeded in developing a high-strength, stress-corrosion-resistant alloy that met the Navy's needs. Algol successfully applied for a patent covering its process for aging and treating its new alloy on February 5, 1971.

When Algol refused to license the patent to its competitor Richards, the latter began to manufacture and sell a high-strength alloy using Algol's patented technology. Alcoa filed suit alleging infringement.

You are Senior Counsel for Intellectual Property Matters at Richards Aluminum. Your defense strategy is limited by the fact that if the Algol patent is valid, your company is undeniably engaged in infringement. Algol gathers evidence that the 33 designees who received Algol's progress reports treated them as highly confidential although they contained no express limitation on access other than the export control notice. Depositions of Richards' own executives reveal that your company kept its copies of the letters in a protected area, screened even from some of its own employees. Such procedures were typical in defense industry circles when a report bearing an export control notice was received. Nevertheless, the absence of any other access restrictions on the letters supports Richards' argument that Richards could have shared the report's contents with every American citizen. Is the patent anticipated by Algol's prior "publication"? If so, under section 102(a), or under section 102(b)?

Analysis

Problem 3-7: This problem is based on *Alcoa v. Reynolds Metals*, 14 U.S.P.Q.2d 1170 (N.D. I.. 1989). Algol (Alcoa) does not "publish" its technology, but discloses it in a "progress letter" mailed to 33 companies (including its client the Navy, its competitors, some other potential customers, and some academics). The letter describing the invention is mailed more than 1 year before the application is filed. The letter is *required* by the Navy, and everyone who receives it treats it as confidential, even though the actual restrictions on distribution are pretty minor. Is this a publication that bars the patent?

There are good arguments on both sides. In favor of treating this as an anticipatory publication, Reynolds might argue that everyone in industry who cared got the letter, so the information was in fact delivered to anyone who would likely be interested; there was no explicit confidentiality restriction on redistribution within the US; if *Hall* is a publication, this should qualify too, as it is much more publicly accessible; and (from a policy perspective) Alcoa should have been more diligent in filing its patent application. On the other hand, the letter was not available outside the circle of 33 in practice, so it was not accessible to the "general public"; even if there was no express restriction on use of the information, a confidentiality restriction could reasonably be implied; and, from a policy perspective, we want to encourage limited disclosures of information consistent with trade secrecy. The court held that this letter was *not* public, primarily because it was treated by the recipients as if it were received under an obligation of confidentiality. In the court's words, "an understood, even though silent, limitation on access can be every bit as effective as an express one." It is interesting to consider this holding in light of the *Egbert* case which follows.

Note that this letter, if a publication, would create 102(b) anticipation, but NOT 102(a) anticipation (since it was by definition after the date of Algol's invention). This point is worth testing, to make sure that students understand the distinction between the two.

Egbert v. Lippmann, page 157, the famous "corset case," teaches that if an inventor gives or sells her invention to another without restriction, limitation or injunction of secrecy; such use is public, even when it is only used by one person, and even if the use does not disclose the structure of the invention to others. The inventor of the corset stay was barred by public use of his invention by his girlfriend. The court is concerned at least in part about reliance by third parties who might deduce that there is no patent when (1) the invention has been marketed for a long period of time, and (2) no patent has ever issued to cover it. Though unusual in some respects (the "slept on his rights" usually produces a chuckle from students – rare enough in the patent section of the course!), many inventions are not readily discernible (e.g., levers, springs) when publicly used. Even so, an inventor may be profiting commercially from their sale; and another important policy here is the prevention of an unwarranted extension of patent term. Long public use, coupled with a subsequent patent, gives the inventor/seller effective exclusivity in the market for the product that far exceeds the statutory patent term. Some inquiry into other practices that achieve the same thing in a perfectly legal way, such as intentionally long patent application pendency periods, should reveal that this is by no means a uniform policy in the law. Note that, after the GATT amendments of 1995, long pendency now involves a tradeoff, since patent terms are measured from the date of filing (with some rather elaborate exceptions in the now-ornate 35 USC § 154).

PROBLEM 3-8

Scientists involved in the field of spectroscopy were being haunted by ghosts. Spectroscopy is the study and analysis of materials to determine their components and molecular structure. One form of spectroscopy, magnetic resonance spectroscopy, works by observing a material's reaction to imposed radiation. A spectroscope bombards the sample material (usually contained in a test tube) with pulses of radio frequency radiation and then records and analyzes the material's response. If the signal response given by the material was weak, the spectroscope would often confuse interfering noise and static for the material's response. Scientists attempted to solve the problem of unwanted frequencies (or "ghost" frequencies) by various mathematical manipulations.

One such scientist was Daniel Murray, a doctoral candidate studying at Oxford under the supervision of Sir William Akeroyd. In the course of his experiments, Murray arrived at a means of "ghostbusting" through shifting the phase of the frequency transmitter at 90 degree angles between pulses, thus avoiding sophisticated manipulations of data. A patent application embodying the Murray invention was filed in the United Kingdom on April 8, 1984 and in the United States on December 21, 1986. Murray secured patent protection in both countries by 1989.

In the spring of 1983, Akeroyd attended a scientific meeting in Boulder, Colorado. On a bus ride during the conference, Akeroyd engaged Dr. Christopher Squire in an informal conversation. Squire headed a research team at the U.S.-based Monsanto Company which developed related technology for use in the company's chemical analyses. Akeroyd informed Squire of the promising results of Murray's preliminary research on the phase shifting spectroscope. By 1985, Squire had updated his spectrometer at Monsanto to include a similar phase shifting transmitter.

Squire immediately applied his improved spectrometer technology to assess whether a particular Monsanto herbicide was safe for release into the environment. This was a project Squire's team had been working on for a full year prior to the improvement in the lab's spectrometer. Excited by the improved results, Squire invited several of his superiors and fellow employees into the lab to observe his data.

Is Squire's use a public use under section 102(b)? Does your analysis depend on any of the following hypothetical facts:

* Dr. Squire was the only person who was permitted access to the Monsanto lab where the updated spectrometer was located.
* Anyone *could* have entered the lab, but in fact Squire was the only one who did.
* The only person who set eyes upon the updated spectrometer besides Squire was a Monsanto custodian.
* Squire left the door unlocked regularly at night.
* The phase shifting transmitter is located deep inside the apparatus and cannot be seen without dismantling the spectrometer.

Analysis

Problem 3-8: This problem is loosely based on *National Research Development Corp. v. Varian Assoc.*, 822 F. Supp. 1121 (D.N.J. 1993), *aff'd in part* 30 U.S.P.Q.2d 1537 (Fed. Cir. 1994). This case points up the difference in standards between public use and publication. Murray invented an improvement in NMR spec. His boss mentions the improvement to a Monsanto employee on a bus, apparently without Murray's knowledge or consent, and Monsanto altered its device to incorporate the invention. Monsanto uses the device to test popular chemicals, and published the test results, but did not publish the invention.

The court saw two basic issues here: (1) was the disclosure to Monsanto made under an obligation of confidentiality, as in the *Alcoa* problem discussed above; and (2) if not, was Monsanto's use of the information "public" because it was in the ordinary course of their business? On the first issue, the court had no trouble rejecting the theory that the disclosure was impliedly confidential, since it was not expressly restricted and in fact was made at a conference designed to promote intellectual discourse.

On the second issue, the court says one use *for profit* is enough to constitute a "public use" within the meaning of section 102(b), even though Monsanto kept the invention confidential (and even though Murray would probably have objected to this use). Only if they had taken extraordinary precautions -- amounting to *not using the invention* in the ordinary course of their business -- would the use not be considered public.

The Federal Circuit notes that "this result furthers the important public policy of discouraging the removal of inventions from the public domain which members of the public justifiably have come to believe are freely available." This problem – perhaps in conjunction with *Egbert* -- provides a useful way to introduce the difficult policy problem of "submarine patents."

Of the cases in the notes, *Pfaff v. Wells* may perhaps merit special attention. The Supreme Court's new "ready for patenting" test in § 102(b) "on-sale bar" cases is worth a moment's discussion. What problem does the new test try to solve? Why is reduciton to practice – clearly the more "certain" moment in the history of most inventions – a poor choice for the beginning of the on-sale bar clock? If the concern is that a patent applicant may strategically delay completion of an invention, two points are worth discussing: (1) non-statutory bar reasons to counsel against delay (being first to reduce to practice confers advantages in interference proceedings, e.g.); and (2) third party on-sale (and other § 102(b)) prior art, over which the applicant has no control. (Consider the *W.L. Gore* case, also discussed in the notes, for an example of a court perhaps stretching to exclude third-party § 102(b) prior art, a move that might be motivated by thre fact that third-party prior art presents challenging issues from the perspective of the goals § 102(b) is trying to serve.)

In *City of Elizabeth v. Pavement Company,* page 163, the Supreme Court created an "experimental use" exception to the public use statutory bar. There was no other way for the inventor to test the durability of his wooden pavement invention other than to use it in public. Here we have another exception to the apparently far-from-sacrosanct policy against long public use prior to filing a patent application. One policy of the on-sale bar is supposedly to protect the public's "reliance interest" on the *non-existence* of a patent; a competitor who observes a product on the market for a long period of time, and diligently checks issued patents all the while, is supposed to be able to conclude that it is safe to imitate the product at some point (long) after it is introduced. Is there any way for such a competitor to find out whether a particular product will be subject to the "experimental use" exception to the statutory bar? Note in this context that the advent of publication of patent applications eighteen months after filing (in effect now in the U.S. for all applications having counterparts filed abroad) may undermine the point somewhat.

Griffith v. Kanamaru is an effective introduction to the vagaries of the U.S. "first to invent" system. It is worthwhile before jumping into the case reviewing several "easy" cases under § 102(g). Posit an inventor, A, who both conceives and reduces to practice before another inventor, B. Note that in this scenario, the respective dates of each activity are all that matters; A's "diligence" under the statute is irrelevant. Diligence – the issue in *Kanamaru* – matters *only* in the special case where B conceives before A, but reduces to practice after A. The following timeline is conventionally used to describe these cases:

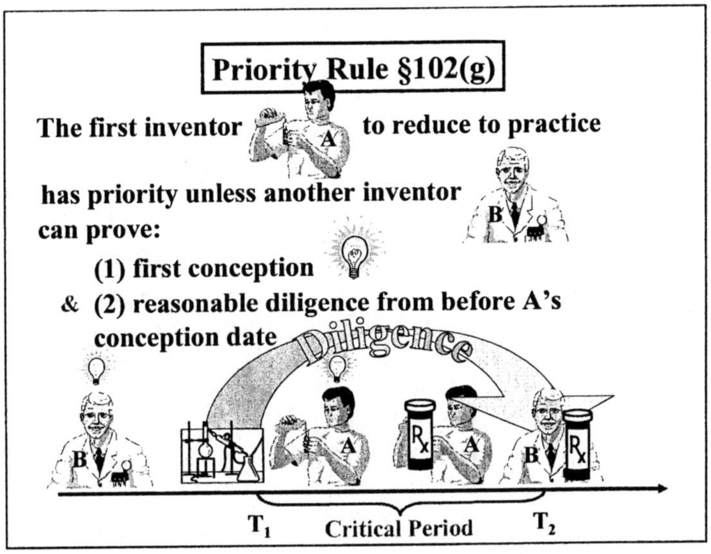

Where T1 is, in the words of the statute, "a time prior to conception by the other," i.e., A here.

After constructing these diagrams, and perhaps exploring for a moment the evidentiary requirements called for by the various rules stated in § 102(g) (e.g., proof of the reason for the delay in this case, waiting for the graduate student), it is worth pointing out that under a first to file rule the case would come out the same way – at far lower cost to the litigants and society (i.e., consider the time invested in interferences by Patent Office officials). A full review of the intricacies of the first to invent system is often the best argument in favor of the simpler first to file rule in place throughout the rest of the world!

4. Nonobviousness

In *Graham v. John Deere,* page 172, the Supreme Court invalidated the patent for a spring clamp in a plow because moving the position of the clamp was obvious to someone with ordinary skill in the art. The Court lists the now-famous factors to consider in determining nonobviousness: (1) the scope and content of the prior art; (2) the differences between the prior art and the current claim; and (3) the level of ordinary skill in the pertinent art. Secondary considerations, we are told, "may be relevant"; these include commercial success, a long felt but unsolved need, the failure of others, copying, and unexpected results. It should be pointed out that these secondary considerations are now treated as a very important and indeed coequal "fourth factor" in many Federal Circuit decisions.

Graham v. John Deere

Is it obvious to move the hinge plate from position A under the shank to position 1 above the shank?

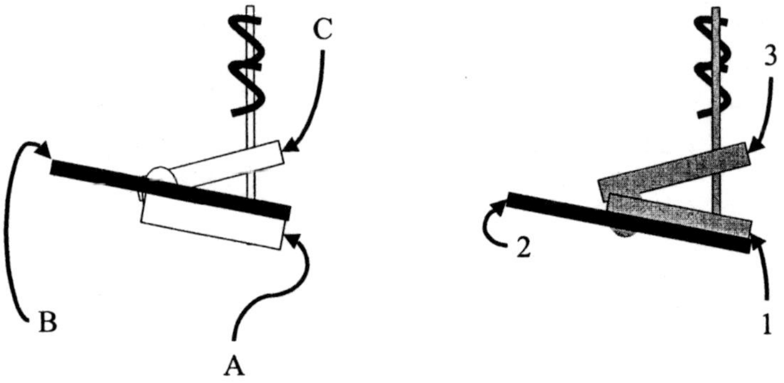

This figure might be used to show how moving the hinge plate would be obvious to one skilled in the art.

In re Vaeck, page 184, involved a genetic engineering technique to produce proteins in cyanobacteria hosts. The court found the invention to be nonobvious because there was no suggestion to combine references in prior art and there was no reasonable expectation of success. One possible explanation for this and other cases: the standard for non-obviousness seems to be low for biotech inventions because research is expensive; inventors need additional incentives to innovate.

You might ask whether *Graham* and *In re Vaeck* are fundamentally inconsistent. It depends on the level of abstraction. Does the art teach away? Did we really need the offer of a patent to induce this kind of research or invention? We may presume that without a patent, many things will not be done because they are too costly. In the *Graham* case it is difficult to use commercial success evidence because we cannot attribute increased sales to a single improved feature; market demand and technical sophistication are not necessarily related. In *Vaeck*, the court did not think the invention was obvious. A lot of people tried but had little expectation of success.

PROBLEM 3-9

You have drafted a patent application for a client claiming a lollipop in the shape of a human thumb. An examiner rejected the claims as obvious over a combination of numerous prior art references. You must now prepare an argument trying to overturn the Examiner's decision by appeal to the Board of Patent Appeals and Interferences. The claimed invention consists of a lollipop filled with a plug of gum, chocolate or food-grade wax. A thumb-shaped elastomeric mold served as the product's wrapper, and after it was peeled from the candy, the user could wear the mold on his or her own thumb. The examiner relied on the following prior art references in rejecting claims to the thumb-shaped lollipop invention:

a) Siciliano shows ice cream in a mold with a stick inserted. The removable mold also serves as the product's wrapper.

b) Copeman shows candy lollipops in elastomeric molds taking "varying shapes, such as fruit or animals." The molds may be used as toy balloons after being removed.

c) Harris shows a hollow thumb-shaped lollipop into which the user's thumb is inserted.

d)	Webster shows a chewing gum entirely enclosing a liquid syrup product. This patent also suggests the greater appeal to consumers of providing two different components in the same confection.

Although some of the references cite at least one other reference, no reference explicitly suggests combining its teaching with that of any other reference. What is your basis for arguing that the invention is patentable?

Analysis

Problem 3-9: This problem is based on *In re Gorman*, 933 F.2d 982 (Fed. Cir. 1991). The prior art references are taken directly from that case, which also includes several other references and attractive diagrams of the thumb lollipop. The court upheld the Board's finding that the invention was obvious. The court first noted that all the elements of the invention appeared in the prior art in different combinations. However, the court found suggestions in many of these references (such as the ice cream mold) that the same ideas could be used in analogous arts. Further, the court considered it important that the purpose of the invention was identical to the purposes of the elements contained in the prior art references.

The problem is a good exercise in actually going through an obviousness analysis, and may introduce students to the ad hoc judgment calls that are made in many of these cases. The case also provides a useful counterpoint to *Vaeck*, suggesting that combining even a large number of references is sometimes permissible.

5. Describing and Enabling the Invention

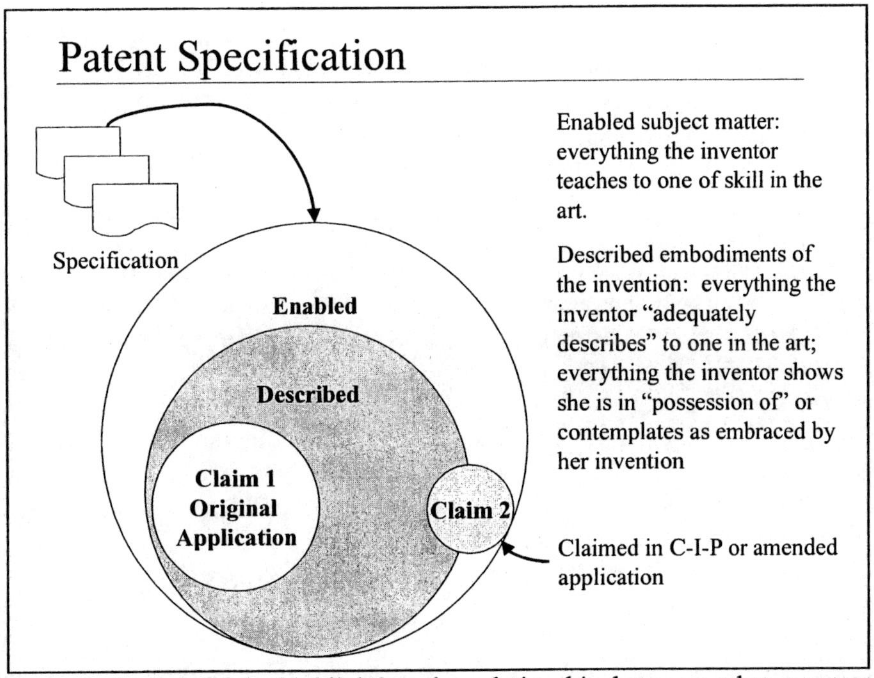

This figure may be helpful in highlighting the relationship between what a patent teaches, what is described, and what is actually claimed. Claim 2 is an example of an amendment that an inventor might make to preclude competitors from entering the market. See *Gentry Gallery*.

The Incandescent Lamp Patent, page 197, illustrates the downside of overly broad claims. There was nothing in the Sawyer/Mann patent that would enable one with ordinary skill in the art to discover the subset of bamboo that Edison found. If the description is so vague and uncertain that no one can find it without independent experimentation to find which of the embodiments work, then the patent is void. The presence of Edison as defendant often produces two mistaken thoughts in the mind of students: (1) that this is an interference, or that Edison's famous light bulb patent is somehow at issue; and (2) that Edison in fact had access to the Sawyer and Mann patent, which failed to instruct him properly in his search for the ideal incandescing material (bamboo). As to the first point, Edison is involved strictly as a defendant. On the second, there is of course no requirement that one skilled in the art *have actual access* to a patent specification; only that *if he or she had*, it would have guided them in the construction of claimed embodiments without undue experimentation. Edison's herculean labors would not have been *reduced* if he had closely followed the specification, in other words; nor would any other researchers have been aided in trying to determine which of the many "fibrous and textile materials" claimed actually worked as effective filaments.

Gentry Gallery v. Berkline Corp.

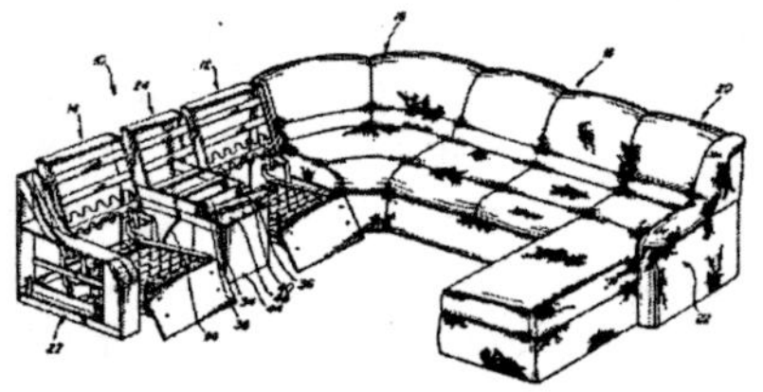

Disclosed: A sectional sofa segment with a pair of reclining seat sections built into it with a console that accommodates the controls. The push button controls may be mounted on the top or sides of the console.

Claimed: A sectional sofa comprising a pair of reclining seats, a fixed console, and a pair of control means mounted on the double reclining sofa seat section.

This figure may be used to illustrate several concepts: (1) the importance of the written specification; (2) the relationship between the specification and the claim; and (3) the canon of claim construction that claims should be interpreted such that the preferred embodiment falls within their scope.

If you are interested, you might do some "armchair" research (so to speak) on the web; check out http://www.berkline.com/duet.html for a good look at the double reclining sofa sold by the accused infringer. Note the center console, sans reclining controls; other photos on the website show controls on the side of various sofas, near but not on the armrests of certain Berkline products. Note that the practice of monitoring competitors' products during the pendency of a patent application is quite commonplace; does *Gentry Gallery* suggest this is no longer worth the trouble – because post-filing amendments will always be held unsupported by the original "written description"?

A good question to ask in this section is what differences there are between the new written description requirement and the old enablement requirement. Do we need two tests?

C. Infringement

PROBLEM 3-10

Slice-O-Rama is a company that makes food preparation items, including cheese slicers. It owns a U.S. patent covering a cheese slicer with a novel twist: the cutting element is a wire, which can be stretched between an end point and a handle. The slicer is well-received by the public, and is even the subject of a national design award. One element in the claim calls for "a cutting wire" stretched between a handle and a fixed point on the base of the cutting element arm (see Figure 3-5).

OmniCorp is a large conglomerate with numerous divisions in various industries. One division, BigChem, Inc., is in the business of developing and manufacturing plastics. In the wake of research on new plastics, BigChem has come up with a plastic that is capable of holding a sharp cutting edge. Deemed "sharpylene," it can be manufactured in a variety of thicknesses, including a very thin version that looks like a wire or piece of string. As part of an internal initiative to encourage various divisions of OmniCorp to work more closely, Fran Fromage, product manager for the food processor and blender product lines in OmniCorp's FoodMulch division comes across a sample of the BigChem plastic. Being familiar with the popularity of the Slice-O-Rama cheese slicer, she hits on the idea of substituting BigChem's new plastic in place of the metal wire. She believes that this cheese slicer would be an important addition to the FoodMulch product line. She is aware of the Slice-O-Rama patent, but as she puts it, "how can that patent stop us from selling blades made from plastic that *we invented*?! Those folks at Slice-O-Rama have never even heard of sharpylene!"

You are a member of the patent department at OmniCorp. Assuming that the FoodMulch cheese slicer will meet all limitations other than the "cutting wire" element in the Slice-O-Rama patent, how would you advise Ms. Fromage?

Analysis

Problem 3-10:

This problem serves a number of functions. Its primary purpose is to introduce concepts related to infringement. (Placement at the beginning of the infringement section will facilitate discussion of the issues on a "first principles" basis – before the admittedly complex infringement doctrines have been introduced.)

The obvious issue here is one highlighted in the Supreme Court's *Festo* opinion – the problem of "after-arising" technologies. Does OmniCorp's cheese slicer incorporating "sharpylene" infringe Slice-O-Rama's patent? The important fact to focus on is that sharpylene had not been invented at the time the Slice-O-Rama patent issued. Hence there is no way that the cheese slicer patent could possibly have been drafted so as to intentionally embrace the use of sharpylene in the blade.

In Problem 3-10, the infringer is also the inventor of the "after-arising" technology. This presents an opportunity for students to debate the relative merits of the patentee and the creator of the after-arising technology. From an economic incentive point of view, what are the effects on the sharpylene inventors of a rule which permits Slice-O-Rama to capture the value of sharpylene used in certain cheese slicers? On the other hand, what if sharpylene is clearly superior to Slice-O-Rama's best alternative cutting wire material? Will a ruling in favor of OmniCorp effectively destroy Slice-O-Rama's market, thus undermining incentives for the *next* inventor trying to create something along the lines of the cheese slicer?

One issue that may arise in a discussion of this problem is whether OmniCorp is entitled to a patent on the *improvement* of using sharpylene in a Slice-O-Rama cheese slicer, and if so, what effect this might have on the problem. A discussion along these lines might provide an occasion for a quick review of patentability doctrines. Any claim in the improvement patent that specifically recites sharpylene will establish novelty, since this element is missing from the prior art. The key issue is therefore likely to be obviousness. This raises an interesting issue in itself – whether the combination of the preexisting Slice-O-Rama elements and the sharpylene blade is different enough from the prior art to deserve a patent. Comparisons with the *John Deere* case may be in order here. How is rearranging the plow shank in that case like substituting sharpylene for the next best blade? (Both changes are motivated by a straightforward desire to improve performance. But sharpylene is an entirely new material, whereas all the plow elements in *John Deere* were old, "off the shelf" components.)

Note that if OmniCorp/BigChem obtains a patent, this is likely to significantly impact any negotiations between that company and Slice-O-Rama. In particular, if the sharpylene improvement provides a significant advantage that is recognized in the market, OmniCorp's patent may prove valuable indeed. Economists call this sort of bargaining situation a "bilateral monopoly" – each side needs the other if either is to tap the market for the improved product. Rational actors may bargain to split the proceeds 50-50, but other strategies – including many that are rational on their own terms – lead to other outcomes. In some percentage of cases, we may even expect the parties to fail to reach agreement. These cases of "bargaining breakdown" are one cost of granting what amounts to a "split entitlement" over the market for improvement inventions.

The problem can also be analyzed in less utilitarian terms. Who deserves to dominate the market for cheese slicers with sharpylene blades? Obviously, both Slice-O-Rama and OmniCorp/BigChem contributed to the availability of the sharpylene cheese slicer on the market. Perhaps it is worthwhile to consider some subsidiary issues. How large is the overall market for sharpylene compared to the market for sharpylene cheese slicer blades? How large is the market for cheese slicers with sharpylene blades compared to the overall market?

The problem may also serve as a useful springboard for discussions of the relationship between enablement/written description and infringement. For this purpose, the key fact to highlight is once again the unavailability of sharpylene at the time the Slice-O-Rama patent was drafted. Surely the Slice-O-Rama inventors were not "in possession" of the sharpylene embodiment when the patent issued – yet they may have a claim for infringement. How can this be squared with the principle of cases such as *Gentry Gallery*, which employ the "possession test" to invalidate claims that go beyond the specific embodiments disclosed in the originally-filed patent specification? Is it fair to permit an embodiment such as the sharpylene cheese slicer to be covered by the Slice-O-Rama patent, while excluding other embodiments that are enabled by the Slice-O-Rama patent specification but not specifically called out as required by cases such as *Gentry Gallery*? Note that the "foreseeability" test of *Festo* may go a long way toward reconciliation here. Looked at from the perspective of *Festo*, embodiments enabled but not "described" are ones that the inventor *could have* described and claimed with precision but chose not to. Compare this to the sharpylene cheese slicer, which the inventor could not possibly have foreseen. (Notice the interaction between the improvement patentability issue mentioned earlier and the foreseeability test: a nonobvious improvement such as the sharpylene cheese slicer is one that is, *a fortiori*, unforeseeable prior to its creation.) If you can get the students to follow out this line of thinking, you may lead them to what appears to be a bit of a paradox: the original property right may be stretched to cover a significant, unforeseeable improvement, but not a minor, straightforward variation.

1. Claim Interpretation

Note on Interpretive Sources

The material in this section is important to an understanding of the Federal Circuit's interpretive approach. At the same time, because the court seems bent on tweaking and even overhauling doctrine in this area on a regular basis, it is difficult to keep this section of the book current. For those who wish to keep their students fully up to date, here is a summary of recent trends since the third edition of the casebook went to press. For those in need of a more general approach, perhaps a broad admonition to the effect that these doctrines are a moving target may be in order.

The main development has been the elevation of dictionaries (and presumably other reference sources) to the "preferred" status of "intrinsic" evidence concerning the meaning or terms used in a claim. A key case in this trend is Texas Digital Systems, Inc. v. Telegenix, Inc., 308 F.3d 1193, 1202-1203 (Fed.Cir. 2002), where the court stated:

> Dictionaries are always available to the court to aid in the task of determining meanings that would have been attributed by those of skill in the relevant art to any disputed terms used by the inventor in the claims. See Vitronics Corp. v. Conceptronic, Inc., 90 F.3d 1576, 1584 n. 6, 39 USPQ2d 1573, 1578 n. 6 (Fed.Cir.1996) ("[T]echnical treatises and dictionaries ... are worthy of special note. Judges are free to consult such resources at any time ... and may also rely on dictionary definitions when construing claim terms...."); Cybor Corp., 138 F.3d at 1459, 46 USPQ2d at 1177 (citing Vitronics for the proposition that a court is free to consult dictionaries, encyclopedias, and treatises at any time to help determine the meaning of claim terms); Vanguard Prods. Corp. v. Parker Hannifin Corp., 234 F.3d 1370, 1372, 57 USPQ2d 1087, 1089 (Fed.Cir.2000) ("A dictionary is not prohibited extrinsic evidence, and is an available resource of claim construction.").

When a patent is granted, prosecution is concluded, the intrinsic record is fixed, and the public is placed on notice of its allowed claims. Dictionaries, encyclopedias and treatises, publicly available at the time the patent is issued, are objective resources that serve as reliable sources of information on the established meanings that would have been attributed to the terms of the claims by those of skill in the art. Such references are unbiased reflections of common understanding not influenced by expert testimony or events subsequent to the fixing of the intrinsic record by the grant of the patent, not colored by the motives of the parties, and not inspired by litigation. Indeed, these materials may be the most meaningful sources of information to aid judges in better understanding both the technology and the terminology used by those skilled in the art to describe the technology. These materials serve as important resources to assist courts in many ways. . . .

As resources and references to inform and aid courts and judges in the understanding of technology and terminology, it is entirely proper for both trial and appellate judges to consult these materials at any stage of a litigation, regardless of whether they have been offered by a party in evidence or not. Thus, categorizing them as "extrinsic evidence" or even a "special form of extrinsic evidence" is misplaced and does not inform the analysis.

The *Texas Digital Systems* opinion has been criticized on one ground: it seems to suggest that courts should consult dictionaries even before looking to the specification of a patent itself. *See* Ben Hattenbach, *Chickens, Eggs and Other Impediments to Escalating Reliance on Dictionaries in Patent Claim Construction*, 85 J. Pat. & Trademark Off. Soc'y 181 (2003). Hattenbach makes the common sense suggestion that the specification be consulted in conjunction with dictionaries. Other Federal Circuit cases take a similar approach. In *Inverness Medical Switzerland GmbH v. Princeton Biomeditech Corp.*, 309 F.3d 1365 (Fed.Cir. 2002), for example, the court states:

[Relevant] dictionaries include dictionaries of the English language, which in most cases will provide the proper definitions and usages, and technical dictionaries, encyclopedias and treatises, which may be used for established specialized meanings in particular fields of art. The parties here do not argue that the term "mobility" has an established specialized meaning in technical dictionaries, encyclopedias, or treatises of the relevant field of art, and we agree that "mobility" has no such specialized meaning. Accordingly, standard dictionaries of the English language are the proper source of ordinary meaning of the phrase. We may look, therefore, to the dictionary definition of the claim term "mobility" as of the date the patents issued. As with most words, the standard dictionaries offered multiple definitions. "[W]here there are several common meanings for a claim term, the patent disclosure serves to point away from the improper meanings and toward the proper meaning." Renishaw PLC v. Marposs Societa' per Azioni, 158 F.3d 1243, 1250, 48 USPQ2d 1117, 1122 (Fed.Cir.1998) . . .

309 F.3d at 1369-70 (footnotes omitted).

Finally, on the question of which dictionary definition should prevail – the one in place whenthe patent was filed, or when it was issued – the suggestion in *Texas Digital Systems* that it is the issue date that wins has now been reaffirmed. *See* Brookhill 1 LLC v. Intuitive Surgical, Inc., (Fed. Cir. June 27, 2003), avail. http://www.fedcir.gov (which also adopts the approach championed in the Hattenbach article cited earlier).

Literal Infringement

In *Larami Corp. v. Amron,* page 226, Larami wanted a declaratory judgment that its Super Soakers were not infringing Amron's squirt gun patent. The court found that the Super Soakers did not literally infringe Amron's patent because the water chambers were detachable ("thereon") and not contained inside the gun ("therein"). You might point out that there may be a strategic reason why Larami would want to talk about its own patents—to highlight that their inventions must be different. You may also want to conduct an exercise to show how difficult claim drafting really is. For example, you can have the students come up with another term for "therein."

Right to Jury Trial at Law

ROLE OF JUDGE	ROLE OF JURY
• determines questions of law	• resolves questions of fact
• claim construction	• whether the claim as interpreted by the judge covers the alleged infringer's product or process
• injunctive relief	• determines damages

You might use this comparison as an introduction to the topic of patent litigation dynamics.

3. The Doctrine of Equivalents

A bit of background may aid in understanding the two recent Supreme Court opinions on the doctrine of equivalents.

Before 1870, patents were not required to have formal claims in the way they do now. Inventors often concluded their specification with a general statement to the effect that their legal rights extended to the invention "substantially as described herein," or the like. Because of this, it was often necessary to compare the detailed description of the invention with the particulars of the defendant's product to determine whether infringement had taken place. A famous example of this – and the earliest generally recognized instance of the doctrine of equivalents – was the case of *Winans v. Denmead*, 56 U.S. 330 (1854). In *Winans*, the patentee had invented a coal car having a cylindrical body. The defendant began making and selling a car with an octagonal body. The Court, speaking in terms of the "substance" and "principle" of the plaintiff's invention, reversed a judgement in favor of defendant, and remanded for consideration of issues deeper than the mere "form" of the invention as described in the specification.

The introduction of formal claiming in 1870 ushered in the modern era of the doctrine of equivalents. Prior to 1870, patents were said to involve "central" claiming: a general definition of the invention was given, and courts were asked to move outward to determine whether an accused product infringed the principle at the center of the claim. After 1870, many commentators believe that patent claims shifted to a system of a "peripheral" claiming: the claims were now said to determine the outer edge or periphery of protection, and only those inventions inside the literal terms of the claims were to be found infringing. The late Judge Helen Nies provided a characteristically clear description of the problem in her dissent in the *Hilton-Davis* case. *Hilton-Davis Chemical Co. v. Warner-Jenkinson Co., Inc.*, 62 F.3d 1512, 1565 (Fed. Cir. 1995) (Nies, J., dissenting), *rev'd* 520 U.S. 17 (1997).

The Supreme Court decisions eventually coalesced around a few broad themes. These were gathered together in the important 1950 decision in *Graver Tank & Mfg. Co. v. Linde Air Products*, 339 U.S. 605 (1950). In *Graver Tank*, the Court seemed to emphasize the *equitable* nature of the doctrine, taking pains to point out, for instance, that the doctrine of equivalents (as non-literal infringement was now known) could not be made "the prisoner of a formula." The question to be asked, according to the Court, was whether the accused product performed substantially the same function in substantially the same way to achieve substantially the same result as the patented invention. This "function-way-result" test was the operative standard until the Federal Circuit got hold of the issue beginning in the 1980s.

Almost from the beginning, the Federal Circuit swung back and forth between liberal and restrictive readings of the doctrine. In cases such as *Pennwalt v. Durand-Wayland, Inc.*, 833 F.2d 931 (Fed. Cir. 1987) (in banc), the Federal Circuit stressed the need for the patentee to demonstrate that every element of a claim was infringed literally or by equivalence; this tended to shrink the application of the doctrine, by eliminating from the zone of infringement accused products which combined or eliminated elements. On the other hands, the notion of an "element" proved somewhat plastic; an example is *Corning Glass Works v. Sumitomo Electric USA, Inc.*, 868 F.2d 1251 (Fed. Cir. 1989), where the Federal Circuit seemed to backtrack from *Pennwalt* by finding infringement where the accused product inverted a series of elements to achieve the same effect as the patented invention. In the years just prior to *Festo*, the Federal Circuit continued to oscillate, most prominently in a series of cases that hinged on whether a doctrine of equivalents argument would "completely vitiate" a particular (perhaps important) claim limitation. *Compare Tronzo v. Biomet, Inc.*, 156 F.3d 1154, 1160 Fed.Cir.1998) (agreeing with defendant's argument that to find infringement under the Doctrine of Equivalents would "completely vitiate" a key limitation in the patentee's claim) *with Overhead Door Corp. v. Chamberlain Group, Inc.*, 194 F.3d 1261, 1271 (Fed. Cir. 1999) (reversing summary judgment of noninfringement: "Although the literal meaning of the 'memory selection switch' [element in the claim] does not cover the software-implemented [accused device], this case does not preclude application of the doctrine [of equivalents] because any application of the doctrine would not leave some aspect of the claim missing from the accused device. Applying the doctrine of equivalents to cover [the accused device] does not vitiate the 'memory selection switch' element."). Note that the Supreme Court in *Hilton-Davis* picked up on the "vitiation" language from these cases.

It is a good idea to test this theme with students when reviewing *Hilton-Davis*. One way to do this is to put aside the prosecution history estoppel issue at the outset and consider only infringement under the doctrine of equivalents. The key issue is whether the lower pH limitation in the claim – "at a pH from approximately 6.0 to 9.0" – is infringed by the defendant's process, which takes place at a pH of 5.0. Does it "vitiate" this element to stretch it from 6.0 to 5.0? What would true vitiation look like here – to find infringement at any pH below 9.0, i.e., to eliminate in effect the lower bound of 6.0 altogether? The conceptual difficulty of applying the "all elements" rule may become clear after some questioning along these lines. One effective technique is to contrast *Hilton-Davis* with another case that tests the limits of the all-elements rule. A good candidate here is the *Hughes Satellite* case, described in the section entitled "Note: What is a Limitation?" on pages 247-250. Pay special attention to the claim elements or limitations from the Hughes patent listed at the top of page 248. It is quite clear that these limitations are not met by the accused spacecraft, because the advent of "on board computers" makes it unnecessary to "provid[e] an indication [e.g., an electronic signal] to a location external to said [satellite] body of the instantaneous spin angle position" of the satellite. In other words, there is no longer any need to send raw data back to a large mainframe computer on earth to do the spin angle calculations. The newer generation of satellites can do the calculations on board. The Federal Circuit was not fazed by the absence of literal infringement of this element, finding in its post-*Hilton-Davis* review of *Hughes* that "the equivalent" of this element was present in the sending of calculation *results* back to earth. What does it mean to say that an equivalent of element (e) in the claim is present in the accused device? What would that device have to look like for it *not* to include element (e) – perhaps it would do all necessary calculations and take all necessary steps to correct the satellite's orientation without communicating with earth at all? Questions along these lines will help probe the actual workings of the "all elements" rule – and may expose some of its weaknesses as well.

In parallel with the doctrine of equivalents, the Supreme Court developed a limiting doctrine, called Prosecution History Estoppel ("PHE"). PHE developed early in the post-1870 "peripheral claiming" era, as a limitation on attempts by patentees to reclaim during litigation what they had surrendered in order to obtain a patent from the Patent Office. The typical PHE case involved three steps: (1) submission of an original claim by the patentee; (2) rejection of that claim by the patent examiner because of patentability concerns, e.g., novelty or obviousness; and (3) submission of an amended claim which had been narrowed from the original claim in order to avoid the patentability concerns raised by the examiner. PHE applied to prevent the applicant from reclaiming – by virtue of a doctrine of equivalents argument – subject matter claimed originally but surrendered subsequently during prosecution. The Supreme Court's decision in *Exhibit Supply Co. v. Ace Patents Corp.*, 315 U.S. 126 (1942) reviewed precedent and laid out this common sense rule.

Warner-Jenkinson marked a shift from this basic rule. First, it adopted a presumption that claim amendments are made for patentability reasons, thus triggering application of PHE by default. (Claims are in fact amended for myriad reasons.) This of course has the effect of expanding the range of PHE, thus liming the doctrine of equivalents. The rationale most often cited for this trend is to give "the public," i.e., the patentee's competitors, better "notice" regarding the actual, operative scope of the patentee's claims. This was certainly the basis for the Federal Circuit's efforts to reign in the doctrine of equivalence through an expansive application of PHE in *Festo*.

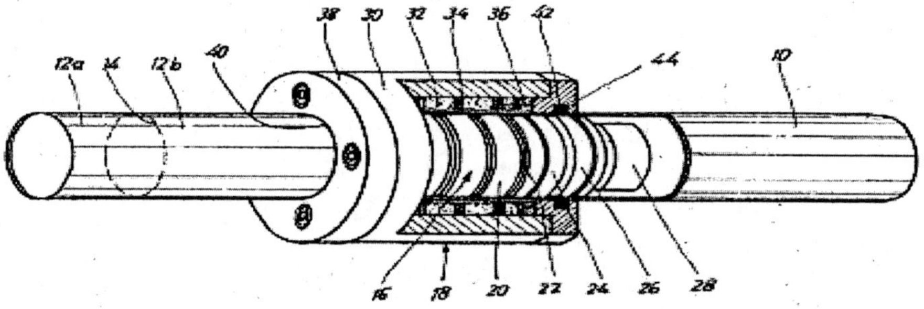

The facts in *Festo* are as follows. The diagram above shows the essence of the invention. The piston (16) is moved by the follower (18) by virtue of magnets in the piston (20) which are coupled to magnets in the follower (30). The entire piston is magnetizable. As the sleeve moves, the piston moves. Wiper rings (26) on either end of the piston prevent dirt and other crud from building up inside the piston sleeve and on its outer edge.

SMC's accused device is a bit different. It employs only a single sealing ring, and in its design the piston itself is not magnetizable.

It is useful at the outset to clarify why, in light of these differences, there is no literal infringement. Then, students may be asked to apply the *Hilton-Davis* test to the facts. Is the elimination of one sealing ring akin to changing the lower bound of the pH range in *Hilton-Davis* – i.e., does this change preserve an equivalent to the sealing ring limitation, or does it eliminate the sealing ring element altogether? For clarification, here is the relevant language from claim 1 of the Stoll Patent (U.S. Patent 4,354,125):

> *first sealing rings* located axially outside said guide rings for wiping said internal wall as said piston moves along said tube to thereby cause any impurities that may be present in said tube to be pushed along said tube so that said first annular magnets will be free of interference from said impurities . . . *second sealing rings* located axially outside said second permanent annular magnets for wiping the external wall surface of said tube as said driven member is moved along said tube in response to a driving movement of said piston to thereby cause any impurities that may be present on said tube to be pushed along said tube so that said second permanent annular magnets will be free of interference from said impurities

Does a doctrine of equivalents argument by Festo "vitiate" one or both of the "sealing ring" limitations? This might be an issue for consideration on remand, and may be worth a brief discussion.

The heart of the case is the PHE issue, however. As the Court points out, both the sealing ring and piston composition (i.e., magnetizability) elements of Festo's claims were amended during prosecution. The Federal Circuit's sweeping opinion provided for a flat bar to all doctrine of equivalents arguments in this context. The Court rejects this approach, and reinstates a more flexible version of PHE.

The first part of the opinion deals with what types of examiner rejections can give rise to the PHE rule in the first place. Here the Court sides with the Federal Circuit's majority view on this issue, which holds that any amendment related to patentability triggers PHE. A brief example of two different motivations for the same amendment may clarify the issue. Imagine the original claim in this case included as an element the phrase "means for keeping the piston/tube [i.e., piston-follower] combination free of dirt," and the examiner rejected this as indefinite or perhaps not fully enabled (both § 112 rejections). An amendment that included the language of the claim as actually issued – i.e., the two sealing ring limitations – would give rise to PHE after *Festo*. The same result would follow if the original claim had been amended to avoid a prior art reference – say, a prior patent with tiny brushes to keep a cylinder free from dirt. Whether the two sealing ring elements were added to flesh out the disclosure or to avoid a prior art reference is now irrelevant after *Festo*. The only exception is what the Court calls "truly cosmetic" amendments. Would this include a change from an original claim reciting "sealing mechanism" to an amended claim using "sealing rings," where the change was made only to maintain consistent terminology in the specification and claims? You can bet lawyers representing patentees are going to be finding many such "cosmetic" changes in future infringement cases!

Part B deals with the meat of the case: the scope of estoppel. Here the Supreme Court rejects the rigid "complete bar" announced by the Federal Circuit. In its place, the Court installs a more flexible bar, centered on the concept of foreseeability. If a patent drafter could reasonably foresee a particular infringing embodiment at the time the claim is amended, yet failed to include that embodiment within the literal terms of the amended claim, PHE applies. When the embodiment is not foreseeable, PHE will not necessarily bar application of the doctrine of equivalents.

At this point it might make sense to review the cheese slicer/sharpylene example from the beginning of this section of the chapter. A quick question on foreseeability here should help establish the continuing vitality of the doctrine of equivalents in the case of "after-arising" technologies.

The Court also establishes two other situations where PHE may not apply: (1) cases where the "rationale for the amendment bears only a tangential relation to the equivalent in question," and a residual category where PHE simply does not make sense ("some other reason"). A few questions on these latter categories might be in order, to help establish that there is still plenty of ground for contention in the equivalents/PHE area. For example, consider a hypothetical claim amendment in *Hilton-Davis* premised on enablement grounds, but made solely to speed up issuance of the patent, perhaps because of a pending product launch. If the patentee in fact believed that the specification was fully enabling with no lower pH bound, yet amended the claim to include the minimum 6.0 pH limitation to avoid a lengthy appeal from the examiner's rejection, would this qualify as a "tangential rationale" when the infringer began selling an embodiment using a pH of 5.0? As for the third, residual category, use your imagination: perhaps an amendment is made to make a claim dependent on a prior claim, simply to reduce Patent Office fees. Should estoppel apply in this case?

The entire equivalents/PHE morass has been described as an attempt to balance two competing policies: clear notice to competitors, and fairness for patentees. A noteworthy recent article by practitioner John Schlicher reviews the entire history of the prosecution history estoppel doctrine, arriving at an interesting conclusion. Contrary to the Federal Circuit majority's view in *Festo*, and consistent with what he says is the brunt of prior Supreme Court caselaw, Schlicher concludes that the "public notice" function of claims is limited to reducing the costs that *courts* bear in interpreting claims – as opposed to costs borne by the competitors of the patentee:

> The Supreme Court [in its older precedent] commonly said prosecution history estoppel arose because an applicant abandoned, surrendered, or disclaimed that the invention and the scope of rights it was seeking included certain types of devices. Whether called disclaimer, surrender, abandonment or something else, the patent owner was deemed to have agreed with the Patent Office during prosecution that the invention was not employed by products that were removed from the scope of the claims by the amendment, and the Patent Office relied on that agreement in issuing the patent. Therefore, the law protected the reliance interests of the Patent Office (that is, protected the government examination and issuing process) by preventing those claims from being construed or applied under the doctrine of equivalents to reach products that would have been within the scope of the claims before the amendment and were not after the amendment. As applied to the doctrine of equivalents, this meant the patent owner gave up the right to show that this category of products employed the invention that justified the issuance of the patent.
>
> The [Federal Circuit] Court of Appeals majority [in *Festo*] said that "The logic of prosecution history estoppel is that the patentee, during prosecution, has created a record that fairly notifies the public that the patentee was surrendering the right to claim particular matter as within the reach of the patent." The Supreme Court's decisions do not explain the reason for prosecution history estoppel as based on protecting the reliance interests of people who read the prosecution history, and reasonably believed the patent owner surrendered the right to sue them for selling certain products. The ability of the public to rely on the prosecution history depends on the what courts say is the effect of that history, not the other way round. If the courts say the law precludes a finding of infringement based upon certain events that occurred during prosecution, then that record does notify the public that the scope of the rights are limited, and the patent owner has surrendered the right to claim certain subject matter as within the reach of the patent. If the courts say that the law does not preclude finding infringement based upon the same events during prosecution, then prosecution does not create a record that notifies the public that certain activities are beyond the scope of the rights. The correct legal principle cannot be determined by simply asserting that the public is somehow entitled to rely on the history of the prosecution as establishing the scope of the rights.

John W. Schlicher, *The Law, History, and Policy of Prosecution History Estoppel in Patent Actions in the U.S. Supreme Court – Implications for* Festo *(Part I)*, 84 J. Pat. & Trademark Off. Soc'y 581, 622-23 (2002).

Johnson & Johnston v. RE Service

The invention here is fairly straightforward: a stiff, more manageable sheet for holding delicate copper sheets used in printed circuit boards. The question in the case centers on the fact that the patentee, J&J, disclosed but did not claim the use of stainless steel as the material for this stiffer "substrate" sheet. The claims were limited to aluminum sheets.

The court resolves a split in its earlier authority by adopting a blanket rule: the failure to claim the disclosed embodiment dedicates that embodiment to the public.

By itself, the rule is simple and seems to make sense. Conceptual problems with it can be explored, however, by comparing it to the reasoning and result in *Festo* and *Hilton-Davis*. To begin this line of analysis, you might want to remind the students that the jury found the stainless steel substrate to be an equivalent of the claimed aluminum material. It was, we may presume, an "insubstantial variation" on the claimed invention. If it had not been included in the specification, the use of stainless steel would have been an infringement. The obvious question is, why penalize the patentee for *disclosing* a variant but reward him or her for *not disclosing it*? Is foreseeability – the touchstone of *Festo* – the answer? If so, then would the result change if the patentee had originally included stainless steel in the specification and later deleted it from the specification without changing the claims? (Note: nothing on the face of *Festo* would suggest that amending the specification gives rise to PHE, though of course an argument along these lines might well be made.)

Another angle of approach is to focus on the strong indications that the opinion is centrally concerned with issues of "notice" to the public. Is this inconsistent with the balancing approach of *Festo*, under which notice and fairness have equal claims in the judicial process involving patents?

Finally, you might wish to consider this issue. If the stainless steel embodiment is "dedicated to the public," no one can obtain a property right to it. If RES tries to patent it, the specification of the J&J will surely stand as a bar. And of course the holding is that J&J does not own it. Does this make sense? Or does it leave an "orphan" embodiment that perhaps no one will have an incentive to develop?

4. The "Reverse" Doctrine of Equivalents

5. Equivalents for Means-Plus-Function Claims

6. Contributory Infringement

PROBLEM 3-11

Mike Molar, a production engineer for Tasty Toothpaste Corp. (Tasty) hit upon a way to make a sanitary, cheap, and small disposable toothbrush. The problem he had been running into was how to keep the toothbrush small while still providing a feature he thought necessary to make it attractive -- a built-in supply of toothpaste. The solution: a small reservoir for holding toothpaste in the handle of the toothbrush. Then the user could squeeze the toothpaste from the reservoir to the brush bristles.

He quickly built a prototype of the invention. To build it, he bought a fountain pen, pulled out the ink cartridge and other parts from the interior, tore the bristles off a toothbrush and glued them onto a hollow tube, poked two holes in the top of the tube between two rows of bristles, fitted up a plastic plunger that slid in and out at the back of the fountain pen body, pulled the plunger all the way out, filled the tube with toothpaste, glued the tube inside the fountain pen body, and pushed the plunger. Voila! Toothpaste came out of the holes more or less onto the bristles, ready for brushing. It worked! He drafted a patent specification that included this passage:

> It is one important object of the present invention to provide a portable toothbrush which is easily carried in the pocket and which is thus available whenever it is required for brushing teeth.

The open end of the device includes a reduced section portion which carries the bristles. The cylindrical body shaft includes an interior passage that extends into the reduced section end (i.e., the one with the bristles). The passage includes two termination openings which are in the area at the base of the toothbrush bristles. An open space for placing toothpaste is provided within the interior passage, and a movable plunger is provided for forcing the toothpaste from this space through the narrow part of the passage and out through the termination openings into the toothpaste bristles for use.

In the preferred embodiment, the body shaft is made of plastic. The invention may be made so as to be disposable. Various means for filling the space with toothpaste are envisioned, including pressure-injection through a small hole in the top of the body, which hole can then be sealed. This would make the toothbrush usablc only once; it would then be disposed.

He concluded with the following claim:

I claim:

1. A pocket toothbrush having an exterior structure resembling a traditional fountain pen case comprising
   [a] a removable cylindrical end cap cover,
   [b] a main cylindrical body shaft over at least one end of which said end cap cover fits and having means for engaging the interior of said end cap cover to retain said end cap cover,
   [c] said cylindrical body shaft having one end which contains toothbrush bristles [the "bristle end"] extending transversely and capable of being confined within said end cap,
   [d] said cylindrical body shaft including an interior passage extending into said bristle end and having at least one termination opening in the area at the base of said bristles,
   [e] a movable plunger extending into said cylindrical body shaft in said main cylindrical body shaft,
   [f] said body shaft including an interior space for the accommodation of a charge of toothpaste to be fed to said bristles by the operation of said movable plunger, said space being at least big enough to hold a charge for a single application of toothpaste.

Once the patent issues, Tasty begins selling a disposable, portable toothbrush that garners a loyal following. Soon competitors begin entering the market. One, KopyCat Industries, Inc. (KCI) begins selling a portable toothbrush that includes a replaceable toothpaste cartridge so that the brush can be used over and over if the user wishes. The cartridges are designed to have a weak plastic closure that easily breaks when the plunger is pushed against the cartridge. This keeps the toothpaste from hardening in the openings to the bristles. Also, instead of a cap, the KCI design has a telescoping retractable cover that remains attached to the nonbristle end of the brush. The cover is collapsed down, the brush used, and then the cover is pulled back into place. The retractable cover is attached very firmly with two tiny screws. The screws can be taken out and the cover removed, but it takes a tiny jeweler's screwdriver and is difficult.

Tasty has threatened to sue KCI for infringement of the Molar patent. KCI has come to you for advice. Focusing on the *claim language* -- and using the specification only to interpret that language -- determine (1) whether KCI runs a serious risk of being found liable for infringing the Molar patent; and (2) what changes KCI might make in its product to avoid a future infringement action by Tasty. In particular, pay attention to these issues: Does the KCI product include a "removable end cap cover"? Is it relevant that KCI improved the design of the replaceable toothpaste cartridge?

Analysis

Problem 3-11: This rather simple claim gives students a good opportunity to do an actual infringement analysis, comparing the claims element by element with an accused device. In this case, note that there are two basic differences between the products -- KCI's brush has replaceable toothpaste cartridge, and it has a telescoping brush cover. The first change is probably most significant, but it probably does not avoid infringement, because the presence or absence of a replaceable cartridge doesn't appear to be a claim element. Indeed, the patent specification seems to contemplate the possibility of replaceable charges of toothpaste, though the patentee did not tell us how to accomplish such an end. The critical point for students here is that patents are defined by their claims, not by what the inventor made: if an improvement is covered by the claims, it still infringes the patent. [Perhaps KCI could argue that the plastic closure protecting the toothpaste prevents the KCI brush from meeting the requirement of an "interior passage." Note that the specification describes an "open space" within the interior passage, which is arguably lacking in the KCI brush during the time a charge is installed.]

KCI's second change will avoid infringement if (but only if) a retractable cover is not a "removable" cover within the meaning of the patent claim. This is an arguable point, on both literal infringement and doctrine of equivalents grounds. In favor of infringement, Tasty might point out that the cover can be removed with screwdriver; that the cover slides back, which is within meaning of "removable" as used in the patent; and more generally that this is an insignificant change to the basic invention of a portable, disposable toothbrush. On the other side, KCI will likely argue that their cover is physically attached, while Tasty's snaps off; that even if their cover performs same "function" as Tasty's, it does so in a different way; and that their cover may in fact be a significant improvement, since the retractable cover can't be lost.

Note that this problem presents the issue of improvements which infringe on the original patent. It is quite possible that the KCI toothbrush infringes this patent, even though it is a significant improvement over the original design. It thus introduces the "blocking patents" idea, as well as the problem of later-developed technologies.

PROBLEM 3-12

Nichols, a scientist who enjoys puzzles, designs a "rotating cube" puzzle in which each face of the cube is composed of a number of smaller cubes, each face is initially of a different color, and the object of the puzzle is to restore the original color scheme once it has been disturbed. Nichols obtains a patent on a method of solving this puzzle, but not on the physical puzzle itself.

Rubik builds and sells puzzles similar to the ones Nichols has designed. Has Rubik infringed the Nichols patent, either directly or indirectly? Does it matter whether Nichols' patent covers the only known solution to the puzzle, or only one among many possible solutions? What if Rubik's product includes a "cheat" sheet advising buyers how to solve the puzzle using a number of methods, including Nichols'? What if Rubik includes a copy of the Nichols patent with each cube sold, ostensibly to advise users how to avoid infringement but arguably with the intent of encouraging them to use the Nichols method?

[see Figure 3-7 in text]

Analysis

Problem 3-12: Rubik's cube presents a classic problem of contributory infringement by device. Rubik's device infringes Nichols' patent on the solution only if Nichols' is the *only* (or at least, the dominant) solution -- if others are possible, or if other uses for the device exist, there is no contributory infringement because there are "substantial noninfringing uses" of the device. Note that even if Nichols proves that his is the "dominant" means of solving the puzzle, he will also have to show that Rubik knew or reasonably should have known of the patent and of the likely infringement. Contrast this knowledge requirement with the normal rule of strict liability for intellectual property infringement.

Regarding inducement, the case is a little different. To be liable for inducement, Rubik must have the ability to control the infringement of others, and must profit from that infringement. Again, if Nichols' is the only solution to the puzzle, these elements should be relatively easy to show -- people buy puzzles from Rubik in order to complete them, and each one who does so infringes the patent. On the other hand, if there are other solutions, inducement is harder to find. In either case, encouraging purchasers to use Nichols' solution is a bad idea from an inducement perspective.

D. Defenses

Motion Picture Patents Company v. Universal Film Manufacturing Co., page 281, involves the famous motion picture patent pool, made notorious in Hollywood lore (and in the now-aging film *Nickelodeon.)* The Edison interests, owner of the patent, tried to exploit its patent monopoly by conditioning the use of the patented projector to licensees who agreed to show only Edison films. The absence of a modern-style inquiry into market power in the market for the tying product (projector) shows that patent misuse represents a less rigorous way than antitrust action to attack anticompetitive behavior. You might give modern day examples of Edison's business strategy of leveraging a key proprietary asset into effective market presence in related markets -- e.g., computer interfaces and operating systems and the market for application programs and web browsers.

E. International Patent Law

F. Remedies

The cases here provide a straightforward treatment of prospective injunctive relief, as well as the basic principles for determining retrospective compensation. In its details, this is a complex area; only a brief overview is possible in the introductory course.

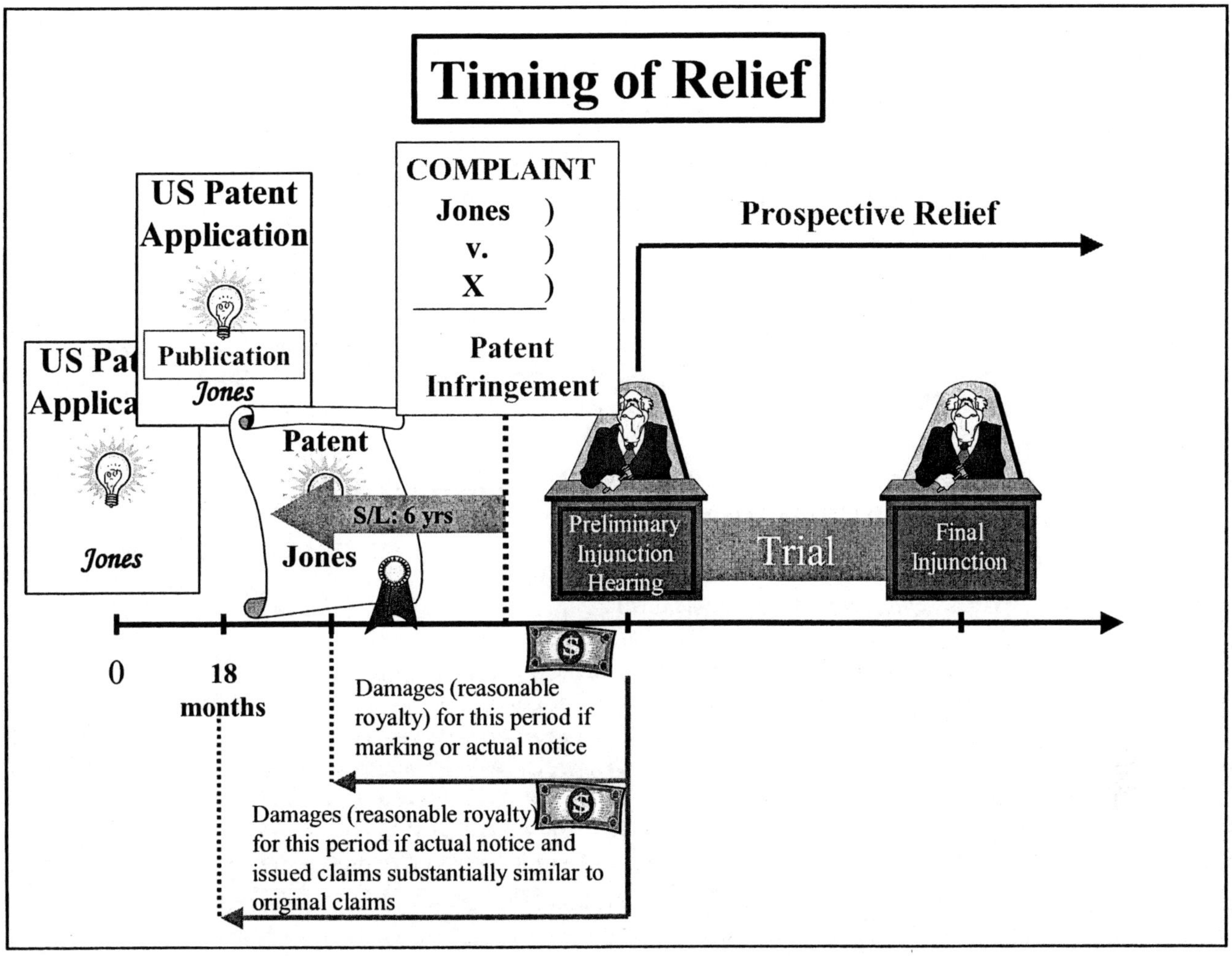

The shift to a more pro-patentee injunction standard, represented by *HH Robertson*, page 299, is worth some discussion; in many cases, an injunction is the main remedy sought, and given the expense and complexity of patent trials, the preliminary injunction determination is often crucial. It is not infrequently the end of the matter one way or the other, as well. In the area of damages, one approach in the introductory course is to compare the main features of damages across the various substantive areas of the course. If this makes sense, you might want to emphasize the *absence* of a disgorgement remedy in the patent statute. The infringer's profits are not available directly to the patentee, even as an alternative measure of the patentee's loss from infringement. Note that various innovations in damages theory can in many cases more than make up for this, however; some are mentioned in the "Note on the Frontiers of Lost Profits Damages."

G. Design and Plant Patents

Chapter 4 Copyright Law

A. Introduction

B. Requirements

Feist, page 329, is the starting point for a consideration of copyrightable subject matter. The barebones facts, and the more-or-less stipulated issue of infringement, frame the question of copyrightability quite clearly. (The issue of the state law mandating production of the phone book is a bit of a red herring; would a state law requiring a summary of a town meeting by itself deprive the summary of originality?) Given this simple structure, the case also invites application of the historical/philosophical points made in the introductory materials. Does a phone directory merit a legal reward? What are the consequences of either granting or not granting a copyright for this type of work?

PROBLEM 4-1

Central Bell, the local telephone utility, distributes both a "white pages" telephone book and a "yellow pages," which lists businesses who have chosen to advertise there. Bell's yellow pages are organized alphabetically by subject matter of the business, and alphabetically within each subject. Bell itself created the subject headings with input from its advertisers. Bell also sells larger advertisements to certain companies for more money.

Christopher Publications decides to create and distribute its own yellow pages directory in competition with Bell. Christopher does this by taking a copy of Bell's yellow pages and calling every business that advertises there, asking each if it would like to advertise in Christopher's publication. Christopher places the resulting ads in its own subject matter listings (which do overlap somewhat with Bell's). Many of the advertisements themselves (which are submitted by the advertisers) are identical to those in the Bell directory. Bell sues Christopher for copyright infringement. Who should prevail?

Analysis

Problem 4-1: The Eleventh Circuit took this issue in the wake of *Feist*. The decision is *Bellsouth v. Donnelley*, 999 F.2d 1436 (11th Cir. 1993).

The key to this case is understanding exactly what information was taken. First, there is some overlap between the headings in the competing Yellow Pages. There is also substantial difference between the two. The court says that while the selection and arrangement of headings is potentially copyrightable, that copyright is thin, because many of the headings are the logical way to organize the book. For example, copying the heading "Plumbers" is reasonable, both because that is a recognized profession people are likely to look for, and because that is the name they are likely to look under.

Second, the information that appears in the final Donnelley Yellow Pages is in some respects identical to that appearing in BellSouth's. However, those similarities result from the necessary facts provided by the advertisers (their names and addresses), or from the ad copy submitted by the advertisers. The court says that Donnelley has not copied original, protectable information in the final directory, since the only information used is that provided by advertisers who chose to participate in the Donnelley directory.

Finally, Donnelley made an "intermediate copy" of all the information in the BellSouth directory, loading it into the database from which it began to call people and produce its own directory. The dissent says that intermediate copying is illegal, even though the original information copied did not make its way into the final directory. Technically, the dissent is correct on this point -- there is no requirement in the copyright laws that an infringing "copy" must appear in a commercial product, or even be shown to anyone outside the defendant. As a practical matter, however, intermediate copying which facilitates the use of unprotectable information, and which does not translate into copying in the final version, is likely to be allowed as a "fair use."

The material on fixation and formalities may best be covered by judicious discussion of the following problem. Consider using one variant on the Problem's facts to get at fixation: what if the poems were merely spoken at various poetry recitals, and never written down? This discussion may also lead to a consideration of unauthorized recordings of the poems – a good opportunity to point out that not all actual "fixations" are legally significant fixations.

PROBLEM 4-2

Which of the following acts would constitute publication under the 1909 Act? the 1976 Act?

a) Penelope Poet brings copies of her latest three poems to the monthly meeting of the Philadelphia Aspiring Poets Society. She distributes copies to the eight people in attendance that month prior to reading the poems.

b) Professor Edgar Edifice assembles a course reader consisting of public domain materials and excerpts he wrote himself. Students in his Advanced Copyright Theory seminar purchase the reader for the cost of reproduction from the school's reprographics service.

c) Arnold Author recently completed a draft of his first novel. He sends a copy to his agent, whom he authorizes to distribute copies to publishing houses for consideration.

Analysis

Problem 4-2: The critical fact for publication purposes under the 1909 Act seems to be whether a publication is "to a limited group for a limited purpose," or is either to the public at large or (if to a limited group) is made with the intent that the work be redistributed or transmitted to the public. Each of these three cases presents variations on this theme.

Penelope Poet did not distribute very many copies of her work to the public. However, the number of copies is not the determinative test. Rather, the questions that will help determine publication here are whether the meeting was open to the public, or on the contrary was limited to members of PAPS, and whether there was an express or implied restriction on the use that recipients could make of the poems.

Edifice's distribution of his course reader (which presumably qualifies for copyright protection, both because of his own contributions and because of the selection and arrangement of public domain works) presents a similar problem. Here, though, it is reasonable to assume that the distribution of the work was intended to be limited to students in his class, as was not therefore open to the public. It is also relevant whether there was an express or implied limitation on redistribution; in this case, though, it seems likely that the work was not given to the students with the intent that it be redistributed.

Author did not distribute his work to the public, but did intend that the agent who received it redistribute it to others. This clearly seems to be distribution "for the purpose of" republication, although the issue is complicated by the fact that the republication expressly authorized is itself to only a limited group.

The 1976 Act defines publication in § 101 in ways which largely track the 1909 approach. Under the 1976 Act, however, publication is far less significant an event, since it does not trigger copyright protection, and since most of the formalities that accompanied copyright under the 1909 Act have disappeared.

C. Copyrightable Subject Matter

Baker v. Selden, page 345, is the cornerstone for computer interface and program infringement suits, and an important case on basic principles of the breadth of copyright protection. Selden created a condensed ledger form and described his accounting system in a book. Baker did not copy Selden verbatim; he described the Selden system in his own words. Does the Baker book infringe the Selden copyright? Looking at the Court's holding in terms of infringement, the opinion can be read to say that such a notion of infringement is too broad. The book copyright is not infringed by the Baker book because not enough protectable expression has been taken. The broader – and more significant – reading emphasizes copyrightability: what Baker did copy (the method of bookkeeping) is not copyrightable. If Selden's book copyright covered what Baker had done, Selden would effectively own the system itself. If Selden were allowed to win, then copyright would become a very powerful weapon for the *indirect* protection of systems, methods, and other "ideas" embodied in a particular expression. Copyright should not have the breadth of patent law, the Court says clearly. This is the first brush with a topic that will recur in this section, and later in the cases on trade dress: intellectual property law's zealous patrolling of the borders between the different statutory systems, in an effort to prevent "backdoor patents."

PROBLEM 4-3

Mediforms designs and sells health care forms to doctors, who submit them to insurance carriers. A sample form is shown in Figure 4-2.

[see Figure 4-2 in text]

The diagnosis checklist contains categories specified by the American Medical Association or government publications (including official code numbers). Mediforms offers a variety of forms, according to specialty, to reflect the illnesses and treatments most relevant to the particular doctor. The forms are personalized to include the doctor's name and address, the nature of the doctor's practice, and the hospitals or clinics at which the doctor performs services. Doctors may use the checklists provided or may customize their own checklists, which most doctors choose to do. The forms also contain brief instructions for filling in each blank and instructions explaining how to obtain insurance reimbursement. The forms were widely praised in the industry and were copied by competitors and individual doctors. Are the forms copyrightable? Should Mediforms be entitled at least to recoup its investment in developing the forms?

Analysis

Problem 4-3: The Mediforms contain somewhat more information than those in *Baker*. For example, they have specific blanks for patient information, short instructions for filling out that information, and a checklist for use by the doctor. Whether anything on this form is copyrightable depends on two factors: whether the form "conveys information", distinguishing it from the forms in *Baker*, or alternatively whether there is original creativity, selection or arrangement in the choice of information requested on the form. Certainly a list of diseases is more likely to be creative and warrant protection than a form which merely asked for the patient's "name, address, and phone number". Note that protection is not guaranteed even in this circumstance, however: (a) part of the information gathered is simply necessary, and therefore is a functional part of the idea of such a form; (b) part of the information conveyed will likely be unprotectable facts -- the address of the doctor, standard code numbers, etc.; (c) there is a definite problem of merger, at least with respect to certain parts. In this respect, it may matter a great deal whether, for example, the list of diseases used in the form is based on the Medicare reimbursement categories?

If a form of this nature is copyrightable at all, it will likely be entitled only to "thin" copyright protection, for example against verbatim copying. In the actual case, the Ninth Circuit held that forms that "convey information" are copyrightable, but this particular form did not, and so was ineligible for protection. *Bibbero Systems, Inc. v. Colwell Systems, Inc.*, 893 F.2d 1104 (9th Cir. 1990). The court reasoned in part that "All forms seek only certain information, and, by their selection, convey that the information sought is important. This cannot be what the Copyright Office intended by the statement "convey information." 893 F.2d at 1107.

On the other hand, assuming that it is not purely functional, or required (by the insurance carrier or by statute, for example), Mediforms should be entitled to copyright its instruction text. Copying of the text therefore constitutes infringement. However, copying of the form without the text should not constitute infringement. Further, if the entire form is copied, it is only the textual copying that should be enjoined. This problem therefore introduces some of the consequences of partial copyright protection, which quite often flow from the "analytical dissection" of copyrighted works.

Morrissey, page 351, gives a quick overview of the "merger" doctrine. It invites inquiry into an important but metaphysically murky distinction between the expressive content of a work and the functional purpose of the work. Look at the language in the opinion: the court distinguishes the expression of the game rules from the "substance" and "subject matter" and "topic" of the game itself. The conventional reading of the case is that copyright won't protect expression where there are only one or a few ways to "achieve the same thing." This seems to make sense here. But a few well-directed questions will illustrate the difficulty that sometimes attends defining with any precision what "thing" the expression is meant to achieve. Consider computer operating systems: if the function is to permit at least some application programs to run on a certain computer, then many different operating systems will suffice. No merger. But if the function is defined as permitting all existing applications programs written for a "standard" operating system to run on a computer, compatibility with the standard becomes the "function." An argument for merger may be made out: only one expressive form permits a work to perform a certain function (compatibility). The point is that much of the action in the merger doctrine is in how you define the "function" of the expression. The function is easily seen in *Morrissey* – "the contest" is obviously separate from the sentences describing the rules. But this will not always be so. Obviously this approach to *Morrissey* highlights issues that recur later in the chapter, viz., the idea-expression dichotomy and functionality doctrines. It is not too soon to stress the conceptual overlap between merger and these other doctrines, however.

PROBLEM 4-4

Insect Representations, Inc., sells a highly successful line of jewelry in the shape of various insects. One of its products is a stickpin in the shape of a bumblebee, made of gold veining and encrusted with a number of white gems. Animal Jewelry Corp. designs and markets a jeweled bee pin that also has gold veining and is encrusted with gems. However, Animal uses a different number of total gems, and some of its gems are colors other than white. When Insect sues Animal for copyright infringement, Animal defends on the grounds that it has taken merely the "idea" of a jeweled bee pin. Who should prevail?

PROBLEM 4-5

Harry Historian had always been curious about the cause of the Hindenberg disaster, the explosion of a German zeppelin in 1938. After carefully investigating records and news accounts of the disaster and interviewing witnesses, Harry concluded that the disaster was caused by a disgruntled crew member who sabotaged the dirigible so as to embarrass the Nazi regime. He then wrote a book developing his hypothesis. The book contained rich descriptions of the events leading up to the disaster, including detailed accounts of German beer hall revelry and the passionate patriotism of German nationals (as expressed in their enthusiastic singing of the German national anthem). Without obtaining the movie rights to Harry's book,

Capitalistic Studios produced a movie of the disaster which featured a crewman-saboteur and many of the richly detailed scenes in Harry's book. Does Harry have a valid copyright infringement claim? Should he have such a claim?

Analysis

Problem 4-4: This problem introduces the tricky issue of "levels of abstraction." Insect wants to copyright a jeweled bee pin. Presumably there is some creative expression in its jewelry design -- the precise shape, the choice of jewels and metals, etc. On the other hand, this creative expression is highly constrained, at least if we define the unprotectable "idea" as that of a jeweled bee pin. The basic shape is determined by the choice of a bee, and the requirements of color and cost may dictate much of the selection of materials. [On the other hand, note how the level of abstraction at which the "idea" is set makes a difference -- if the unprotectable "idea" is jewelry, or even "representational jewelry", Insect might well be able to exercise control over *all* jeweled bee pins.

While there is probably some expression in Insect's work, the merger doctrine presents a real problem for copyright protection here. There are only a limited number of ways to represent a bee using jewelry, and some of those may be constrained by cost factors. Thus, the court in this case held that the jeweler was not entitled to any copyright protection, despite the existence of original expression. *Herbert Rosenthal Jewelry v. Kalpakian*, 446 F.2d 738 (9th Cir. 1971). The court notes the difficulty of doing more in this area than restating your conclusions, and quotes Judge Learned Hand's singularly unhelpful statement that "Obviously, no principle can be stated as to when an imitator has gone beyond copying the idea, and has borrowed its expression." *Peter Pan Fabrics, Inc. v. Martin Weiner Corp.*, 274 F.2d 487, 489 (2nd Cir. 1960). One factor that may have been driving the court's conclusion was the fact that the pin was separately protectable under the design patent laws, which have no similar merger doctrine. For a discussion of the overlap between patent, copyright, and trademark in the design field, see Chapter 5.

Problem 4-5: This problem is based on *Hoehling v. Universal City Studios*, 618 F.2d 972 (2d Cir. 1980). The problem presents the classic issue of copyright protection for factual works. The court acknowledges the substantial similarity of the two works, but denies relief because it concludes that the copying was primarily of unprotectable "facts" uncovered by Hoehling's research. The court does acknowledge that there is some "thin" protection to Hoehling's work, however. It notes that a virtually identical copy of Hoehling's book would be infringing.

In *Brandir International, Inc. v. Cascade Pacific Lumber Co.,* page 356, the Second Circuit applied the useful article doctrine to a bicycle ribbon rack. The majority determined that the rack possessed no aesthetic qualities and thus was not copyrightable. The majority reasoned that the design of the bike was influenced by utilitarian concerns. Here form and function were inextricably intertwined. You might analogize Brandir's bike rack to Baker's accounting system in that they are both useful things. If you use copyright law to protect useful things, you are effectively granting a "backdoor patent." The *Baker-Brandir* pair permits exploration of a number of important issues. The cases often stress the connection between design choices and copyrightable expression. The exercise of choice or discretion implies that what results is copyrightable expression. By contrast, utilitarian objects are the product of rigid, ineluctable constraints. This can be explored through a number of hypotheticals: an ultra-realist painter rendering a still life, versus an engineer designing an auto engine who may choose between any of five configurations for the cylinders; a journalist writing a run-of-the-mill obituary, versus a software engineer designing the overall configuration of a complex computer program.

PROBLEM 4-6

The Walt Disney Company markets a line of telephones in the shape of the cartoon characters Mickey and Minnie Mouse. The telephones resemble the characters standing up, with push buttons on the torso and the telephone receiver resting on the hand. Are these designs copyrightable?

PROBLEM 4-7

Armond Artist designs a belt buckle cast in gold and silver which is generally recognized as a work of abstract art. The shape of the buckle is the key artistic component. The buckles retail for $200 to $6,000 at high-fashion jewelry stores. Some of the designs have been made a part of the permanent collection of the Metropolitan Museum of Art. Is the buckle copyrightable, or is it merely a "useful article"?

PROBLEM 4-8

Versace Fashion Display Inc. has developed a collection of original sculptural forms in the shape of the human torso. They are life-size and anatomically accurate, but without neck, arms, or a back. Versace supplies these forms to clothing retailers for the display of fashion clothing. These forms became popular in the market. Versace customers found the distinctive lines of the forms to be visually attractive and effective in selling blouses, shirts, and sweaters displayed on the forms. Discount Display, Inc., began to notice a decline in their mannequin sales after Versace entered the market. Thereafter, Discount Display expanded its catalog to include forms that it copied from Versace. In response, Versace registers its forms with the Copyright Office and sues Discount Display for copyright infringement. How should a court resolve this dispute?

Analysis

Problem 4-6: Disney markets a Mickey Mouse telephone, which works as a telephone. Part of the mouse sculpture -- e.g. the hands -- function as the telephone handset. The threshold question is whether the Mickey Mouse character is copyrightable. The answer is unquestionably yes. Not only is the phone a sculptural work, but the character is a literary or graphic work that receives strong protection in whatever form it appears. The second question is whether there is any reason to reject copyrightability under the useful article doctrine. The phone is a useful article. Applying the different tests for separability produces the following results: (1) the phone is arguably physically separable from the mouse, certainly to the same extent as the lamp held protectable in *Mazer v. Stein*, 347 U.S. 201 (1954). (2) there is no question that it is conceptually separable -- both telephones and Mickey Mouse are well established in the public consciousness. (3) the "original intent" of the artist was probably not to produce a functional work, and the mouse has not been significantly adapted for functional reasons; (4) the primary purpose and economic contributions of the work are unclear -- people by this both for its function and for its appearance. In practice, there seems no question that Mickey Mouse is copyrightable in this form.

Problem 4-7: The belt buckle at issue in this problem is extremely expensive, and is occasionally displayed as art, but is clearly a belt buckle. Copyrightability is tougher here than in the Mickey Mouse case. There is clearly not physical separability -- the artwork is integrated into the buckle itself. There is probably also no conceptual separability either: the basic form of the work is driven by its function, and the remainder of the work is rather abstract, nonrepresentational art. The same argument can be made to some extent about all expensive jewelry. [Of course, if the conceptual separability test means nothing more than "can you visualize it hanging in an art museum", the answer is probably yes].

On the other hand, the primary purpose of the buckle is ornamental, not functional. The economic value of the work clearly derives from its artistic nature -- people would not pay $6000 for an "ordinary" belt buckle. The Second Circuit held that the buckles were copyrightable under the primary purpose or economic effect test, reasoning that the buckles have "conceptually separable sculptural elements" which predominate over their "subsidiary utilitarian function." *Kieselstein-Cord v. Accessories by Pearl*, 632 F.2d 989 (2d Cir. 1980). This result seems right, even though there is arguably neither physical nor conceptual separability here. Note that *Brandir*'s test -- the intent of the artist -- would most likely render the work protectable as well.

The dissent rejects this distinction, concluding that the buckles are uncopyrightable because of the artist's "success in completely integrating the artistic designs and the functional aspects." 632 F.2d at 994 (Weinstein, J., dissenting).

Problem 4-8: This problem is based on *Carol Barnhart Inc. v. Economy Cover Corp.*, 773 F.2d 411 (2d Cir. 1985). The majority rejects the mannequins as uncopyrightable, relying on the lack of physical separability between the artistic and functional elements of the mannequins and on their primary purpose, which is unquestionably utilitarian. The dissent criticizes the majority's test as indeterminate, and pushes a strong form of the "conceptual separability" test. Should the mannequins be copyrightable? Most people would say no -- based on the clear utilitarian purpose, and the dubious artistic value of the mannequins themselves standing alone. Note that *Brandir*'s test would most likely reject a finding of copyrightability.

PROBLEM 4-9

To celebrate the bicentennial of the federal court system, the Administrative Office of the United States Courts commissioned KPBS, a public broadcasting station, to create a television series dramatizing famous early federal cases. The production contract assigned all copyright interests in the works to the federal government. The History Channel seeks to air these programs. Must it obtain a license from the federal government? Would your analysis differ if there were no assignment clause? What if a historian employed by the Administrative Office of the United States Courts served as a consultant to the television series? What if federal public officials -- including Supreme Court Justices and the Solicitor General -- provided commentaries about the famous cases?

Analysis

Problem 4-9: Had the federal government, its employees, or contractors operating within the scope of the "works made for hire" doctrine created the broadcast, it would not be copyrightable. Here, however, a private organization created the work at the request of the government, and assigned the copyright to the government. 17 U.S.C. § 105 permits the government to hold copyrights it receives by assignment. Thus, anyone wishing to use the broadcast must obtain copyright clearance from the U.S. government. The participation of government officials acting in the scope of their employment does not change this result, though the contribution of original expression by such an individual will not itself be the subject of copyright, and hence can be freely copied.

PROBLEM 4-10

The New York Arrows, a professional soccer team, hired Sports Images, an advertising firm, to develop a logo to advertise the team. Sports Images developed the accompanying logo (Figure 4-4).

[see Figure 4-4 in text]

After a dispute with the team about fees, Sports Images submitted an application to the Copyright Office to register the work. Is the work copyrightable? By whom?

Analysis

Problem 4-10: This problem is analogous to the "short phrases" issue in literary works. Are there some pictorial works that are sufficiently simple that copyright protection should be denied? The analysis seems to track Problem 4-10 closely, and the copyright-trademark channeling issue is also present here.

The problem also presents an issue of copyright ownership, if we decide the work is copyrightable. That issue is perhaps better deferred until after considering the section on ownership, below.

PROBLEM 4-11

At the 1995 Pan-World Figure Skating Championships in Denver, Colorado, skater Kurt Klutzinovich performed the first series of quadruple lutzes ever seen in competition. ABC sports commentator Bill McKay proclaimed it the "klutz," "Kurt's patented move." At the 1996 Championships, Kurt's coach threatens to bring a copyright infringement action against any other skater who performs a "klutz." Is Kurt's series of moves protectable as a choreographic work? If so, would another skater's performance of a klutz infringe Kurt's copyright?

Analysis

Problem 4-11: We have previously addressed the issue of sports moves in the context of *patentable* subject matter. One could certainly view a series of figure skating moves as a "choreographic" work within the subject matter of copyright. A quadruple lutz, however, is sufficiently constrained by functional goals and limits that anyone who succeeds in performing one will probably do it in approximately the same way. Thus, unless we were to give Kurt protection for the *idea* of a quadruple lutz, we would have to deny protection under the merger doctrine for the way in which it was performed.

On the other hand, an entire figure skating routine is clearly a choreographic work, and taken as a whole may have sufficient original expression that one skater could prevent another from copying her routine wholesale.

PROBLEM 4-12

Assume that West Publishing Company, which has published both official and unofficial reports of federal and state court decisions for over 100 years, and Mead Data Central are the only competitors in the market for computer legal research databases. Because cases (especially in the federal courts) are cited by the West's volume and page number, Mead decides to copy West's pagination in its computer database. West sues, arguing that the arrangement of its cases in its reporters is copyrighted. Does West have a valid copyright?

PROBLEM 4-13

The Bond News and Investor's World are both financial reporting services. Each provides to its subscribers a weekly update of all municipal bonds that have been "called" by the city, and several pieces of information about the bonds: the bond series, the call price, the date of the call, and the address and phone number of the calling agency. Bond obtains this information by having researchers cull through published notices in 250 newspapers nationwide each day. Bond, suspecting that Investor's is copying its data rather than conducting a similar search, plants false information in its updates. When Investor's publishes the same false information in its update, Bond sues. Investor's admits copying the data but claims that it had a right to do so because the data were not copyrightable. Who should prevail?

Analysis

Problem 4-12: This case was litigated and decided in 1986. *West Publishing Co. v. Mead Data Central*, 799 F.2d 1219 (8th Cir. 1986). There was no dispute that the opinions themselves could be copied, and that Mead could use the original case citation. That rule had been established quite early. *See Callaghan v. Myers*, 128 U.S. 617 (1888); *Wheaton v. Peters*, 33 U.S. 591 (1834). Similarly, there was no dispute that West *could* copyright its "headnotes," but that the headnotes were not copied in this case. The only dispute was over the use of "pincites." The court upheld an injunction preventing Mead from using West's page numbers, concluding that they were "the result of considerable labor, talent, and judgment." While it acknowledged that the page numbers were facts, ordinarily not copyrightable, the court concluded that the "wholesale appropriation" of West's work was actionable.

West was controversial when it was decided, and almost certainly does not survive *Feist*. Indeed, the *West* court compared the page numbers in West's books to phone numbers in a telephone directory, which at that time were protectable in some circuits. The organizational scheme of the pages in West's reporters is that of any book -- increasing sequential order -- and is no more original than alphabetizing names. Further, the placement of words on a page is purely an accident of typesetting, once the (concededly unprotectable) beginning page for a case is set. A recent decision concludes that West lacks copyright in its internal case pagination after *Feist*. *Matthew Bender v. West Publishing Co.*, 158 F.3d 674 (2d Cir. 1998). *Contra Oasis Publishing v. West Publishing Co.*, 924 F. Supp. 918 (D. Minn. 1996) (concluding that *Feist* is consistent with the decision in *West v. Mead*, and finding that West's internal pagination of cases "easily" meets the requirement of originality).

The other point worth mentioning about *West* concerns the economic consequences of the decision. Granting West an injunction gave it a competitive advantage in an extremely lucrative product market. Further, because the data West used were data they created themselves, and which had been officially sanctioned by the courts, Mead had no alternative means of acquiring or developing a similar advantage. This may be a case in which the right to access or concerns about competition ought to outweigh whatever weak rights West might possess in its data.

Lexis does use West's pincites today, apparently as a result of a settlement with West. But other legal publishing companies are currently litigating this issue. *See supra*.

Problem 4-13: This case is loosely based on *Financial Information, Inc. v. Moody's Investors Service, Inc.*, 808 F.2d 204 (2nd Cir. 1986). In that case, Moody's denied copying FII's data. The court found FII's updates uncopyrightable because it had merely filled in five facts about each bond call taken directly from the newspaper advertisements on each card, and that "little independent creation was involved." *Id.* at 208. The court explicitly reserved the question, however, of whether Moody's would be liable if it had engaged in "wholesale appropriation." We have modified the problem to present that issue squarely.

The logic of *Feist* suggests that Investor's should not be liable, regardless of the level of its appropriation. Bond published all bond calls, rather than selecting some and rejecting others. Bond published all public information necessary to redeem a bond, and nothing else. Neither the organization nor the selection of facts appear sufficiently original to qualify for protection, therefore.

Interestingly, Moody's did include significant proprietary information in its updates, and also selected only certain calls for publication. If FII had done the same thing, copying such original selection and arrangement would be infringement.

It is instructive to compare *FII* to *Eckes v. Card Prices Update*, 736 F.2d 859 (2nd Cir. 1984), referred to in *FII*. In that case, the court held that a baseball card price book was copyrightable because "appellants exercised selection, creativity and judgment in choosing among the 18,000 or so different baseball cards in order to determine which were the 5,000 premium cards." *Id.* at 863. Presumably SportsCard made this selection based on price. If the prices themselves are not copyrightable, what is being protected here? The idea of separating the cards in price order? The choice of the number 5,000? In either case, the protection appears pretty thin, which may be the point of all the factual compilation cases.

D. Ownership and Duration

1. Initial Ownership of Copyrights

Community for Creative Non-Violence v. Reid, page 380, can be used to explain the work made for hire doctrine and to review what constitutes an employee. In this case, the sculptor created a modern day nativity scene. The Court concluded that Reid was an independent contractor and that CCNV was not the copyright owner. The many factors in the Restatement of Agency boil down to three main concerns: how close to conventional employment is the arrangement (salary, benefits, etc.); who owns the "means of production," i.e., tools etc.; and who controls the action, a "commissioning party" or the person commissioned to create the work? In this area, metaphysical questions about the exercise of creative judgment are not as important in some of the originality cases; even an employee who is instructed about what goal to achieve is usually left with a host of "design choices" in carrying out orders. But here the abstract question "who is the creator of a work?" yields to more pragmatic concerns. What would happen if all employees owned copyrights in their work product? What would the negotiations look like among the fifty or so animators who work on a typical Disney cartoon film?

At the end of the day, the Court remanded to determine whether the sculpture in *CCNV* was a joint work. You might point out the pitfalls of a joint work. First, there are the practical problems of having more than one owner (e.g., competing tours, downstream transactional hurdles (like termination of transfer, duration)). Also, with each additional author/owner, the transaction costs multiply – multiple permissions, clearances, and licensing negotiations. Should the law express a preference for unified ownership whenever possible? How far should this goal be allowed to go – would it undermine individual incentives?

In most settings in which two or more people contribute to the creation of an economically significant work of authorship such as a major motion picture, the producers and/or collaborators agree in advance how ownership be held and how income will be divided. As noted above, motion pictures are among the 9 enumerated categories of work eligible for work for hire treatment. Therefore, motion picture producers typically have all contributors to the project execute employment and/or work made for hire agreements ensuring that ownership of the work vests *ab initio* in the hands of the producer.

Aalmuhammed v. Lee, page 387, illustrates the complications that can potentially arise if a contributor to a motion picture is not brought into the project through a clear "work made for hire" arrangement. In this case, Denzel Washington, the lead actor in Spike Lee's early 1990s production of the film Malcolm X, asked Jefri Aalmuhammed, a person knowledgeable about the character Washington was to portray, to assist him in preparing for the role. During the course of his work, Aalmuhammed suggested extensive script revisions aimed at ensuring the religious and historical accuracy of the portrayal of Malcolm X. After being denied a writing credit for he film, Aalmuhammed claimed status as a "joint author" of the motion picture. Were he to be deemed a joint author in the absence of any contractual agreement regarding his rights, he arguably would have the power to license the film (non-exclusively) and share in the proceeds of the project on a per capita basis.

The court side-stepped that potentially messy circumstance by finding that Aalmuhammed, although arguably a contributor of original copyrightable expression, did not qualify as a "joint author" as that term is understood under the 1976 Act. Drawing upon a line of Second and Seventh Circuit authority, the Ninth Circuit focused on three factors: (1) the degree of creative contribution; (2) the intention at the time the work created as to authorship; and (3) control over the ultimate product – who "superintended" the work. The court found that although Aalmuhammed may have contributed copyrightable expression, there was never an intention by the producers of the work that he would be deemed a "joint author" and Spike Lee, the director of the film, had exclusive control over the final product.

In exploring this case, it is worth asking how the motion picture studio got into this mess – Aalmuhammed presumably did not qualify for treatment as an employee (refer to *CCNV* factors) or a commissioned independent contractor (failure to execute a "work made for hire" agreement). With these concepts reinforced, the discussion can move to the court's interpretation of joint authorship. You might want to have students examine the rather terse definition on which the court bases its decision: "A 'joint work' is a work prepared by two or more authors with the intention that their contributions be merged into inseparable or interdependent parts of a unitary whole." Has the court imposed a "super" originality standard on jointly authored works? Why shouldn't the burden be on the motion picture producer to execute the appropriate documents if it wants to be the sole "author"?

PROBLEM 4-14

Smith, a graphic artist, is employed full time by ADCO to design and flesh out illustrations for advertising campaigns. In his spare time, at home and using no materials taken from work, Smith designs an ad campaign for another company on a freelance basis. Who owns the copyright in Smith's freelance work?

PROBLEM 4-15

Edwards, a playwright, wrote three short plays to be produced by a community theatre company. The plays were written on a tight budget, and Edwards made a number of revisions to the script during rehearsals. Some of the changes, including the reconstruction of two scenes, were made at the suggestion of actors during rehearsals, and the new scenes were worked out largely by consensus.

After a creative disagreement, the theatre company performs the plays without Edwards' permission. Edwards sues for copyright infringement, and the actors claim that they are joint authors with a right to perform the work. Who should prevail?

PROBLEM 4-16

Bable comes up with an idea for a toy car with an integrated circuit that responds to commands as well as speaking and singing songs. Bable founds a company called Up and Running, Inc. to market her "talking car" concept. Bable finds several people to record some new material for the talking car.

* The first is Sally Singer, who agrees to record a children's song she has written called "Red Light Go, Green Light Stop -- Woops!" for use on the car. Bable has Sally sign an agreement giving Up and Running "all ownership in the song." The song becomes a hit, and Bable licenses the song to Warner Kids Records for inclusion on an album of children's songs. Sally protests, saying she had planned to release her own album with the song on it.

* The second is Telly Talker, a multilingual kids' storyteller who enters into a "long-term requirements employment" contract with Up and Running. Telly's job is to record translations of the songs and slogans that the toy car says into as many languages as Bable requires. The Japanese version of the toy car becomes a big hit, and Telly informs Bable that he is planning to license his recorded voice to a third party, Toyco, for use in their Japanese talking Bear product.

* The third is Gary Guitar, a musician who records guitar music for Up and Running. His practice is to record a snippet of music in whatever genre (bluegrass, jazz, etc.) Bable requests. Bable then sends a

check with a standard form legend saying "cashing this check confirms your employment relationship with Up and Running, Inc., and the latter's ownership of the copyright in the music paid for hereby."

Who owns what copyrights in the car's songs and slogans?

Analysis

Problem 4-14: The key issue in this problem is whether the employee has acted within the "scope of his employment." On the one hand, Smith acted "on his own time" and without using the resources (or presumably the name) of ADCO. On the other hand, Smith's freelance work was directly competitive with his work for ADCO. Particularly if Smith was a salaried employee, ADCO is likely to expect that all Smith's advertising work is done for their benefit. The ultimate resolution of this problem will depend on principles of labor, agency and fiduciary law.

At this point, it is relevant to refer back to the discussion in the trade secrets chapter about employment agreements which seek to control off-site work of employees. Several states, including California and Massachusetts, have statutes limiting an employer's rights to an employee's off-site work. See that section of the text and teacher's manual for a further discussion.

Problem 4-15: Can the theatre company who helped revise a playwright's work be considered a joint author of that work? The Seventh Circuit says no in *Erickson v. Trinity Theatres*, cited in the notes in the text. The court explicitly adopts Professor Goldstein's test, requiring both the intent of the parties to merge their contributions, and the contribution of copyrightable expression by both authors. Both of these present potential problems here. At the time he wrote the play, the playwright did not intend to merge his contributions with those of an unselected group of actors. Further, it is not clear from the facts of the case whether the actors have contributed actual copyrightable expression, as opposed to ideas.

The policies behind the limits on joint authorship are worth raising at this point. Why should the intention of one author prevent joint status on the part of others who make copyrightable contributions? What happens to the others' work? The reason for limiting joint authorship is that the tenancy-in-common rules impose difficult obligations on both sides to account to the other for profits, and may make licensing more difficult by muddying the issue of who owns the copyright.

In *Erickson*, any copyrightable expression contributed by the actors presumably resulted in the creation of a derivative work (the revised script), ownership of which will then have to be decided. Does this approach further the goal of simplicity? Arguably not.

Problem 4-16: Sally signed over "all ownership in the song." This doesn't make the song a work for hire, given the rules set out in *CCNV v. Reid*, but it does validly assign the copyright to Bable. So Bable can then license it to Warner. Sally has no further rights in the song [except for the 35-year termination provision established in section 203 of the Act].

Telly records translations, on an "as-needed employment" basis. If Telly is an employee, these recordings are works made for hire and are owned by Bable. Even if Telly is not an employee, they may still be works made for hire under section 101(2) as a translation *if* the parties agreed to treat them as such. Either way, Bable and not Telly owns the translations, and Telly couldn't sell them to a third party. On the other hand, if Telly was not an employee *and* there was no agreement to treat the translations as a work made for hire, Telly retains the copyright in the expression he has added.

Gary sells music recordings to Bable, and is paid by a check which alleges an employee relationship. If this establishes such a relationship, the work would be for hire, but it is doubtful that there is an employer-employee relationship here. Under *CCNV*, the courts would look to a variety of factors to determine whether such a relationship exists, including the payment of taxes, and the location of the working relationship. Even if there is no such relationship, Gary has still assigned or licensed the rights in the song to Bable. The only question that remains, therefore, is whether there is some moral right the author retains even after assigning the copyright. In the United States, the general answer is no.

PROBLEM 4-17

After graduating from law school and passing the bar examination in 1994, George Jones joined the law firm of Blaketree, Hickman, and Charles (BH&C). He signed a standard associate employment contract stating that he would provide legal services on behalf of BH&C in exchange for a compensation package (salary plus bonus tied to billable hours, bar dues, health benefits, contribution to retirement plan). George rotated among a variety of practice areas during his first two years – IP litigation, trademark prosecution, corporate transactions. He received solid evaluations. He particularly liked the trademark group and requcsted to specialize in that department, which already had four partners, six associates, and four paralegals. Glenda Elston, the lead attorney in the department, viewed George favorably and he joined the department full-time early in his third year with the firm.

Six months into his third year, George began to feel that the trademark prosecution work was becoming monotonous. He increasingly recognized that many aspects of his work – validity analysis, record keeping, correspondence, etc. – could be usefully automated through the use of computer macros. In addition, he felt that the efficiency of the office could be vastly improved by creating an integrated database that all members of the trademark department (and clients) could access and use. He mentioned this idea at a department lunch and received mixed reactions. A few members of the group liked the idea and wanted to hear more about it. Glenda noted that there was a tremendous work load and that she did not want this type of project to distract George from his prosecution responsibilities. Without discussing the matter further with his colleagues, George decided to pursue the project in his spare time. He had taken some computer classes while in college and had kept up with advances in microcomputers, network computing, web-based computing, JAVA, and HTML. He liked fooling around with computers and began chipping away at this project at home. Using his own computer and software he purchased with his own funds, George developed a prototype of the program over the next year. He worked round the clock, putting in regular hours at the office and then spending evenings and weekends in his home office. George occasionally accessed the law firm's website and filed in developing the program and eventually ported a version of the program onto his office machine. He also tested the program with his office files. As the program components reached the operational stage, George began using (and refining) the program at the office. His productivity increased, as did his enjoyment of work. The challenge of automating his practice brought tremendous satisfaction. After more than a year of effort, George completed a prototype for what he called "TM Prosecution Toolkit." The program stores general information on clients and their applications, provides a check-list/expert system for assessing the applicability of § 2 bars to registration, identifies necessary actions for trademark prosecution, records information on actions taken, generates draft forms and correspondence for use in prosecution, calculates prosecution deadline dates, and alerts responsible individuals to impending deadlines.

George demonstrated the program to the trademark group on February 12, 2000 at a department-wide planning retreat. By that point in time, the department had grown to almost 20 attorneys. Everyone was duly impressed. Glenda recommended that the system be implemented throughout the department immediately. BH&C touted the use of the program on its website and promotional materials. The materials referred to the program as BH&C's innovative TM Prosecution Toolkit™. Steven Roland, the webmaster at the firm, adapted aspects of George's program so that clients and attorneys could gain access to the firm's trademark database through a password protected portal. The firm touted this new service as its TM Fileshare℠.

George received a particularly large bonus the following December. He was initially quite pleased by the reaction of the firm and colleagues, but was chagrined when Glenda informed him that BH&C planned to register the copyright and trademark in the program under the firm's name and market the programs to other law firms and trademark consulting firms. She informed George that BH&C owned all rights in the programs and that the firm intended to exploit this market edge aggressively. She invited George to serve on a committee that she was forming to guide Steve Roland and the firm's computer staff on improving the products and services. Although there were some other programs of this general type available, the firm considered George's program to be the best available – its user interface (designed by George) and networking features (originally designed by George, but later augmented by Steve Roland) went well beyond the competing programs.

George has come to you for advice. (You work at another IP law firm in town.) A prominent trademark search firm, TM r Us, has approached George about acquiring the program. In addition, Shiply and Elrod, another law firm in town specializing in IP is interested in bringing George on board in a lucrative "Of Counsel" capacity, which would allow George to develop a business around the TM Prosecution Toolkit. (Although George still enjoys practicing law, the past two years have surfaced a latent entrepreneurial streak in him. The Shiply and Elrod opportunity provides what he considers to be an ideal mix of legal practice and entrepreneurship. In addition, his income would go up significantly.) Shipley and Elrod would, however, want George to license the program (on a non-exclusive basis) to the firm and charge relatively high fees to any other firms (including BH&C, a principal competitor) using the software.

a) Who owns copyright in "TM Prosecution Toolkit"? "TM Fileshare"?
b) Could George prevent BH&C from further use of the programs?

Analysis

Problem 4-17: George v. BH&C

A. Computer software qualifies for protection under the Copyright Act. Although the scope of such protection is limited by various doctrines (most notably the idea-expression dichotomy (§102(b); see Chapter 7), a complex program of the type described would undoubtably qualify for some protection under copyright law.

TM Prosecution Toolkit

George is clearly the author of the "TM Prosecution Toolkit." Therefore, the critical question is whether his "authorship" falls to BH&C under the "work made for hire" doctrine or whether his rights were transferred to BH&C through assignment.

WMFH: BH&C will argue that George prepared TM Prosecution Toolkit as an employee within the scope of his employment. (They would have trouble asserting WMFH status under the "commissioned work" prong of the test because there does not appear to be any express agreement signed by George stating that the software was prepared as a WMFH and it is doubtful that this software fits within any of the enumerated categories.) George could rebut this assertion on the grounds that he was hired as an attorney to provide legal services and that BH&C actually discouraged his work on the TM Prosecution Toolkit. Under the Restatement 2d of Agency §228, to which the Supreme Court alluded in *CCNV*, the scope of employment encompasses three elements: (1) the copyrightable work falls within the type kind of work the employee is hired to perform; (2) the effort expended occurs substantially within the authorized time and space limits; and (3) the work is actuated, at least in part by a purpose to serve the master. The first two considerations favor George (he was hired to perform legal services and he prepared the software on his time while at home), while the third is ambiguous – George felt that his software development served BH&C, whereas BH&C actually discouraged such work. A very similar issue is posed in *Quinn v. City of Detroit*, 988

F.Supp. 1044, 1049 (E.D. Mich. 1997), cited on page 385, where the court held that computer program for tracking litigation developed by an attorney/supervisor was not a work made for hire. Similarly, George will likely prevail on this issue.

Assignment: BH&C could argue that George transferred, licensed, or donated the TM Prosecution Toolkit to the law firm. Any transfer of copyright ownership would have to be in writing (signed by George). BH&C may have a stronger argument that George voluntarily licensed the software to the firm through his actions. (His "particularly large" bonus could be viewed as compensation for providing this software to the firm.) George could possibly revoke such license. BH&C could also argue for a state law "shop right," although it appears that George did not conduct the work on BH&C's premises.

TM Fileshare

A. Assuming that George owns copyright in TM Prosecution Toolkit, he could assert "TM Fileshare" violates his derivative work right §106(2) to the extent that it "recasts, transforms, or adapts" TM Prosecution Toolkit. BH&C could argue George consented to the creation of the derivative work by his active involvement. BH&C could further argue that George's work on this project with within the scope of his employment (which by that point in time had expanded to included software design.) Assuming that George's work on TM Fileshare was not deemed a WMFH and that he actively collaborated with Steven Roland in developing this program, George would likely be viewed as a joint author with BH&C (Roland's work falls within the WMFH doctrine because he was the firm's webmaster). This would turn on factual issues relating to intent and collaboration.

B. Assuming that BH&C lost on the WMFH argument, it would contend that George consented to BH&C's use of the programs (and in fact was paid in the form of the bonus). The scope of any such implied license would have to be determined. In addition, George could revoke the license.

2. Duration and Renewal

PROBLEM 4-18

Determine the duration of copyright in the following cases:

* Arnold Author completes his novel *You'll Be Mine 'Til the End of Time* on February 28, 1996. The next day, February 29th, Arnold is hit by a bus and dies instantly. On what day does his copyright expire?

* While working for the New Englander Magazine, Arnold Author writes a story entitled "You'll Always Be Mine." The story is finally published by The New Englander in 2010. When does the copyright expire?

* Arnold Author began work on his greatest novel, *Time Is on My Side*, in 1990. In 1991, he completes the first three chapters. In 1992, he writes the middle three chapters. In 1993, he completes the final three chapters. In 1995, he signs an agreement with Time/Life Books to publish the novel. The contract assigns all copyright interests to Time/Life Books in exchange for 20 percent royalties based on the wholesale price. The book is finally published on January 1, 1996. Arnold dies on February 28, 1996. On what day does the copyright expire? Does your answer change if you assume that Arnold entered into a contract with Time/Life Books before writing the novel?

* At the time of his death on February 29, 1996, Arnold Author has completed three-fourths of his novel *Time Lives On*. His will leaves all his property to his spouse, Angela Author, who is also a writer. She plans to complete the novel by 1999. Time/Life Books has agreed to publish the completed manuscript in the year 2000. Assuming that all goes according to plan, when will copyright in "Time Lives On" expire?

PROBLEM 4-19

What is the duration of copyright in the following cases?

* Loretta Wrighter composed and sent a letter to her friend, Emily Johnson, in 1961. Emily has saved the letter in her correspondence file since that time. Loretta died in 1970. What is the term of protection for this work?

* Stephen Morris published his first novel, "Child's Play," at the age of 15 in 1920. He is still alive today. What is the term of protection for this work?

* Anita Author published (with proper notice) her novel entitled, "The Winds of Change," in 1970. She died three years later. What is the term of protection for this work?

* Penelope Painter painted her masterpiece entitled "Garden of Wildflowers" in 1953. She distributed copies with notice of copyright in 1955. She renewed the copyright in 1982. She died the next year. When does the copyright expire?

Analysis

Problem 4-18: Author's novel is an individual work created in 1996, so the duration of its protection is the life of the author plus 70 years. Under 17 U.S.C. § 305, the term runs to the end of the calendar year in which it would otherwise expire. Thus, the copyright should expire December 31, 2066.

Author's article for New Englander magazine was written "while he was working for" the magazine. While more facts would be helpful, it is reasonable to assume that the article was a work made for hire because it was done within the scope of his employment. Copyright in a work made for hire subsists for the lesser of 95 years from publication or 120 years from creation. In this case, the expiration date is 95 years from publication, or December 31, 2115. [However, if Author had written the article before 1985, the copyright would expire 100 years after he wrote it].

Author's novel is an individual work created between 1991 and 1993. However, the date of creation does not matter, because the copyright expires 70 years after the author's death, or December 31, 2066. An advance contract to write the book does not change this result, since it cannot make the novel into a work made for hire under 17 U.S.C. § 101(2).

Author's novel completed by his wife is probably not a joint work under *Erickson v. Trinity Theatres*. While both authors have contributed copyrightable material, there is no evidence that Author intended to merge his contribution with his wife's at the time he wrote his portion of the novel. Thus, his portion of the finished product is an individual work whose copyright expires 70 years after his death, on December 31, 2066. His wife's contribution is a derivative work which is separately copyrightable under 17 U.S.C. § 103, and the copyright in her contribution expires 70 years after her death. However, her copyright cannot prevent the use of his contributions after 2066. [If the authors were deemed to be joint authors, the copyright in the entire book would expire 70 years after her death].

Problem 4-19: Wrighter's letter presumably has not been published prior to January 1, 1978. Thus, under 17 U.S.C. § 303, it is entitled to the term of protection granted in section 302 -- the life of the author plus 70 years, or until December 31, 2040. However, section 303 provides that if the letter is published before December 31, 2002, the term of copyright protection is extended until December 31, 2047.

Morris's novel was published in 1920. Assuming he complied with the requisite formalities, he obtained a 28-year term of protection under the 1909 Act. In 1948, he was eligible to renew his copyright for an additional 28 years, giving him protection until 1976. The copyright would have expired in 1976, since the 1976 Act granted extended protection only for works in which copyright subsisted "at any time between December 31, 1976 and December 31, 1977." 17 U.S.C. § 304(b).

Author's novel was published in 1970, entitling it to protection under the 1909 Act. Under 17 U.S.C. § 304(a)(1), Author is entitled to 28 years of copyright protection (until December 31, 1998), and she or her successors are further entitled to renew and extend the copyright term for an additional 67 years, or until December 31, 2065.

Painter's publication occurred in 1955, giving her protection under the 1909 Act until 1983. She renewed in 1982, within one year before the expiration of the initial term, entitling her to 67 additional years of protection under 17 U.S.C. § 304(a)(1)(C). Thus, her copyright expires on December 31, 2050.

Division, Transfer and Termination

This is highly "technical" copyright material. Detailed treatment might best be saved for a more in-depth course on the subject. For those who think it essential – either because of intrinsic importance (which is nontrivial, especially in the entertainment industry) or theoretical interest (e.g., in the "second bite at the apple" policy of §§ 203 and 304) – the material here provides the barebones basics. The obvious supplementary case would be *Stewart v. Abend,* 495 U.S. 207 (1990) (the "Rear Window" case).

E. Rights of Copyright Owners

1. The Right to Make Copies

Arnstein v. Porter, page 404, illustrates the two kinds of copying: (1) the physical act of duplicating, and (2) copying that constitutes improper appropriation. This is an important distinction to drive home. Independent creation is a full defense to copyright infringement. But "substantial similarity" means more than "lack of completely independent creation." As for the evidentiary and litigation issues in the case, the role of expert testimony should be explored. Technical testimony – especially in music and software cases – can sometimes indirectly prove access. This is a close case on access, which raises the possibility that the law/fact distinction can be manipulated so as to keep a case from the jury.

PROBLEM 4-20

Scooter, a ventriloquist, performs a travelling show with a dummy that vocalizes the catchphrase "You Got the Right One, Uh-Huh." Scooter has performed this show since 1984. His performances have primarily been at elementary schools and Job Corps camps, but he did have a pavilion at the 1984 World's Fair in which he used the phrase. Scooter also attempted to promote his show by mailing unsolicited information packets to corporate executives. Included in these packets were letters that referred to his catchphrase. He mailed one such packet to a Pepsi executive in Baltimore in 1988, but the executive cannot recall ever receiving it.

In 1991, Pepsi starts a massive advertising campaign using Ray Charles singing "You Got the Right One Baby, Uh-Huh" with similar voice inflections. Scooter sues for copyright infringement. Does he have a case?

Analysis

Problem 4-20: Scooter's travelling ventriloquist show featured the catch-phrase "You Got the Right One, Uh-Huh." Scooter sued Pepsi after it came out with a remarkably similar ad campaign, and proves some remote possibility of access (an unsolicited packet mailed to a Pepsi executive in Baltimore, but which the executive cannot recall receiving). Should he prevail? *Takeall v. Pepsico*, 29 U.S.P.Q.2d 1913 (4th Cir. 1993) says "striking similarity" is not enough to preclude the need for any evidence of access. The mere assertion of access cannot overcome sworn testimony that there was no access. The dissent says that Scooter's public use of the phrase provides the necessary inference of access. In rejecting the idea that striking similarity precludes any need for evidence of access, the Fourth Circuit thus lines up with the Seventh Circuit [*Selle v. Gibb*, 741 F.2d 896, 901 (7th Cir. 1984)], and against the Second Circuit's rule in *Arnstein* and *Gaste v. Kaiserman*, 863 F.2d 1061 (2d Cir. 1988)

There is a second problem with the plaintiff's theory in this case: the "copying" is entirely of a short, though memorable, phrase. Short phrases are ordinarily not protectable under copyright law, and the *Takeall* court suggests in dictum that this phrase is not copyrightable. Even if it is copyrightable, however, it seems unreasonable to call the near-literal copying of such a short phrase "striking similarity." The Fourth Circuit might feel differently if several pages of text were found to be almost identical.

Nichols v. Universal Pictures Corp. is the famous "levels of abstraction" case. It is the classic vehicle for exploring the idea/expression dichotomy. A series of questions tracing the court's approach might be helpful. What "patterns of increasing generality" can be imposed on the plaintiff's play in the case? It might be helpful to construct a triangle or pyramid diagram to illustrate the point. The bottom of the triangle represents the literal text of the copyright owner's work, the work alleged to be infringed. The top represents the most general description of the work – "a boy-meets-girl play," for example, or "a cook book." Somewhere in the middle is "the" line separating the "idea" from the "expression." If the similarities between the copyrighted work and the defendant's work are at too general a level, they will be said to share only a common "idea." Another way to put it is to state that the key issue is the shared qualities held in common by the two works. If these qualities are numerous, and specific, they may be said to share expression. If they are few in number and more general, they may be said to share only a common idea. The one thing to watch for in this discussion is to keep two distinct issues separate: (1) the "patterns of generality" fitted onto the copyrighted work; and (2) the comparison between the copyrighted work and the allegedly infringing work. The key to *Nichols*, especially in the Introduction to IP or overview course, is that is quite nicely connects the early material on "copyrightability" or "protectability" with the later issue of infringement. The "patterns of abstraction" test can be restated in these terms: we cannot find infringement in this case because to do so would in effect protect an "idea" rather than "expression." That is, we begin by asking, "if we found infringement here, what would we *in effect* be saying was copyrightable (or protectable)." If we would have to find copyrightable something we think ought not be copyrighted, then there is no infringement, in other words. One can use this line of thought to show that infringement just carries forward basic policies already explored in the cases on copyrightability (e.g., *Baker v. Selden*).

The *Steinberg* case that follows provides ample room to explore these same themes. For students who learn better with a "visual" presentation, the two illustrations in the text will tell the whole tale. Here again, the question of whether the movie poster infringes the magazine cover drawing can be restated: how broad is plaintiff's copyright if we do find infringement? Likewise, how narrow if we don't? To show that it easier to frame and discuss the issue than to decide it, note that several of the casebook authors have made a habit of showing the two illustrations to federal judges when making presentations at judicial conferences. We always ask whether the judges would find infringement or not. The instructor will be happy to know that with many dozens of judges' votes now in, the judiciary seems split right down the middle! Some solace for the student struggling to predict outcomes in this area, at least.

PROBLEM 4-21

Dinopets markets a line of stuffed animal toys for children. The line includes five popular dinosaurs with exaggerated facial features (e.g., large droopy eyes, long teeth, rounded noses), cheerful pastel colors (pink, blue, green), distinctive stitching, and a soft cuddly cotton texture. About a year after Dinopets were on the market, Gigatoys, Inc., a leading toy manufacturer, developed a line of stuffed dinosaur toys. Its line, the Dinomites, featured the five dinosaurs in the Dinopets line as well as three others. Dinomites are about 25 percent larger than comparable Dinopets. Dinomites feature cute facial features (including droopy eyes and long teeth) and come in earth-tone colors (light brown, clay, sand, and stone). They are made of a suede-like material (somewhat coarser than the Dinopets). Dinopets sues Gigatoys, alleging copyright infringement. How would the analysis be conducted? What result?

PROBLEM 4-22

The Stunted Intellectuals, a psychedelic punk rap jazz fusion band, write songs by taking digital "samples" from previous compositions of a number of different genres, juxtaposing or superimposing them, and laying an electronic beat under and continuous rap commentary over the mixture. Some of the "samples" are from works in the public domain; of the remainder, some are identifiable and unaltered, some are identifiable but altered, and some are unrecognizable as a prior song. No sample lasts for longer than four seconds in any song, but some are repeated within the same song. Have the Stunted Intellectuals infringed the copyright on any of the songs they sample? On all of them?

PROBLEM 4-23

In preparing a biography of the reclusive author J.D. Salinger, Ian Hamilton gained access to letters Salinger wrote to a number of notable people that had been donated to university libraries. Through these letters and other sources, Hamilton constructed his biography of Salinger's life. Out of concern for copyright infringement, Hamilton quotes barely more than 200 words from the letters throughout the entire biography. Nonetheless, the letters are quoted or otherwise drawn upon in approximately 40 percent of the 192-page biography. To accurately describe events and emotions, impart some of Salinger's distinctive style, and avoid "pedestrian" reporting, Hamilton follows some of the passages from the letters closely.

The following examples illustrate Hamilton's use of the letters to present Salinger's life. In a 1943 letter to Whit Burnett, Salinger's friend, teacher, and editor at *Story* magazine, Salinger expressed his disapproval of the marriage of Oona O'Neil, with whom Salinger had been romantically involved, and Charlie Chaplin, the silent screen film star.

Salinger's Letter	Hamilton's Biography
I can see them at home evenings. Chaplin squatting grey and nude, atop his chiffonier, swinging his thyroid around his head by his bamboo cane, like a dead rat. Oona in an aquamarine gown, applauding madly from the bathroom. Agnes (her mother) in a Jantzen bathing suit, passing between them with cocktails. I'm facetious, but I'm sorry. Sorry for anyone with a profile as young and lovely as Oona's.	At one point in a letter to Whit Burnett, he provides a pen portrait of the Happy Hour Chez Chaplin: the comedian, ancient and unclothed, is brandishing his walking stick -- attached to the stick, and horribly resembling a lifeless rodent, is one of Chaplin's vital organs. Oona claps her hands in appreciation and Agnes, togged out in a bathing suit, pours drinks. Salinger goes on to say he's sorry -- sorry not for what he has just written, but for Oona: far too youthful and exquisite for such a dreadful fate.

In another letter to Burnett, Salinger expresses his disfavor of presidential candidate Wendell Wilkie.

Salinger's Letter	Hamilton's Biography

<table>
<tr><td>He looks to me like a guy who makes his wife keep a scrapbook for him.</td><td>[Salinger] had fingered [Wilkie] as the sort of fellow who makes his wife keep an album of his press cuttings.</td></tr>
<tr><td colspan="2">In another letter describing Parisians' adulation of American soldiers at the liberation of Paris, Salinger writes that the Parisians would have said "What a charming custom!" if:</td></tr>
<tr><td>Salinger's Letter</td><td>Hamilton's Biography</td></tr>
<tr><td>we had stood on top of the jeep and taken a leak.</td><td>the conquerors had chosen to urinate from the roofs of their vehicles.</td></tr>
<tr><td colspan="2">Has Hamilton infringed Salinger's copyright in his letters?</td></tr>
</table>

Analysis

Problem 4-21: As copyrightable subject matter becomes more highly constrained, the analysis of nonliteral infringement claims becomes more difficult. While there are undoubtedly similarities between the two lines of toys, not all such similarities are relevant in an infringement analysis. The court must first "dissect" -- remove from consideration -- those elements of the copyrighted work that are unprotectable, because they represent the idea of the stuffed dinosaur, because they are functional, or because they are *scenes a faire* endemic to the genre. What remains is the expression that must be compared to the infringing works. Presumably the color and some of the facial features (if altered from the historical dinosaur record) will fall into this latter category.

Arnstein and *Krofft* both suggest that the comparison for similarity is to be made by the "ordinary observer," and indeed in this case arguably by young children. This presents a real problem for copyright analysis. These ordinary observers may well make impermissible judgements of similarity based on uncopyrightable elements. To prevent this, courts in complex copyright cases have increasingly (1) decided factual questions such as this as a matter of law, and (2) permitted expert testimony regarding similarity to be given to the jury, despite the statements in *Arnstein* and *Krofft*.

Problem 4-22: The "digital sampling" of pieces of music, common in the rap genre and increasingly in other areas of music, presents a problem of "fragmented literal similarity." The question here is not whether there has been copying: everyone would agree that the defendants have literally copied from the plaintiff's sound recording. Rather, the question is generally whether this copying is sufficiently *substantial* to rise to the level of unlawful appropriation, or whether on the other hand it is de minimis. Two cases to consider the issue have found musical sampling to be *qualitatively* significant copying (and therefore infringement), even though in one case the copying was only of three words from the plaintiff's song. *Jarvis v. A&M Records*, [cite]; *Grand Upright Music v. Warner Bros. Records*, 780 F. Supp. 182 (S.D.N.Y. 1991).

It is helpful to illustrate this point by playing some examples of sampling, including the ones listed in the two cases above. In both cases, the focus seems to be on whether the material taken from the *plaintiff's* work is quantitatively or qualitatively significant. In theory, there is no reason to focus on the extent to which that material is used in the defendant's work, though in fact that turns out to be a relevant consideration.

What does this focus on the plaintiff's work say about artists like Koons (art) or Negitivland (music), whose entire works consist of samples, but frequently from a wide variety of different sources? These groups are walking a fine line, but if nothing they take from any one copyrighted work is significant, they should be OK. Further, they are probably entitled to a compilation copyright, assuming their material doesn't infringe the copyright of another.

Problem 4-23: This problem is based on *Salinger v. Random House, Inc.*, 811 F.2d 90 (2d Cir. 1987). Salinger is a reclusive author who does not give interviews or grant permission for his works to be used by others. He sued the author of an unauthorized biography, claiming that the biographer's use of letters violated his copyright in those letters. The first issue this problem presents is the copyright status of Salinger's letters. Contrary to the common assumption of most people, sending a letter to someone does not relinquish copyright in that letter. As a result, Salinger had a copyright in the letters on display in the university archives.

The next issue is whether the letters were actually copied. The court found numerous instances, including the ones cited in the problem, in which the biographer either quoted or closely paraphrased from several lines of a letter. It found that this was an easy case for nonliteral copyright infringement, therefore.

The *Salinger* case also presents a difficult issue regarding the alleged fair use of private letters in biography. We discuss that issue in more detail in the fair use section.

2. The Right to Prepare Derivative Works

As noted in the text, the scope of copyright has gradually expanded through the recognition and growth of the "right to prepare derivative works." In one sense, this right can be viewed as no more than the right to reproduce the copyrighted work in that courts require that there exist "substantial similarity" between the alleged derivative work and the protected work. Thus, in *Litchfield v. Spielberg*, the plaintiff claimed that screenplay she had written and submitted to Steven Spielberg about a cute alien entitled "Lokey from Maldomar" was infringed by Spielberg's blockbuster hit, "E.T." The Ninth Circuit considered the two works in detail and affirmed the district court's determination that defendants had not violated Litchfield's exclusive right to make copies (§106(1)) of her work because the two works were not "substantially similar." The court then considered Litchfield's alternative contention that E.T. was a derivative work of Lokey from Maldomar. As noted in the main case (*Anderson v. Stallone*), the Ninth Circuit rejected this effort to use §106(2) as merely a less exacting version of §106(1): "A work will be considered a derivative work only if it would be considered an infringing work if the material which it has derived from a prior work had been taken without the consent of a copyright proprietor of such prior work. . . . To prove infringe, one must show substantial similarity. Litchfield's arguments that section 106(2) radically altered the protection afforded by the law of copyright are frivolous."

If the right to prepare derivative works turns upon a showing of substantial similarity, then it can be argued that it is superfluous. Any violation of §106(2) can be brought as a violation of §106(1). Even if it is not doctrinally distinct from §106(1) in terms of the elements that need be proven to establish infringement, there is good reason to think about the right to prepare derivative works as distinct from the standpoint of the commercial reality surrounding the exploitation of many mass market copyrightable works. As George Lucas so clearly established in building his Star Wars empire, there is as much or more money to be made in merchandising (toys, video games, commercial tie-ins) and certainly sequels and prequels than in the primary market exploitation of the work in question (the film Star Wars). The ability to exploit these related markets vastly expands the financial rewards (and financing potential) for copyrightable works. The right to prepare derivative works makes explicit the opportunity to exploit collateral markets.

The *Stallone* case illustrates one of the key "scope" issues raised by the right to prepare derivative works: the copyrightability of "characters." It is well established that graphic (e.g., cartoon) characters receive protection under copyright law. Only the Disney Corporation can make or authorize others to make Mickey Mouse cartoons, subject of course to the fair use doctrine. Any comic strip or film depicting Mickey would infringe the §106(1) right and the §106(2) right. What has been more complicated is whether a literary character – such as "Sam Spade", "James Bond", "Superman", or "Rocky" – can also be protected, even if set in a new plot. By tracing the roots of the character protection doctrine, the *Stallone* case provides a wealth of examples for exploring the contours of this doctrine. What would be so terrible if others were allowed to produce their own story lines surrounding James Bond, Rocky, or the Seinfeld characters? In fact, there is growing body of "fan fiction" on the Internet and secondary literature about popular culture. Some copyright owners vigilantly police such unauthorized uses (see e.g., Castle Rock Entertainment, Inc., v. Carol Publishing Group, Inc., 150 F.3d 132 (2d Cir. 1998) (objecting to the publication of a trivia book about the Seinfeld show entitled "The Seinfeld Aptitude Test), while others welcome it (e.g., the creator of "The Sims" software allow others to market "skins" and other enhancements; Microsoft allows others use screen shots in developing guides for its software.) MGM, the owners of the James Bond franchise, contends that allowing such derivative works by others would undermine their development of the character. But isn't this more of a trademark problem? MGM would still be able to say that they are the "original" producers. But as the *Stallone* case implies, there may be only so many good plot twists and Sly should not have to compete with others in view of his having created the franchise. Others can create their own rags to riches hero.

Although it gets ahead of the lesson plan to some extent, it should be noted that the fair use doctrine (particularly the parody line of cases) allow some berth to use characters. Although the pre-1976 Act case involving Mickey Mouse did not afford much room, later cases suggest that parody remains a viable avenue. See, e.g., Suntrust Bank v. Houghton Mifflin Company, 268 F.3d 1257 (11th Cir. 2001) (allowing the use of the Gone with the Wind characters in a retelling from the perspective of slaves on the plantation). Mel Brooks' hilarious "Spaceballs" captures the parody concept well.

PROBLEM 4-24

Garamon, a French author, wrote a successful novel in French. The novel is copyrighted in France in 1954. Garamon authorized an English translation of his novel but failed to comply with the formalities then required under U.S. law to obtain a U.S. copyright in the translation. Thus the translation fell into the public domain. Subsequently, Oaktree Press photocopies and distributes the English translation of the novel in the United States. Garamon sues for infringement, not of the translation, but of the copyright on the underlying French novel. Who should prevail?

PROBLEM 4-25

A graphic artist for World Enquirer magazine is asked to produce a seamless integration of two photographs, so that it appears that two figures from separate photographs were in the same picture. To accomplish this, he uses digital imaging technology. He feeds both photographs into an optical character reader, or "scanner," and stores both images separately in the computer. Using a commercially available graphics program, he merges the pictures.

Assume one picture was copyrighted, and the other was in the public domain. What rights do the photo owner and World Enquirer have in the resulting image?

Analysis

Problem 4-24: This case occurred during the heyday of U.S. copyright formalities, when the accidental loss of copyright rights was relatively common, particularly for foreign authors. Garamon copyrighted a novel in French, but lost copyright for an authorized English translation because of his failure to comply with the U.S. notice requirement. The translation was therefore in the public domain. Oaktree duplicated the (uncopyrighted) translation and distributes it. Clearly this is not an infringement of the copyright in the translation, for there is none. Instead, Garamon sued for infringement of the *derivative* right on the *original* (still copyrighted) novel. In *Grove Press v. Greenleaf Publishing*, 247 F. Supp. 518 (E.D.N.Y. 1965), the court says Oaktree infringed the copyright in the original, because it created a substantially similar work.

As a policy matter, this is a difficult question. On the one hand, the derivative work is what was copied, and that is unquestionably in the public domain. If one accepts the policy arguments in force at that time, that work should be freely copyable. Further, because it entered the public domain for lack of a copyright notice, the accused infringer could presumably expect to rely on that lack of notice as evidence that the work wasn't copyrighted. On the other hand, Oaktree is copying not only the derivative translation, but effectively copying the copyrighted original work as well. The problem seems to be this: either Garamon can effectively protect both works, or (at least in English) he can effectively protect neither. Which outcome is preferable is a policy choice.

It may also be worth raising the issue of copyright restoration under 17 U.S.C. § 104A. If the court had gone the other way in *Grove Press*, Oaktree would presumably now be forced to stop publishing, since Garamon could apply to restore his copyright.

Problem 4-25: Digital manipulation of photos is increasingly common. Other manipulation is coarser, placing one image in a scene created for another (as in the movie Forrest Gump, for example, or the Coca-Cola ads featuring Humphrey Bogart. Either of these works is presumably a "derivative" of the original copyrighted photograph, though liability is easier to find when there are some pieces that remain identical in the two photos (as in the Forrest Gump example). Liability under section 106(2) should therefore be relatively easy to establish. A harder question is whether the digital manipulator owns any rights in the final product of the manipulation. Under section 103(a), the "portion" of the work used unlawfully cannot be copyrighted. In the example given in the text, the parts of the two images have been merged into an inseparable whole, and so courts would likely deny the infringer copyright entirely. Further, if the creative expression exists in the manipulation or alteration of the photos, that creative expression will almost by definition be in the "portion" of the work using infringing material.

Of course, if an artist manipulates her own photos, or is licensed to do so by the copyright owner, they can separately copyright any creative expression in the manipulated photo as a derivative work.

The Distribution Right

Quality King Distributors, Inc. v. L'anza Research International, Inc., discussed on page 437, illustrates a copyright owner's distribution right. Importer lawfully purchased shampoo overseas but reimported product into US. L'anza wanted to block these imports. The first sale limitation terminates the distribution right; therefore L'anza didn't have any right to sue. You might point out that this is an example of arbitrage in a gray market. From a business point of view, the importer was taking advantage of L'anza's price discrimination strategy by purchasing at lower price abroad and selling the same product domestically at lower price than MSRP.

PROBLEM 4-26

Lee, a law student, attends an expensive private school. After buying the books for his first-year classes, he underlines key passages in the books and takes some notes in the margins. At the end of the first year of law school, Lee sells his books back to the law school bookstore. The bookstore in turn sells them to incoming law students the next fall as "used books." Under what theory might Lee or the bookstore be liable for copyright infringement? Should they be?

Analysis

Problem 4-26: Clearly Lee has not made copies of the book -- he has merely sold back the original work, albeit with changes. Selling the book to the bookstore unaltered would be protected under the first sale doctrine, as would the bookstore's subsequent commercial resale. [This is why used bookstores can exist].

The question raised by *Mirage v. Albuquerque A.R.T.*, cited in the text on page 445, is whether alterations to the book change that result. Under *Mirage*, *any* changes to the book would be infringing derivative works -- conceivably including things such as bent pages or broken spines. Professor Goldstein's approach, which would require a derivation to contain copyrightable material to be infringing under section 106(2), seems the better approach. Note however that margin-noting a book may still constitute the preparation of a derivative work, assuming copyrightable expression was created in the notes -- which seems likely. Thus, Lee would be liable for infringing the copyright owner's right to prepare derivative works, *even if he never sold the book at all.* [Under *Midway v. Arctic*, by contrast, one could argue that the interlineations were not derivative works because they had no economic value. The test is troubling in theory, though, and probably unworkable in practice].

So far, the results above can be reached without reference to the distribution right. The *bookstore's* liability is what hinges on distribution. The bookstore did not prepare the derivative work. However, if the work is infringing, and if *Mirage* is correct that the first sale doctrine does not apply to derivative works, then the bookstore is presumably liable for reselling the infringing derivative work.

These results seem troubling, and they suggest some of the problems with stretching the derivative works right too far.

3. Public Performance and Display Rights

PROBLEM 4-27

Ralston Hotels, a national hotel chain, offers guests an "in-room video rental" service. A menu is displayed on the guest's interactive television screen, and the guest can select both a movie and a starting time by using his remote control. Portland Pictures, a major movie producer that owns the video rental rights to its movies, sues Ralston, alleging that each selected movie is a "public performance" and demanding royalties. Who should prevail?

PROBLEM 4-28

Buford, the owner of the Pumpwell service station on a busy commercial street, receives approximately 20 calls each day from customers. Because of the volume of repair work that Pumpwell does, it frequently must put callers on hold. Buford decides to provide those callers with music while they are holding, so he patches his radio into the telephone. When a call is placed on hold, the caller hears a station selected by Buford until the call is picked up again. ASCAP sues Pumpwell for copyright infringement, claiming that Pumpwell is publicly performing its songs. Does ASCAP have a case?

Analysis

Problem 4-27: Can a hotel offer its guests "movies-on-demand?" Playing the movie in a VCR is unquestionably a "performance," so the only issue is whether it is "public." The courts have focused on whether the hotel room is "open to the public." The Third Circuit said yes in two cases involving Columbia Pictures: *Columbia Pictures v. Redd Horne*, 749 F.2d 154 (3d Cir. 1984) and *Columbia Pictures v. Aveco*, 800 F.2d 59 (3d Cir. 1986). These decisions -- which involved private viewing studios rented for a limited time -- reason that the public is invited into the studio (albeit at various times). By contrast, the Ninth Circuit held that the viewing of movies rented to individual hotel guests did not constitute a public performance in *PREI v. Columbia Pictures*, 866 F.2d 278 (9th Cir. 1989). The court distinguished the Third Circuit line of cases by concluding that a hotel room is no longer "open" once it has been rented, a conclusion which would seem to apply with equal force to the viewing rooms in the Third Circuit cases. On the other hand, the Ninth Circuit also said that if the movie could be played to multiple guests *simultaneously*, unlike a rented video which is physically delivered to one room at a time, it is a public performance. This suggests that current video-on-demand systems in hotels require performance licenses.

Under the Third Circuit's rationale, is a hotel guest liable for singing in the shower?

Problem 4-28: This problem tests the limits of *Aiken* under the 1976 Act. Under section 110(5), the relevant question is whether Buford's "patch" is a device commonly found in ordinary homes. The answer is unclear. Both radios and telephones are found in homes; if Buford had done nothing more than play the radio near the telephone receiver, he clearly would not be liable. Does it make sense that the result should change if he wires the two together *to produce the same result*? [There is also a question whether this is a "public" performance at all, given that only one person at a time *can* hear it. That question seems to track problem 4-30, above.]

The court in *Prophet Music v. Shamla Oil,* 26 USPQ2d 1554 (D. Minn. 1993) found infringement on the grounds that Buford is "retransmitting" and therefore falls within the limitation of section 110(5)(B). On this rationale, Aiken also seems clearly liable for retransmitting.

Moral Rights

Contributory and Vicarious Infringement

Although the Copyright Act does not expressly provide for contributory or vicarious infringement (unlike the Patent Act), the courts have long extended the reach of the copyright to acts which contribute to or vicariously benefit from copyright infringement by others. This issue has become particularly important in the digital age. Although *Fonovisa* relates to a physical world means of contributing to and vicariously benefitting from the infringing acts of others – the organizers of a swap meet providing space to vendors selling unauthorized reproductions of audio tapes – it provides the foundation for the Napster case which we present in the "Digital Copyright Law" section of the chapter. It provides a clear discussion of the evolution of the indirect liability doctrines and applies them to a somewhat new context. The critical issue is how far should this reach should extend. Knowledge in the case of contributory infringement and control in the case of vicarious infringement are the touchstones, but neither concept is self-defining. With this foundation, students will be better prepared to take the next steps into the Napster and Grokster cases discussed later in the chapter.

PROBLEM 4-29

Industrial Music Co. (IM) develops and produces a device known as a digital music filter for home and personal use. The filter allows individuals with access to audio tapes to "remix" those tapes themselves, and create new works in which sounds from existing works are speeded up, slowed down, added to or subtracted from, or combined with other preexisting works. IM markets its filter as a device for amateur musicians who want to edit their own works, but IM knows that approximately half of the filters it sells are used for "sampling" or otherwise copying copyrighted works without authorization. Is IM guilty of contributory infringement? If so, with every sale, or only with some sales? Can the sale of the filter be enjoined?

Analysis

Problem 4-29: This problem provides an interesting transition into the next section, dealing with fair use. At least some digital sampling is illegal, and some of that illegal sampling will take place on IM machines. Given this, should it be illegal to sell "sampling machines"? The legal answer is to define a certain threshold as contributory infringement. Determining that threshold divided the Court *Sony v. Universal City Studios*, cited in text *infra*. The majority said a device does not contribute to infringement if it is "capable of a substantial noninfringing use," which is the test in patent law. The four dissenters would have required that it have a "predominantly noninfringing use," a standard which would have made VCRs illegal. [The government's NII White Paper endorses a standard similar to the dissent's view -- a "primary purpose or effect" test -- in the limited context of Internet copying devices].

The problem is set up so that the test chosen determines the outcome. Because 50% of samples are illegal by hypothesis, IM is not infringing under the current test, but would be infringing under the dissent's test.

F. Defenses

Fair use is many respects the most important and vague of copyright's many defenses and for those reasons we devote substantial pages to explicating its boundaries. Although the 1976 Act offers a four factor codification of the doctrine, its boundaries cannot be appreciated without a review of cases from the various categories of disputes in which the doctrine arises. We begin with the classic case of *Harper & Row*, page 451, which illustrates the general method of applying the four factor calculus. The case itself is easily disputable. The defendants "scooped" a rather small part (less than 300 words) of large work of great public interest (former President Ford's explanation for his historic decision to pardon his predecessor, Richard Nixon). On the other hand, this scoop adversely affected the market for exclusive articles based on this authorship. Although the case itself raises more questions than it answers, it provides one of the Supreme Court's principal explications of the 1976 Act's fair use formulation.

We then move on to other important fair use cases that establish important ground rules for competition in a range of contexts. In *Sony v. Universal City Studios,* page 462, the Supreme Court imported into copyright law patent law's "staple article of commerce" defense in concluding that Sony was not liable for contributory copyright infringement because its Betamax video cassette recorder was capable of substantially noninfringing uses. The Court weighed the use of the machines and reasoned that the Betamax could be used for noncopyrighted material (e.g., live feed of a town council meeting) and consensual copying. Also, consumers would be using the Betamax to "time-shift" for personal use and thus the market would not be substantially impacted. You might point out that the studios went after Sony under an indirect cause of action because of the negative publicity that would have resulted from "Universal City Studios v. John Doe, TV Viewer [and filmgoer]".

The "market failure" rationale for fair use discussed in the case has been under fire recently, as cases such as *American Geophysical Union* make clear. If electronic clearance mechanisms and collective rights organizations become ubiquitous, fair use will either wither away or have to be rethought. The latter project is an active one in the academy right now, with numerous thoughtful scholars trying to reconnect this area of the law to the policies historically animating it, viz., forthrightly favoring certain classes of uses and users. These ideas are worth discussing, in light of the pressing issues of digital content on the internet and Congress' rush to legislate strong (fair use-proof?) protections, e.g., in the Digital Millenium Copyright Act of 1998.

Campbell and the "Air Pirates" problem illustrate the parody branch of fair use jurisprudence and are good vehicles for exploring the limits of the market failure rationale for fair use.

PROBLEM 4-30

A home movie taken by a witness named Zales captures the shooting of President John F. Kennedy in Dallas in 1963. Only days after the shooting, Earth magazine buys the exclusive rights to the Zales film. It subsequently publishes some Zales frames in a magazine special on the assassination. The Zales frames are also appended to a government report by the Whitewash Commission on the assassination. Stone, a writer who is convinced that the Whitewash Report is flawed, unsuccessfully seeks permission from Earth to reprint the Zales pictures in his book alleging a conspiracy to kill the president. Undaunted by Earth's refusal, Stone breaks into Earth's offices and photocopies the pictures, which he then publishes in his book. Earth sues for copyright infringement. Stone defends on grounds of fair use, and offers to turn over all profits from his book to Earth. What result?

PROBLEM 4-31

Garrison, a scholar who believes that Lee Harvey Oswald acted alone, is incensed by Stone's book. Garrison publishes a book that he styles *A Rebuttal to Stone*. In it, Garrison follows Stone's organization in detail, presenting and refuting each of Stone's arguments. In doing so, Garrison quotes liberally from Stone's work. Garrison does not use the Zales pictures, however. Stone sues for copyright infringement. Is Garrison's work fair use?

PROBLEM 4-32

Refer back to the Salinger-Hamilton case (Problem 4-23 above). Can Hamilton successfully argue a fair use defense?

Analysis

Problem 4-30: The facts are based on *Time, Inc. v. Bernard Geis Associates*, 293 F. Supp. 130 (S.D.N.Y. 1968). Geis surreptitiously photographed the Zapruder pictures from Life's offices after having been refused permission to use them (though in the actual case he did not break into the building). Nonetheless, the court found that Geis' use was fair. While the court noted that "Fair use presupposes good faith and fair dealing," it concluded that Geis could have obtained the pictures from public sources, including the Warren Commission report. The court concluded that there was a strong public interest in promoting scholarship on the Kennedy assassination, and that Life was not injured directly because it did not sell the Zapruder pictures and did not compete with Geis. Central to the court's conclusion appears to have been Geis' offer to turn over to Time all of the profits from his work.

Interestingly, the court did not analyze the amount and substantiality of the portion used, now a section 107 factor. While Geis used only a few frames in his book, it is fair to assume that they were the most significant ones. Further, if each individual frame was copyrighted, then Geis has used several of Zapruder's works in their entirety.

Further, it is open to question whether or not Life has suffered economic injury from Geis' use. Surely Life found some value in owning the film and in its exclusive story on the assassination. Does that value dissipate once the story is published?

The case is also notable for the proposition that having asked for permission and been refused *does not* affect the fair use analysis.

Problem 4-31: This problem raises the fair use question in the context of "thin" copyright protection. Stone has created a factual work which embodies a number of facts and ideas which are unprotectable, along with protected expression. [Reference back to *Hoehling* is probably appropriate at this point]. Copying the facts and ideas will not be infringement, so the copyright claim will have to be limited to those portions of Stone's book which are (a) protectable expression and (b) actually used by Garrison.

Applying the four factors from section 107 produces the following results:

1) Garrison's book was written for scholarship, and his use of Stone's copyrightable material appears to be for the purposes of criticism or comment. These are public interest, transformative

uses which favor a finding of fair use. On the other hand, Garrison's work is probably also commercial in nature, which cuts against a finding of fair use, at least to some extent.

2) Stone's work is published and factual, both considerations that support a finding of fair use.
3) This is a critical factor here. How much copyrightable expression is taken is not easily determinable from the problem. In addition to the quantitative and qualitative significance of the taking, determination of this factor may also depend on whether Garrison's use was reasonable and necessary for the effectiveness of his technique, borrowing the "reasonably necessary" test from the parody cases. This factor could go either way.
4) The market analysis is complex. The books may or may not directly compete for sales, depending on whether subject matter or viewpoint is the determining factor in purchase decisions. Garrison's criticism of Stone's book may reduce Stone's sales, but that substantive effect is not actionable under copyright law.

It is not at all clear how courts would come out in this instance. The determining factors will probably be the amount taken, and the evidence of market effect on Stone's book.

Problem 4-32: This problem is based on *Salinger v. Random House, Inc.*, 811 F.2d 90 (2d Cir. 1987), discussed above. In that case, Hamilton and Random House published an unauthorized biography of J.D. Salinger which included quotations and paraphrases from his letters. The Second Circuit preliminarily enjoined the publication of the biography, after concluding that Hamilton's was not fair use. Applying the four statutory factors, the court concluded that Hamilton's work did implicate a public interest in biography of public figures. However, the facts that the letters were unpublished and Salinger intended them to remain so, that a large part of the letters had been taken, and that the letters occupied a prominent place in Hamilton's biography counseled against a finding of fair use. [The market impact factor was largely neutral; it is worth noting that the court inquired into market effects in spite of Salinger's determination that he would never avail himself of that market opportunity]. The opinion is highly recommended reading.

PROBLEM 4-33

ReplayTV has introduced a digital video recorder (DVR), a digital version of the VCR. Thanks to digital technology, the ReplayTV 4500 offers consumers the ability to instantly skip over commercials with the click of a 30-second advance fast forward button. In addition, the large storage capacity of the ReplayTV 4500 hard drive enables consumers to store up to 60 hours of content, making archiving of content much more convenient than on VCRs. Consumers can use an automated feature to bypass commercials. A recent survey of DVR owners finds that 35 percent say they never watch commercials while nearly 60 percent say they watch them only occasionally. The television industry fears that these capabilities will make advertisers much less willing to support their broadcasts. They sue to enjoin sale of ReplayTV's DVR. How should the court rule on this case?

Analysis

Problem 4-33: This case, based on actual litigation brought against ReplayTV by a number of media corporations, should be analyzed along the lines of the distinct capabilities bearing on the reproduction and distribution of copyrighted works: (1) the 30 second advance/commercial skip feature; (2) capacity to record (and archive) television programming. In many respects, the ReplayTV technology at issue here is a much more effective (faster, greater storage capacity, and more user-friendly) form of the VCR which the Supreme Court found to be permissible under copyright law.

The problem can effectively be used to discuss the extent to which an interpretation of copyright law based on one generation of technology (an early form of analog video recording) should be applied to a more advanced form of technology (digital video recorders). The language of *Sony* is quite broad – immunizing the seller of technology from contributory copyright infringement where its products can be shown to be "capable of substantial non-infringing uses." The record in the *Sony* case was quite different from the facts in the ReplayTV context: (1) relatively few consumers skipped advertisements (and typically had to view them to some extent in order to fast forward through them); (2) relatively few consumers archived programming (and it was costly and inconvenient to do so); and (3) a market had not yet formed for rental of movies and other content. Should these factors play a significant role in assessing the legality of DVRs? Should the *Sony* analysis be reconsidered in light of technological advances?

It is worthwhile to reconsider the "staple article of commerce" doctrine developed in *Sony* as well as its application of the fair use test to unauthorized time-shifting (and commercial skipping).

PROBLEM 4-34

Greenwich Systems is a software company that sells the world's most popular "screen saver." (A screen saver is a computer program that blanks a computer screen after a certain period of inactivity and then replaces the old screen with another. Screen savers are highly creative and are designed to entertain the viewer as well as to protect the integrity of the screen). Greenwich's screen saver, called "flying toasters," shows pop-up toasters with wings flying across the screen.

Delaware, a small start-up company, licenses the popular "Bloom County/Outland" characters Opus and Bill for use in its own screen saver. Its program contains a number of humorous replacement screens, including one screen in which Opus shoots down flying toasters with a shotgun. The flying toasters look very similar to Greenwich's. Greenwich sues for copyright infringement, and Delaware defends on grounds of parody. Who should prevail?

PROBLEM 4-35

Air Pirates, a publisher of counter-culture adult comic books, developed a series of comic books cynically depicting popular children's cartoon characters, including Mickey and Minnie Mouse, Donald Duck, and Goofy, as promiscuous, drug dealing rogues. One of the magazine covers had the accompanying image (Figure 4-7).

[see Figure 4-7 in text]

Should Air Pirates' use be considered fair use?

Analysis

Problem 4-34: This problem is based on *Berkeley Systems v. Delrina*, a case filed in the Northern District of California in 1993. Clearly, the idea of Opus shooting down flying toasters is a parody of the original. But it is also commercial. The effect of this parodic content is similar in many respects to *Campbell* -- first factor somewhat favors fair use, because the parodic, transformative character outweighs the commercial value. The copyrighted work is artistic, and the taking is substantial, both of which oppose fair use. Finally, it is the market effect factor where this case differs from *Campbell.* Because these products compete directly, Berkeley loses sales if Delrina's product succeeds, because the customers buy Delrina's product rather than Berkeley's. Thus, the fourth factor cuts against fair use, and that should make the difference in this case.

In the actual case, the court issued a preliminary injunction against Delrina's use of the flying toasters, and Delrina switched to images of Opus shooting down helicopter toasters. The opinion is unreported, but some of the details of the case can be found in the court's opinion in *Jefferson Airplane v.*

Berkeley Systems, 886 F. Supp. 713 (N.D. Cal. 1994), a suit which involved the rock band Jefferson Airplane's claim to own the original copyright in the flying toasters.

Problem 4-35: This case is *Walt Disney Productions v. Air Pirates*, 581 F.2d 751 (9th Cir. 1978). Disney sued, claiming that the parody of Mickey Mouse injured the image of its copyrighted character. The court found the parody infringing, concluding that the defendants took more than was necessary to "conjure up" Mickey Mouse in the minds of readers, and that that fact was determinative. Under *Campbell*, that result is at least open to question.

This case also presents a related issue: should the effect of the parody, rather than its substitutability, be a relevant factor in parody cases? Here the effect was to "tarnish" the wholesome nature of the Disney character. Is that actionable, or is it merely the equivalent of a "scathing review" which reduces the demand for the original? Presenting the issue in this way makes for a nice transition to the trademark cases, where reputational effect turns out to be important.

G. Digital Copyright Law

The expansion of copyright law to encompass the digital age led us to add a new section to the copyright chapter intended to integrate this rapidly expanding dimension of the field. In addition to raising issues that fall within the traditional provisions of copyright law – such as whether the posting of a literary work to a website constitutes an infringement of the right reproduce and the right to distribute – the digital revolution has brought about entirely new copyright-like protections, such as the Digital Millennium Copyright Act (DMCA) which is intended to augment the traditional protections afforded by copyright law.[5] It would be a mistake, however, to characterize these new dimensions as mere extensions of copyright law. The DMCA's anti-circumvention provisions do not, for example, give way to fair use. Rather, the statutory framework builds in exceptions, most of which are far narrower than the fair use defense.

The materials in this section read somewhat more like a textbook than a casebook in that we wanted to describe the technology at issue, the historical development of this new branch of copyright-like law, and the various regimes applicable in the digital copyright arena. Students should be able to appreciate the evolutionary process in part because this field of law is far from an angle of repose. We expect continued rapid evolution of this body of law. Just in the few months since the book has appeared, the Central District of California has found that a new peer-to-peer architecture used by Grokster and Morpheus is not liable for contributory or vicarious liability because the software distributors lack the degree of control that the Napster technology used. Metro-Goldwyn-Mayer Studios, Inc. v. Grokster, Ltd., 66 U.S.P.Q.2d 1579 (C.D. Ca. 2003). Furthermore, another court has upheld the constitutionality of the subpoena provision of the DMCA, which is being used by the record industry to identify the identity of users of peer-to-peer software who make available copyrighted works without authorization. This escalation of legal tactics will characterize the digital copyright field for the foreseeable future.

It is worth spending some time exploring the structure and provisions of the DMCA, summarized on pages 499-502. The anticircumvention provisions and the OSP safe harbor are among the most complex aspects of the intellectual property field.

The *Napster* case, page 505, marks a particularly important development in the evolution of digital copyright law. This case provides a good vehicle for exploring the limits of the *Sony* staple article of commerce doctrine as well as the application of indirect liability in the digital domain. The Ninth Circuit's

---

5 Note that we deal separately with copyright protection for computer software in Chapter 7. The Digital Copyright Law unit deals with means that have been developed to secure the distribution of traditional copyrighted works within digital networks.

handling of the OSP safe harbor defense was less than satisfactory so we address that issue in the first note following the case.

PROBLEM 4-36

Even before Napster was shut down, a range of more decentralized peer-to-peer architectures – most notably, Morpheus, KaZaa, and Grokster – had developed substantial followings on the Internet. Unlike Napster, these architectures do not store any file names on central servers. Rather they merely provided software that permits participants in a file sharing network to connect to other participants. Their software enables searches for files on these other computers, but none of the file names pass through the software providers' servers. They earn income through banner advertisements that are sent out to network participants. The record labels have sued these companies. How should a court rule on their claims of vicarious and contributory liability?

PROBLEM 4-37

Return to problem 4-33 regarding digital video recorders and consider the following additional feature of the ReplayTV 4500: consumers can connect their device to the Internet and send files of television broadcasts to others owning ReplayTV devices. How should this feature be analyzed? Does it depend on whether any premium channel content (e.g., HBO) can be distributed in this manner?

Analysis

Problem 4-36: This problem was answered in Metro-Goldwyn-Mayer Studios, Inc. v. Grokster, Ltd., 66 U.S.P.Q.2d 1579 (C.D. Ca. 2003). The analysis for this case logically starts with *Napster*, but the decentralized nature of the Grokster and Morpheus peer-to-peer schemes strongly affects the issues of knowledge (affecting contributory liability) and supervision/control (affecting vicarious liability).

Contributory liability requires actual or constructive knowledge of specific infringing activity and substantial/material contribution to the infringing activity. The *Napster* opinion makes it clear specific knowledge, whether actual or constructive, is required. Under *Sony's* "staple article of commerce" doctrine, the mere fact that an article has infringing uses is not by itself enough to find liability. Napster's centralized search system was sufficient to provide it with actual knowledge of infringing activity. Grokster uses FastTrack, a pre-existing network which predates the service itself. (At this point, it may be worth taking the opportunity to discuss the "nodes" and "supernodes" network paradigm to demonstrate how and why Grokster has no centralized directory). Morpheus uses an open-source sharing system known as Gnutella and is even less centralized; there are no supernodes at all. The lack of easily compiled collections of user information led the Central District of California to find this degree of knowledge to be insufficient to create actual knowledge. Note that the information was not *impossible* to collect; the court merely did not find a duty upon Grokster and Morpheus to go to the lengths necessary to collect this information. (Though, as noted below, the issue of "designing around" as a form of "willful blindness" should arise through discussion)

The Central District of California also reiterated *Napster* and *Sony* in holding that the mere provision of a product or service which *can* be used for infringing purposes is not enough. The court did suggest that if Grokster or Morpheus actively provided assistance or support to specific users knowing that they, specifically, were engaged in identifiably infringing activity on an individual basis, that would probably constitute material participation. The requirements for contributory liability appear to have strong requirements, and fairly high bars.

As to vicarious liability, the court was less forgiving, but still found no liability. The prong of direct financial interest was fairly easily proven; the quantity of advertising revenue is directly linked to the frequency of use, and given that a substantial proportion of end users were engaged in infringing activity, this had the direct effect of increasing Morpheus' and Grokster's revenues. The court found this bridge easy to make and easy to cross. Even so, the defendants were granted summary judgment because the decentralized network structure gave far less ability to supervise or control end user behavior than Napster possessed. (This was found to be so even given that Streamcast, which owns Morpheus, had access to the software source code and could have installed various filtering mechanisms in the code. It was not stated whether this was because the precautions were actually infeasible or whether liability does not actually extend that far)

The actual outcome does not, however, close the door on discussion; there is much reason to believe that these decentralized architectures were designed to circumvent the legal points of liability which resulted in Napster's ultimate destruction. Though intent is often alluded to in the analysis, it is not a formal element and has little formal evidentiary weight in the opinions. Is this proper? Is the Holmesian "bad man" encouraged to skirt the boundaries of these doctrines? Do these lines effectively permit or proscribe certain underlying behaviors, or does it only circumscribe the manner in which they may be performed? The use of these services is largely transparent; most end users notice little functional difference between using Napster and using Morpheus, KaZaa, or Grokster. Just as narrowly worded patents can be "patented around," so too can narrow legal rules be "coded around" by ingenious programmers. Is this desirable? Would a broader "50-yard rule" appealing to general principles of tort be preferable, or would it inefficiently chill the network benefits that so define the utility of the Internet itself? You might explore with the class how they would argue an appeal to the Ninth Circuit. How would the content providers get around the *Sony* staple article of commerce doctrine? Should that doctrine be restricted to the facts of *Sony*? Was the Court legislating in *Sony* or merely implementing a conservative doctrine of shifting the burden to Congress to restrict technological progress in the name of copyright protection?

Problem 4-37: The technology at the center of this problem highlights the general trend of digital technology toward ease of reproduction and distribution of content. When television was first introduced, the signal could be controlled at the point of origin. Digital technology has now shifted that point of control downstream to the consumer. The *Sony* case was a midpoint along the way. VCR technology allowed consumers to record content, but did not provide an effective means for distribution. With advances in data compression (codecs) and rollout of broadband, consumers can, with the technology described in this problem, nearly effortlessly distribute television programming throughout the Internet.

This problem calls into play the *Sony*, *Napster*, and *Morpheus/Grokster* cases. It is worthwhile asking whether students need to know more about the technology. On the surface, the DVR seems to be just a more versatile version of the VCR and should therefore fall within the staple article of commerce defense. But the technology is different from the VCR in potentially significant ways. For example, indirect liability might turn on whether ReplayTV servers play any role (as did the Napster servers) in the distribution of content. Another issue is whether the content would be redistributed with television commercials omitted. As regards traditional over the air broadcasting, ReplayTV could well argue that its technology actually increases the market for commercial supported programming (assuming that commercials are not removed). The argument is much harder to make for premium channel programming, such as HBO. This feature of the technology would clearly have an adverse effect on subscriptions.

H. International Issues in Copyright

The subject of international copyright law is vast and complex. This brief section is intended to summarize the principal treaties harmonizing copyright law on the international stage and to highlight the choice of law issues involved in international disputes. It is important to emphasize that unlike patent law, which is largely territorial in scope, copyrights are recognized in almost all nations of the world without formalities (registration), although U.S. court must at times apply foreign law to disputes arising in the

United States. Adequate coverage of this complex body of law requires a full course on international intellectual property law or international copyright law.

I. Remedies

The material on remedies is necessarily brief. It is worthwhile to provide students with an overview of the various remedies available:

- Injunctive Relief
- Monetary Relief
    - actual damages and infringer's profits (from such infringement); or
    - statutory damages (if work registered prior to infringement) for each work (all parts of a compilation or derivative work constitute a single work)
    - $750 < court award < $30,000
        - if innocent infringement, then lower bound is $200
        - if willful infringement, then upper bound is $150,000
- Criminal Prosecution
    - No Electronic Theft Act
- Costs and Attorney Fees (if work registered prior to infringement and within court's discretion (to prevailing party)

Sheldon v. MGM, page 523, provides the framework for establishing an infringer's profits from infringement. All the plaintiff need do is place the defendant's gross revenue into evidence and then the burden shifts to the defendant to pare down this amount to that which is attributable to the infringing act.

Chapter 5 Trademarks and Unfair Competition

A. Introduction

B. What Can Be Protected as a Trademark?

1. Trademarks, Trade Names, and Service Marks

2. Color, Fragrance, and Sounds

Qualitex Co. v. Jacobson Products, page 538, is a good case to introduce the major themes of the chapter. The case involves a seller of dry cleaning pads (which look much like disposable ironing board covers). The seller sold pads of a certain color; a competitor introduced similar pads of the same color. The Court held that this was actionable as a violation of the first seller's trademark rights. Dry cleaners associated the seller's color with a particular source. The doctrine of functionality does not create an absolute bar to use of color alone as a trademark. Other examples of unusual trademarks include Owens Corning's pink insulation, NBC's three chimes, and the MGM lion roar.

One might well begin by addressing the basic differences between trademarks and the other areas of IP law studied up to this point in this course. Here a quick series of questions about what is *not* required to secure trademark protection will probably do the job. Creativity? Originality? Nontriviality? No; the goal is not (primarily) to stimulate the creation of new product-identifiers. Protection of the mark itself is an indirect consequence of the primary goal: protecting the *consumer*. Here at the outset is a good time to explore the ways in which trademarks are and are not like the statutory property rights covered in Chapters 3 and 4. There is ample room here for practical comparisons as well as theoretical exploration; the precise mix is a matter of taste.

The wide-ranging but clear opinion in *Qualitex* provides the foundation for a number of issues beyond these basics. The choice of which to emphasize might depend on how one plans to teach the chapter as a whole.

There are enough colors available to suppliers to permit a single color to become associated with a particular source. Using this point, you may wish to lay a foundation for a more thorough discussion of functionality later. The idea of "color depletion" – a species of functionality – provides a good starting point. If color depletion were in fact an issue, who would it affect? Competitors of the trademark owner, of course. So this trademark doctrine brings competitors of the trademark owner into the picture. Highlighting this point will permit later development of the idea that functionality limits trademark rights by expanding the analysis beyond the simple "dyad" of the consumer and the supplier. The effect of trademark protection on competitors is another variable that must be considered. It asks about the effect *on competitors* of protecting a single seller's trade symbol. Emphasizing the point here, where it is first introduced, may smooth the way later. When the student encounters the seemingly difficult notion of "non-reputation related advantages" as the key to functionality, he or she will not be as daunted by the confusing verbiage. One way to square the discussion with the consumer association-oriented holding in the case is to stress the reason that trademark law is concerned about excessively limiting the competitors' range of product-identifier choices: which is, of course, the maintenance of robust competition, presumably for the benefit of consumers. There is thus a tradeoff hidden in these issues: between lowering consumer search costs (by protecting trademarks), and keeping competitors' entry costs low (by guarding against overly expansive trademark protection for product labels and features).

C. Establishment and Extension of Trademark Rights

1. Distinctiveness

Zatarain's is a solid introductory case on the issue of the "spectrum" of trademark distinctiveness. The goal here is to explore how the general policy of protecting consumers against confusion translates into detailed doctrinal considerations. The decidedly undistinctive "Fish Fri" label provides a good vehicle for discussion of the policies behind a disfavored category of protection (descriptive marks) and a prohibited one (generic marks). It is also only a shade different from "Chick-Fri," yet that shade makes a difference. A series of questions can be posed here to explore the effect of decisions such as *Zatarain's*. What of the consumers who had, despite the odds, come to associate Fish Fri with a single source? How are thresholds set in trademark law, for example to determine how many consumers' individual mental associations add up to "secondary meaning"? Note too the geographic element here; *where* was secondary meaning explored? And why should validity of a federally registered mark – good against subsequent adopters nationwide, for all practical purposes – be determined by consumer surveys in one geographic area? The relationship between priority issues (discussed next) and distinctiveness can be mentioned here, without going into too much detail.

If the "circularity" issue has not yet arisen, it may well here. The problem is the relationship between *associations in fact* and *legal protection*. If legal protection is given only after associations in fact have grown up, then what of associations that are only "in the making"? Substantial investments may have been sunk, yet the full, protectible association between a mark and a producer may not have been solidified yet. An obvious response is to recognize legal protection "earlier," rather than "later." On the other hand, if legal protection is recognized early on, the law may be seen as creating (or at least creating the conditions for) protection, rather than simply recognizing it. In the context of cases such as *Zatarain's*, this issue arises because the achievement of "secondary meaning" is not a discrete event, it is instead a continuum. But the law demands at least the appearance of precision. Trademark theory insists that legal recognition (at least for descriptive marks) come "after the fact" of an established association. (Note the lesser standard for "stronger" marks; is this the work of a presumption – more distinctive marks by assumption are more likely to have fostered consumer associations – or a backdoor recognition that trademark rights are at least in part awarded "in advance" in some cases?) The slipperiness of the factual event of consumer association invites policy considerations into the analysis. The earlier in time the law moves the moment when trademark rights vest, the more these rights look like a property right awarded as an incentive, and the less they look like an ex post recognition of established consumer associations.

Two Pesos presents some good facts in the trade dress area. As it may be the students' first exposure to protection of trade dress, a moment on exactly what is being copied (and hence, what plaintiff is attempting to protect from copying) is in order. The Courts' framing of the issue provides room for analysis. It takes standard trademark protection as a baseline or benchmark; compares the appellate court's treatment of restaurant décor; and asks whether there is any statutory or policy reason in trademark law to treat the two differently. Finding none, it does away with the old notion that trade dress is different, and always requires secondary meaning to be protected. One aspect of this, the discussion of "the start-up of small companies" (p. 596), bears exploration. One reading of this is that it seems to suggest that trademark protection is a form of incentive to encourage entrepreneurs. Seen in this light, the comment invites discussion of whether this is a legitimate goal of trademark law. This may even open the way for a discussion of the transition of trademark law, from an older "consumer protection" rationale to a newer "property right" rationale.

The expansive interpretation of trade dress protection reflected in *Two Pesos* and to a lesser extent in *Qualitex* raised concerns that trade dress would become a backdoor to the type of strong product protection reserved for patented products. Trade dress could become a generalized misappropriation doctrine for protecting product design. Not surprisingly, a number of lower court cases applied the distinctive analysis for word marks to the protection of product packaging and design. When the Second Circuit found children's dresses with cute appliques to be inherently distinctive, the Supreme Court granted certiorari and recalibrated the threshold for trademark protection of trade dress. *Wal-Mart Stores, Inc. v. Samara Bros.* (page 565). The Court divided trade dress into three categories: (1) product packaging (e.g., the box or ribbons in which a product is sold); (2) product configuration or design (such as a children's dress); and (3) *tertium quid* (something in between product packaging and product configuration – such as the classic shape of the Coca Cola bottle). As a means of raising the threshold for trade dress protection for product design, the Court held that trademark protection is only available if secondary meaning has been established – i.e., product design can not be inherently distinctive (or more accurately, secondary meaning must be established even if the design is inherently distinctive). In furtherance of this policy of raising the bar for trademark with respect to product attributes, the Court held that trade dress falling in between product packaging and product design – *tertium quid* – should also be held to the more exacting standard of proving secondary meaning.

It might be worth pushing on the objectivity of the Supreme Court's new classificatory system. How should the *Two Pesos* trade dress – the decor of a Mexican-style restaurant – be classified? The Supreme Court in *Wal-Mart* notes that "the decor of a restaurant, seems to us not to constitute product design. It was either product packaging – which, as we have discussed, normally is taken by the consumer to indicate origin – or else some *tertium quid* that is akin to product packaging and has no bearing on the present case." This conclusion seems questionable. And given that it seems to fall somewhere in between product packaging and product design, shouldn't the Court have applied its "cautionary" principle[6] noted in the penultimate paragraph of *Wal-Mart*?

Some students may feel it is unfair that Wal-Mart could, in effect, piggyback on someone else's successful product. Others may feel that the consumer benefit of less expensive clothes outweighs these considerations. It should be recalled that trademarks must identify a product's source. Is it ever possible for a new line of clothing to immediately be associated with a distinct source? If not, companies may hesitate to innovate, for fear popular products will just be copied. A discussion of how else Samara may have protected their designs (Copyright? Design Patent?) may prove fruitful.

PROBLEM 5-1

Alice Richland, a gourmet chef world-renowned for her chocolate desserts, designs a new line of chocolate products. Called "Chocolate Shells," these products are made of dark chocolate flavored in special ways with a combination of ingredients Alice hit upon after months of work in her kitchens. The use of the special ingredients imparts a unique flavor to the Shells, and has the additional property of making the usually soft chocolate feel sandy or grainy to the touch. The Shells are made in the shapes of different seashells native to the Florida coast, and each shell is colored in a different, unusual pattern. On the advice of her lawyer, Alice files a trademark application seeking to register each of her shell designs. What aspects of the Shells are entitled to registration? To section 43(a) protection?

Analysis

Problem 5-1: Can you protect the "look and feel" (literally) and taste of chocolate seashells? The problem provides an interesting way to explore the "fit" between the classifications used to describe the strength of word marks and the product configuration/trade dress cases. If one tries to apply the classification scheme literally, the look of the shells is presumably arbitrary with respect to desserts; so is the physical "feel", assuming that the ingredients used to produce this effect are not also responsible for the taste. By contrast, taste is the point of the dish. This probably makes it functional, an issue we consider *infra*. [Note -- under aesthetic functionality doctrine, "look" and "feel" might be considered functional as well.] From a classification perspective, the taste of the shells would have to be considered at least "descriptive" of the shells themselves.

6 "To the extent there are close cases, we believe that courts should err on the side of caution and classify ambiguous trade dress as product design, thereby requiring secondary meaning. The very closeness will suggest the existence of relatively small utility in adopting an inherent-distinctiveness principle, and relatively great consumer benefit in requiring a demonstration of secondary meaning."

Under *Samara Bros.*, the shells are product configurations that would receive no protection at all unless they indicated the source of the goods to consumers. This approach is arguably inconsistent with *Two Pesos*, however, since there is nothing in the trademark act which suggests any reason to distinguish between trade dress and product configuration protection.

2. Priority

Zazu Designs presents good facts for a close call on priority. The opinion itself provides a good summary of the case against the hair salon, Zazu Hair Design, on the issue of use of the Zazu name on hair care products in interstate commerce. A different perspective on the case is provided by a telephone interview with one of the Zazu Hair Design founders, Sam Segretto; the interview was conducted on March 27, 1996, by our former Research Assistant, who is now a Professor of Law at the University of Wisconsin, Dr. Pilar Ossorrio. Here is an edited version of Dr. Ossorrio's notes:

> It was an extremely difficult and long experience. What I learned is that just because you may feel you are right, and even if you verify your thoughts with a group of attorneys, it doesn't really mean anything. People will do what they want, law doesn't mean anything, it can always go either way. There are a lot of crazy people out there -- including some judges and lawyers.
>
> We were really unlucky in the judges we got; two of them were judges that we didn't want, in fact, one [Easterbrook?] had been the student of the other [Posner?]. Many of the facts that the appeals court included in their opinion were not properly researched, although I don't know if they would have changed their minds if they had the facts right. From the very beginning in court, they did not give our attorneys a chance to speak on our behalf. [referring only to the appellate court proceeding.] We were in the process of trying to expand interstate, but we were very small. It seemed to play into the appellate decision that we were very small and had only expended a small amount of money, whereas they [L'Oreal] were very large and had expended quite a lot of money. The appeals court seemed to take the position that why should a little business like ours get in the way of a big company's plans?
>
> It threw a big curve into our plans for business. . . . When we were doing this it was when our industry was just beginning to see products coming into the market from hair salons. Now, any really big selling product across the country has come from a salon. That's where we were headed. . . . . It took away a lot of energy and really threw a curve into our plans. To try to go back and recapture where we were is too difficult. And I'm not sure I would really want to. My business is still going well but... I'm not really trying for a big national expansion any more . . .
>
> Here is an example of the way they treated us: To let them know that we really were serious about using our mark, they were apprised that there was a lawsuit in the wind. They asked us not to jump to any conclusions, said we could work this out. They came out to our place of business and talked for hours. At the end of that conversation their solution was that they would pay us to change the name of our business, they would come hang a new sign on our door and buy us 5000 business cards. But that was not acceptable to us. The next day we were served with papers for a suit that they brought against us in New York. That suit had been filed before they came to talk with us. When we were served, the date on the papers was the day before they came to talk. When they were talking with us they knew that the suit had been filed. They just offered to come talk to stall us from filing against them in Illinois. They wanted to get us in court in NY because they knew what pressure it would be on a business of our size to have a trial in New York. [The strategy evidently failed; the trial was in Illinois. – Eds.]
>
> I'm really happy with our lawyers, they did an excellent job. Our lawyers used their study against them, proved by their own research that our business impact was more far reaching then they said. I can say that our lawyers were great. They really worked very, very hard. We were with them many nights 'til 11 o'clock going over things, and I have a lot of respect for them. I wouldn't do anything differently. I still

stand behind the reasons that we did it, and we had good representation. I still think we did the right thing, but it was very, very difficult.

[Products now sold by Segretto and co-founder Koubek under the Zazu label: shampoo and styling gel. As this manual went to press, the hair salon appeared to still be in business; see http://www.cybur-hinsdale.com/sv_beauty_hair.htm#Zazu Hair Designs.]

PROBLEM 5-2

Preco Industries began using the term "Porcelaincote" for its porcelain resurfacing material in 1966. Preco concedes that, at the time it began use, the "Porcelaincote" mark was unprotectable because it was descriptive. Preco continued to use the mark for a relatively minor product line. In 1977, Ceramco began to use the identical mark for identical goods. [Both companies sell their products on a nationwide basis.] In 1979, Ceramco began a nationwide advertising campaign using the "Porcelaincote" mark. Shortly thereafter, in 1980, Preco began a similar campaign. In 1981 the parties filed complaints against each other for trademark infringement. The court determined at trial that Ceramco established secondary meaning in 1979, and that Preco established it in 1980.

Assume that neither party ever registered its mark. Who should prevail in the lawsuits? Does either party have rights against a third company that began using the name in 1990? Does your answer to either of these questions change if one or both parties registered its mark on the Principal Register?

Analysis

Problem 5-2: This problem is based on *Perma Ceram v. Preco Industries*, 23 USPQ2d 1134 (TTAB 1992). Here, Preco first used the "Porcelaincote" mark in 1966; Ceramco in 1977. But the marks were descriptive at the time they were introduced by both parties, and neither party acquired secondary meaning until later. The Board held that priority turns on who acquired distinctiveness first, not on who used the mark first. In the hypo, that is Ceramco. This result seems right as a matter of trademark policy, but it leaves open the possibility that one could "steal" a descriptive mark from another.

The problem also raises issues of fair use. Even if Ceramco is entitled to register the mark, having first made it distinctive, can Ceramco now prevent Preco from using its mark? Such a claim might be subject to the "fair use" defense, since Preco can argue that it is simply using the descriptive term it adopted before Ceramco's first use. On the other hand, the purposes of trademark law might be served by preventing Preco's use, especially since it is now advertising the mark as well, and consumers are likely to be confused. Finally, it is possible that the parties could engage in "concurrent use" of the mark if they were to so agree.

PROBLEM 5-3

In May 1989, Shalom Children's Wear begins advertising and planning a line of clothes to be called "Body Gear." In November 1989, In-Wear Corp. files an intent-to-use application for the mark "Body Gear." Shalom files an intent-to-use application for the same mark in December 1989 and begins selling its products in February 1990. Is either party entitled to register the Body Gear mark? (Assume that the mark is otherwise protectable.) Does the result change if In-Wear fails to begin selling its clothes by November 1992?

Analysis

Problem 5-3: This problem is based on *Shalom Children's Wear v. In-Wear,* 26 USPQ2d 1516 (TTAB 1993). Shalom began advertising, displaying, manufacturing, and taking orders in May 1989, but did not sell goods until Feb. 1990. After Shalom began these efforts, but before Shalom either started selling clothes or had filed its own application, In-Wear filed an intent-to-use application. The issue before the Board was who has priority. In-Wear clearly does, unless Shalom's pre-sale activities give them a priority date.

In the case, the Board held that Shalom had engaged in "use analogous to trademark use," which gives them priority even though it would not have constituted "use in commerce" allowing Shalom to register its mark under pre-1988 trademark law. This result is troubling as a legal matter. Arguably, a "use analogous" rule simply replaces "use in commerce" with a new, more lenient test allowing token uses. And the decision certainly seems inconsistent with *Zazu*, where ZHD took similar measures.

On the other hand, one can make a strong policy argument for the Board's position. Particularly if In-Wear was aware of Shalom's activities, their actions seem designed to capture the mark, and perhaps also the benefit of Shalom's pre-sale advertising. From a property perspective, Shalom does not seem less entitled to own the mark because it has not yet begun to sell goods under the "Body Gear" name. Thus, the problem raises the conflicting policies of preventing "mark reservations" and preventing "capture" of marks.

3. **Trademark Office Procedures**

Harjo v. Pro-Football, page 593, is a fascinating case. Washington Redskins trademarks were cancelled under Lanham Act section 2 for disparaging Native Americans. It might be relevant to point out that public interest groups usually have a difficult time getting standing. Here, the parties did a good job of showing they were representative of the group that would be disparaged. You might wish to explore the extent and limits of trademark law's concern with the "third party effects" of protecting certain marks. Functionality is arguably one manifestation of this, cases like *Harjo* another (though very different) one. Interesting follow-up questions might include which well-known sports trademarks seem in jeopardy after *Harjo*, and why the Washington, D.C. NFL team has not yet changed its name. What other forms of protection are available to the team? Will the policy issues underlying the cancellation decision surface in state trademark cases or federal antidilution cases?

In re Nantucket is a concise statement of some of the issues that arise in cases involving geographic names. An established or traditional association between a geographic place name and a product type will be "protected" by a prohibition on use of that place name on goods that do not in fact come from that place. What about plans to *establish* such a connection in a region not traditionally associated with a certain good? Should trademark law take an interest in this situation? Recall the Supreme Court's discussion of the (negative) effect on "start up companies" of the secondary meaning requirement in trade dress cases, mentioned earlier in connection with *Two Pesos*. Are there other ways besides federal trademark law to pull this off? Appellations of origin are one; and note the post-TRIPS worldwide trademark regime is more supportive of this approach.

PROBLEM 5-4

Ernest & Julio Gallo are the nation's largest seller of wine. They sell their wine under the "Gallo" label, and have advertised that trademark heavily. Ernest & Julio's younger brother Joseph Gallo runs a company called Gallo Cattle Co. Gallo Cattle begins selling cheese and salami under the name "Gallo Cheese" and "Gallo Salame." If Ernest & Julio Gallo wish to stop their brother from marketing meat and cheese under the Gallo name, what must they be able to show at trial? If they win, how should a court craft the injunction granting relief; what should it forbid and permit?

Analysis

Problem 5-4: Under what circumstances can the Gallo family prevent their brother Joseph from using his name for closely related goods? In *E. & J. Gallo Winery v. Gallo Cattle Co.*, 967 F.2d 1280 (9th Cir. 1992), the court held that while there is a judicial reluctance to enjoin the use of a personal name, the goal of preventing consumer confusion is paramount. The court held against Joseph Gallo in part based on his apparent intent to trade on the goodwill of the Gallo name. But it also suggested that an injunction would be appropriate even absent such intent, because the goods were similar and the likelihood of public confusion was so high. It is instructive that the court engaged in a full-blown likelihood of confusion analysis before enjoining the mark.

4. Incontestibility

Park 'N Fly deals on its face with a narrow question of statutory interpretation. Yet it is also a good vehicle for exploring incontestability. The practical effects of an incontestable mark are well described. And buried in the list of defenses that do (and by implication, do not) survive incontestability are some interesting issues. Why must genericide survive as a viable defense, but not some of the other objections to trademark protection at time of initial registration? Why should the trademark statute concern itself with "clarity of title" issues, when trademarks are not supposed to be property rights? (Is there any reason to believe that well-established trademarks are more likely to be attacked repeatedly by competitors or prospective entrants?)

D. Infringement

1. Likelihood of Consumer Confusion

AMF v. Sleekcraft Boats, page 614, is much-cited for its list of confusion factors. AMF used Slickcraft boats first but federal registration came after use of Sleekcraft boats. The parties did not want to divide up the submarkets (general family recreation vs. high speed recreation) because a national market for boats exists into which they each might expand. The court concludes that the goods are related but not competitive and examines other factors to determine whether there is likelihood of confusion. You might discuss what can be used as proof of confusion in litigation. Anecdotes and affidavits are better than nothing but can be attacked based on poor memory or not being representative. Surveys serve as better proof if the survey is written well. Generally, a showing that 10-15% (or more) of respondents are confused goes a long way to proving consumer confusion.

PROBLEM 5-5

Bristol-Myers, a major pharmaceutical company, markets "Excedrin" pain reliever. Since 1968, B-M has marketed "Excedrin PM," which is a pain reliever that does not interfere with sleep. Excedrin PM tablets are sold in a solid blue box whose color fades from dark to light from top to bottom. The box contains the words "Excedrin PM" in large white letters across the top third of the box. In the bottom right-hand corner of the box is a depiction of two tablets labeled "PM." B-M also sells Excedrin PM capsules, which are packaged identically except that the background is green and the two capsules in the picture read "Excedrin PM." Both the mark Excedrin PM and the dress of both boxes are registered with the Trademark Office.

In 1991, McNeil Pharmaceuticals introduced "Tylenol PM," a pain reliever chemically identical to Excedrin PM. Tylenol PM tablets are sold in a solid green box whose color fades from dark to light from top to bottom. The box contains the words "Tylenol PM" in large white and yellow letters across the top third of the box. In the bottom right-hand corner of the box is a depiction of two tablets, one labeled "Tylenol" and the other labeled "PM." McNeil also sells Tylenol PM capsules, which are packaged identically except that the background is blue and the two capsules in the picture both read "Tylenol PM."

B-M sues McNeil, alleging that both its use of the term PM and its trade dress are likely to confuse consumers. Who should prevail?

PROBLEM 5-6

Ivory Soap is sold for approximately $1.00 a bar. It is a heavily advertised brand name, which identifies itself as "99.44% pure." Whitewash Soap Co. makes and sells counterfeit Ivory Soap bars, which are packaged identically to Ivory (using the Ivory name and trade dress) and which contain chemically identical bars of soap. These counterfeit "Ivory" bars are sold for $.50 each. If a consumer buys the Whitewash soap thinking it is Ivory, how has he been injured? Hasn't he been benefited? Is there any reason to protect Ivory's trademark against infringement at the expense of consumer welfare?

Analysis

Problem 5-5: This problem is based on *Bristol-Myers Squibb Co. v. McNeil-PPC, Inc.*, 973 F.2d 1033 (2d Cir. 1992). The court divided the analysis of trademark infringement into two different parts: the use of the letters "PM," and the overall trade dress of the products. As to the letters PM, the Second Circuit found that they were descriptive of a medical product to be taken at night, because no leap of imagination was required to go from "p.m.," meaning evening, to "PM." Because Bristol could not demonstrate secondary meaning, it could not prevent the use of "PM" on the Tylenol packaging.

Regarding the overall trade dress, the court found that *as a whole* the packaging was a strong trademark and had secondary meaning. However, this was largely because of the word "Excedrin" (itself a strong trademark) emblazoned in large letters across the front. Despite finding that McNeil acted in bad faith in copying Bristol's color scheme, that consumers were unsophisticated, and that the products were intended to be directly competitive, the court refused to find likelihood of confusion. Central to this conclusion were two factors: Bristol's failure to present competent survey evidence showing actual confusion, and dissimilarity of the trade dress as a whole (given the large "Excedrin" and "Tylenol" marks on the front of the respective packages).

The case is important for teaching the integrated nature of trademark infringement analysis. Courts will not consider isolated elements of a trademark or trade dress. Rather, they look to the product as it would be seen by consumers. Thus, unlike copyright law where adding noninfringing material won't prevent a finding of infringement, in trademark courts take account of disclaimers and dissimilarities between the marks or trade dress taken as a whole.

Problem 5-6: if the quality of the counterfeit goods is identical to that of the original goods, as in the Ivory hypothetical, consumers benefit from getting those counterfeits. The only reason Ivory costs $1.00 and the counterfeits 50 cents is because Ivory has built monopoly power on a (false) reputation that its products are better than its competitors'. From a consumer protection perspective, it is reasonable to question why we would want to protect Ivory in such a situation. While someone would have to determine that the products were in fact identical in quality and other attributes, it would certainly be possible to enforce trademark law only against counterfeiters of lower quality.

On the other hand, if one approaches this problem from an unfair competition or a property perspective, that result seems undesirable. One problem is that if imitation is permitted, there may be less reason to invest in product quality in the first place. A related problem is that Ivory's brand differentiation surplus is a result of its investment in goodwill, perhaps through quality products and word of mouth, but perhaps through advertising. Allowing competitors to free ride on that goodwill would discourage companies from investing in goodwill. Even if they continue to make quality products, they may have no particular incentive to advertise their brand name, increasing the search costs of consumers.

2. Dilution

The enactment of the Federal Trademark Dilution Act of 1995 has raised a host of interpretive issues. As the Second Circuit's first significant encounter with this federal law, *Nabisco v. P.F. Brands*, page 629, works through a number of these linguistic puzzles left ambiguous by Congress. Pepperidge Farm Brands, the maker of the well-known goldfish shaped cracker, sought an injunction against Nabisco for marketing a fish-shaped cracker among other characters in its new line of Cheez-its crackers tied to the popular Nickelodeon Television Network show "CatDog." It is worth pausing for a moment to explore why this case did not turn on a traditional trademark claim. (Pepperidge Farm did unsuccessfully assert this claim.) The lower court was skeptical of such a claim on the ground that consumers would not likely be confused into thinking that the Nabisco goldfish cracker was produced by Pepperidge Farm because it came packaged with the CatDog shaped cracker as well as a bone-shaped cracker (only about 25% of the crackers in any Nabisco branded package were goldfish).

The passage of the FTDA gave Pepperidge Farm another line of attack – that Nabisco's use of an orange, bite-sized, cheddar cheese-flavored, goldfish-shaped cracker would dilute the distinctive quality of Pepperidge Farm's orange, bite-sized, cheddar cheese-flavored, goldfish-shaped cracker. The court accepted the lower court's determination that Pepperidge Farm's goldfish-shaped cracker was indeed "famous" – the record established extensive advertising over many years that the product was the second-largest selling cheese snack cracker in America and number one in sales. The court therefore focuses upon what it means to "cause dilution of the distinctive quality of the senior mark." Contrary to the interpretation of Professor McCarthy, the leading commentator on trademark law (see footnote 2 on page 631), Judge Leval reads the FTDA to require an independent finding of "distinctiveness" (in addition to "fame") as an important limitation built into the statutory framework. Therefore, otherwise famous marks – such American for airlines, United for airlines and truck lines, Merit for oil, and Ace for hardware – are not eligible for dilution protection because they are not inherently distinctive (notwithstanding the fact that they have acquired distinctiveness through the acquisition of secondary meaning. It is worth pausing at this point to discuss the method and reasonableness of the court's interpretation. Professor McCarthy's alternative approach certainly seems plausible. The FTDA is hardly a model of legislative clarity – e.g., "commercial use in commerce"; "in determining whether a mark is distinctive and famous, a court may consider . . . the degree of inherent or acquired distinctiveness of the mark . . ." We suggest focusing in detail upon the language in section 43(c)(1) and pushing students to make sense of the muddle.

Regardless of your assessment of this semantic puzzle, Judge Leval's conclusion that the Pepperidge Farm Goldfish mark is reasonably distinctive and hence eligible for dilution protection makes sense. The court then puts forth an eight factor test – that is similar to the likelihood of confusion analysis – for determining whether a junior user has a dilutive effect. After marching through these factors, the court concludes that Nabisco's goldfish-shaped crackers are highly likely to dilute the distinctive quality of the senior user's nearly identical mark.

The court concludes with a discussion of whether the FTDA merely requires a showing of likelihood of dilution (analogous to the general trademark standard of likelihood of confusion) or a showing of actual dilution. The Fourth Circuit in *Ringling Bros.-Barnum & Bailey Combined Shows, Inc. v. Utah Division of Travel Dev.,* 170 F.3d 449, 464 (4th Cir. 1999), opted for the latter standard based on the statute's use of the language "causes dilution." Judge Leval concluded that Congress did not intend for injury to have occurred before a dilution action could be brought. Shortly after our edition went to press, the Supreme Court resolved this circuit split in favor of the Fourth Circuit's literal interpretation. See *Moseley v. V Secret Catalogue, Inc.*, 123 S.Ct. 1115 (2003). The case will be available in our statutory supplement.

PROBLEM 5-7

Mead Data Central is the owner of the registered trademark LEXIS for a legal and business-related electronic database. The service is extremely well-known among lawyers, but not among the general public.

A decade after the first use of the Lexis mark, Toyota names its new luxury car the "Lexus." Mead sues for dilution of its Lexis mark. What result? On what facts does your decision depend?

Analysis

Problem 5-7: This problem is based on *Mead Data Centra v. Toyota Motor Sales*, 875 F.2d 1026 (2d Cir. 1989). In that case, which predated the Federal Trademark Dilution Act and was based on New York state law, the court held that LEXIS was not diluted by Lexus. The court used a variant of the test for likelihood of confusion, and found that LEXIS was not particularly strong, both because of its linguistic roots and because it was well-known only among lawyers. The court also concluded that the two marks were pronounced differently, and therefore were not too similar. The opinion is notable as well for making clear that despite the abolition of the confusion requirement, dilution is not possible unless there is at least some *association* between the two marks in question.

The problem presents a number of tough issues for dilution law:

- Is partial or "industry-specific" fame sufficient to support a dilution claim? There are lots of marks that are "famous" within their industry, but unknown outside it. To protect those marks would dramatically expand the list of marks eligible for protection. Further, because dilution applies regardless of competition, these "quasi-famous" marks would preclude use of a similar mark even in unrelated industries. [The problem is made more difficult here by the partial overlap in customers between legal services and luxury cars].
- What degree of similarity is required? The original conception of dilution envisioned identical marks. More recently, however, dilution protection has been expanded to encompass variants on a mark. This in turn raises some of the same problems present in ordinary trademark cases – how close is too close? – without the ability to use consumer perception as the touchstone to resolve the issue.
- What factors should go into a dilution infringement case? *Mead* used the factors from the likelihood of confusion test, but this seems wrong. At the least, some of those factors should properly be irrelevant in a dilution inquiry, and others would have to be modified. At the same time, new factors might be relevant (as the *PF Brands* decision suggests).

3. Extension by Contract: Licensing and Franchising

4. Domain Names and Cybersquatting

In 1999, Congress enacted the Anticybersquatting Consumer Protection Act (ACPA) to address various abuses of the Internet domain name registration process associated with trademarks. In most cases, these abuses did not fall squarely within existing trademark protections and some courts saw fit to stretch traditional trademark protection and the new anti-dilution protection in order to address these concerns. The ACPA focused directly on the problem by enabling trademark owners to prevent others from registering their marks as domain names with bad faith intent to profit. Courts have been called upon the determine the precise limits of this new form of trademark protection.

The *Shields* case (page 648) illustrates one area in which the statute is less than explicit. In what has come to be known as typosquatting, John Zuccarini registered a variety of domain names that could best be described as typographical errors of valid trademarks. Imprecise typists who found themselves at Zuccarini's websites would then be bombarded with pop-up advertisements. If they clicked through to one the advertisers' sites – often offering sexually explicit content – Zuccarini would earn a penny or two. The scale of his activity, however, brought him hundreds of thousands of dollars annually. Drawing upon the language of the ACPA and its legislative history, the court held that Zuccarini's variations on valid trademarks were "confusingly similar to" the marks and imposed liability.

The *PETA* case (page 654) addresses the threshold for protection and a tension between the ACPA and the First Amendment. In an attempt to poke fun at the animal rights organization "People for the Ethical Treatment of Animals," Doughney registered the name PETA.org and established a web page titled "People Eating Tasty Animals." Although web surfers who found themselves at Doughney's site quickly realized that it was a parody and could easily move to reorient their search, the court nonetheless held that the rather modest degree of initial interest confusion was sufficient to support the action. Furthermore, the court showed no leeway for a parody defense.

5. Contributory Infringement

6. False Advertising

PROBLEM 5-8

A popular "cult" movie includes characters who have tattooed famous brand logos on various parts of their bodies. The practice quickly catches on, first among "avant garde" artists, and then among college and high school students.

Post-Modern Concepts, Inc. (PMC), seeing an opportunity, opens a storefront tattoo parlor in a popular retail mall in the Midwest. Here PMC applies popular logos as tattoos. At first, customers are primarily interested in the ironic use of logos, as in the film; the logos are primarily used as a spoof or commentary on consumerism. One popular tattoo, for instance, includes the famous "Calvin Klein" wordmark and logo, drawn inside a red circle with a slash. Soon, however -- perhaps predictably -- the ironic intent of the original practice is lost as it becomes very chic to have a logo tattoo. Thus many people begin to request tattoos without the red slash and circle. The most popular trademark logo tattoos are "Rolls Royce," "Nike," the original "Calvin Klein," and "Harley-Davidson."

Success is instantaneous. In response to torrid demand, PMC sets up franchises all over the country.

Owners of the trademarks begin to notice PMC. They are concerned primarily about lost revenues, because PMC has never taken out any trademark licenses. But some trademark owners are also concerned that pictures of people with logo tattoos are beginning to appear in the press. Even some famous celebrities, such as popular musicians and sports stars, have tattoos in prominent places. When their picture appears in the newspaper, the logo -- or part of it -- does too. Other trademark owners are concerned that logo tattoos are being applied on parts of the body traditionally covered by clothing. These owners fear that when pictures of people with logo tattoos in these places appear -- sometimes in press outlets not fit for family viewing -- the trademarks are denigrated.

What hurdles will the trademark owners have to clear to enforce their rights? (Are these marks attached to a product? Also, PMC will undoubtedly argue that sports team fanatics have long painted their faces in team colors, or drawn the team logo on their faces; and that even before PMC, some permanent tattoos consisting of corporate logos were popular, such as "Chevy," "Red Sox Forever," or, perhaps most common, "Harley Davidson."). Are there any risks to letting the practice continue without any enforcement efforts? Does PMC, or its customers, have a defense not based in trademark law?

Analysis

Problem 5-8: When a logo is removed from its corporate context, does its creator/"owner" have any continued interest in it? There are theories of consumer confusion which might be applicable (i.e. viewers might think that the corporation sponsored or approved the tattoos), but they seem to stretch traditional trademark theories. Instead, the trademark owner's approach seems to be one of property ownership -- asserting a right to control all uses of "their" logo. As we will see *infra*, though, some uses of a trademark (such as newspaper reports and some parodies) are "nontrademark uses" -- they are not in connection with the sale of goods, and so are outside the scope of trademark laws.

The problem of disembodied logos presents a difficult question for trademark theory. On the one hand, it seems equitable to give sports associations or corporations control over the use of their logo in commercial contexts, even if the use is not to sell competing products (or indeed any product other than the logo itself). On the other hand, when the use is divorced from the commercial setting, the right of control seems more troubling. Corporate uses of marks for purposes other than goods-identification also raise problems of unsupervised licenses, discussed *infra*.

E. Defenses

1. Genericness

Murphy Door Bed Co. presents a good, simple genericide scenario. Important points to stress here are (1) that genericide is distinct from abandonment; that the mark owner can lose rights notwithstanding the most diligent of efforts; and (2) genericide is a potent defense, precisely because a generic term is in some sense the antithesis of a valid trademark. Groundwork can also be laid for the forthcoming cases: in addition to abandonment, there are also elements of functionality in the genericness defense – what might be termed "linguistic functionality." Third party effects are again the key. And the "reliance" issue at the heart of abandonment plays a role here as well.

2. Functionality

As noted earlier, the Supreme Court's *Two Pesos* and *Qualitex* decisions as well as a host of lower court decisions represented a sort of apogee for the use of trade dress as a means of limiting competition through trademark protection. The *Wal-Mart* case partially reined in the doctrine by requiring those seeking trade dress protection for product configurations to establish secondary meaning regardless of the inherent distinctiveness of the product design. In *TrafFix Devices*, page 686, the Supreme Court reinforced the functionality limitation on trade dress protection by imposing a strong presumption that product features that were the subject of an expired utility patent cannot be later claimed as trade dress. The presumption is not absolute, but accorded strong evidentiary weight that the claimant must overcome. Echoing to some extent the cautionary principle discussed in *Wal-Mart*, the Court warned against allowing "backdoor patents" through appeal to the other regimes of intellectual property.

PROBLEM 5-9

Ferrari is a world famous maker of upscale sports cars. It limits the number of cars it produces, and each car costs approximately $200,000. Ferrari's cars have the same general features as normal cars -- wheels, chassis, etc. -- but they also have a distinctive look that is easily recognized. They are sleek and low to the ground, a fact that may make them accelerate more quickly and that makes them more attractive to look at.

Roberts sells a fiberglass kit that replicates the exterior features of a Ferrari, though not the engine or performance. When sued for trade dress infringement, Roberts defends on the grounds that the Ferrari design is functional. Is it?

PROBLEM 5-10

Eighteen years ago, Spartan Laboratories invented and patented a new pain-relieving drug called asperol. During the term of the patent, Spartan retained the exclusive right to sell asperol, which it manufactured in bright orange capsules. After the Spartan patent expired, a number of other companies began making generic asperol. Each of these companies sells the generic asperol in the same bright orange capsules as Spartan. Although the orange capsules are not visible inside the manufacturers' boxes (which do not resemble each other), asperol is sold only by prescription, and pharmacists invariably remove the drug from its original packaging and repackage it in their own bottles. The result is that the consumer sees only the name "asperol" and the orange capsules, regardless of who makes the drug.

Spartan filed suit under section 43(a) of the Lanham Act, alleging that the other manufacturers had infringed its trade dress protection by coloring the capsules orange. At trial, Spartan proves that the color orange is protectable because it is distinctive and because, over the seventeen years of the patent, pharmacists and customers had come to equate orange with Spartan's asperol. The generic manufacturers defend the suit on the grounds that the color is functional. In support of this claim, they present survey evidence that patients, particularly elderly patients, may become upset if the color of the drug is changed, and may refuse to believe that the drug is in fact asperol. The generic manufacturers present further evidence that pharmacists rely in part on color in making sure that they have packaged and labeled drugs correctly. Is the color orange functional?

Analysis

Problem 5-9: This problem is based on *Ferrari S.P.A. v. Roberts*, 944 F.2d 1235 (6th Cir. 1991). The shape of the Ferrari is a product configuration. In deciding whether it is protectable, it is useful to distinguish three different aspects of the appearance of the car. First, certain attributes of the car are necessary or directly related to desirable performance characteristics. These include the obvious attributes -- four wheels, a chassis, etc. -- but also some aspects of the body shape, to the extent that they make the car more aerodynamic or allow it to corner better, for example. Aspects of the car design that fall into this first group are clearly functional.

A second group of attributes do not affect the performance of the car, but make it aesthetically attractive. The paint job and detailing may well fall into this category, but so may some of the features that contribute to its "sleekness." These features -- which would attract people to the car even if they had never heard of Ferrari -- fall into the category of aesthetic functionality. Courts have sometimes been willing to protect designs even though they are "aesthetically functional." *See RommArt Creations v. Simcha Int'l*, 786 F. Supp. 1126 (E.D.N.Y. 1992) (finding protectable trade dress in an artist's overall style of painting). However, the better view is that such features are unprotectable because they are functional. People may buy beautiful art in preference to ugly art, without any necessary association with the source of the works, because one of the primary reasons to buy art is that it looks attractive.

Aesthetic functionality alone does not explain the appeal of the Ferrari, however. An identical car without Ferrari's name or cachet would not sell for the same price. This is because Ferraris are sold in part on the name, and the look contributes to the name. That additional value is based in source identification: consumers desire the car *because it is a Ferrari*. Trademark law clearly should protect this.

Problem 5-10: The issue here is whether orange is a functional color for prescription medicine. Two arguments favor a finding of color functionality -- pharmacists rely on it in sorting/labeling, and patients rely on it to sort/are comforted by it. Note that both of these arguments are a function of the association Spartan has built up between the color and the drug during the period of its exclusive use. In *Inwood Labs v. Ives*, 456 U.S. 844 (1982), the district court held that pill color was functional because people associated the color there (blue) with soothing effects. The Supreme Court held this finding was supported by substantial evidence, though the Court's later decision in *Qualitex* suggests that determinations of functionality must be done on a fact-specific, case-by-case basis.

Spartan has a reasonable argument that any functionality in the color has been *acquired* as a result of its efforts. Should this matter? Arguably not -- functionality can be acquired as a result of changing consumer expectations, just as marks can "become generic." Nonetheless, we should arguably be more cautious in refusing to protect functional attributes where those attributes themselves result from goodwill built by the trademark owner. This issue is closely related to genericide, discussed below.

3. Abandonment

PROBLEM 5-11

Until 1972, the Humble Oil & Refining Co. was one of the largest producers and sellers of gasoline in the world. In that year Humble decided to change its name to Exxon, an arbitrary mark it had selected for the purpose. The company invested an enormous amount of money advertising the new name, and placing its new brand on all its products, services, and correspondence. However, the new Exxon also started a "brand maintenance program" under which it continued to make a few sales every year under the Humble name. It sent certain invoices on Humble letterhead, and bulk oil was sometimes sold in Humble barrels. Exxon continued this program throughout the 1970s.

In 1975, a new oil exploration company decides to call itself the Humble Oil Exploration Co. The new company picked the Humble name because they hoped to trade on residual goodwill left in the name, and because they believed Exxon had abandoned its old name. Can the new company use the Humble name?

PROBLEM 5-12

IBM Corporation is a world-famous maker of computers and other business machines. For decades, people have informally referred to IBM as "Big Blue," both in conversation and in published articles and papers about the company. However, IBM does not itself use or claim the name "Big Blue." It has never registered the name Big Blue, its employees are forbidden by company policy to use the name in referring to the company, and at one point an exasperated company spokesperson is reported to have said "We're not Big Blue -- please don't call us that. We want nothing to do with the name." Nonetheless, the nickname persists.

In 1994 a small repair shop that specializes in fixing IBM computers decided to call itself the "Big Blue Repair Shop." After BBRS started using the name, IBM sent it a cease-and-desist letter alleging that IBM owned the rights to the name Big Blue, since people used it to refer to IBM. Who has priority in use of the Big Blue mark?

The Major League Baseball case is an entertaining foray into abandonment. Although the court is perhaps too willing to consider "Brooklyn Dodgers" and "L.A. Dodgers" as completely distinct marks, its decision is unassailable on another level: what better example of abandonment, in the colloquial sense, is there than the notorious removal of the Brooklyn Dodgers to Los Angeles? (Caveat: some of the authors of your casebook are serious San Francisco Giants fans, and thus notoriously unable to resist a "dig" at the ex-Brooklyn team.) Is the evidence of abandonment – the limited use of the Brooklyn Dodgers name and logo – convincing?

The case suggests a strategy that might be explored: "nominal" but nontrivial trademark use, to keep rights to a trademark "alive." How would the cases on priority, e.g., "use in commerce," figure in here? Are different policies at work in establishing a mark, versus keeping it alive?

Analysis

Problem 5-11: This problem is based on *Exxon v. Humble Exploration, Inc.*, 695 F.2d 96 (5th Cir. 1983). The issue of abandonment presents a fascinating problem in trademark theory. In *Exxon*, the oil company clearly intended to cease use of the "Humble Oil" name, with the exception of certain token uses designed purely to reserve trademark rights. The court ignored these token uses, finding an abandonment of the Humble name. However, theoretical justifications for the abandonment doctrine are hard to come by. From a property perspective, there is no reason Exxon should not be permitted to keep the old name (and whatever goodwill is associated with it). From both a consumer protection and an unfair competition perspective, it is troubling to award the Humble name (which unquestionably retained some goodwill) to a random competitor.

Problem 5-12: This problem presents many of the same issues as does *Exxon*, except that in this case IBM never claimed rights in the Big Blue name. Thus, it is reasonable to conclude that they have no continuing property interest in the name. Should consumer associations of the "Big Blue" name with IBM be sufficient to grant it what would effectively be an "involuntary trademark"?

The case was actually litigated in the Trademark Office, though not reported. The PTO awarded the Big Blue mark to Big Blue Products in late 1995, finding that IBM had disclaimed and therefore abandoned any interest in the name, and that Big Blue Products was entitled to the trademark. While the Board's conclusion on abandonment may be reasonable, it seems more troubling to give another company exclusive rights to a name consumers associate almost exclusively with IBM. News reports indicate that the company is considering competing with IBM under the Big Blue name. *See* Eric Hausman, *IBM is no longer Big Blue*, **Comp. Reseller News**, Dec. 4, 1995, at 2.

Dawn Donut is a good, comprehensive account of the abandonment defense in the franchising/licensing context. It is a good entre to the general topic of the role of trademarks in licensing contracts, franchising arrangements, etc. This is an important area in legal practice.

Nontrademark (or Nominative) Use, Parody, and the First Amendment

The *Mattel* case, page 710, summarizes a variety of cases that trim the scope of trademark and trademark dilution law in order to avoid conflict with First Amendment interests in free expression, criticism, and truthful presentation of a product. It might be worth asking students how the *Mattel* analysis would apply to the *PETA* case (page 654).

PROBLEM 5-13

Toho, Inc. is the owner of the copyrights in several Japanese "Godzilla" movies, as well as the registered U.S. trademark "Godzilla." Toho granted a license to a major American movie company to use the name and the monster in its recent high-budget film and various related products and promotional efforts.

Capitalizing on the hype surrounding the new Godzilla film, Edgar publishes a book cataloguing the history of Godzilla in film and print. He titles his book "Godzilla," and places a picture of the monster on the cover. Toho sues for trademark infringement.

How should the court rule? Would it matter if Toho had licensed a different writer to produce an "authorized" history?

Analysis

Problem 5-13: The district court granted a preliminary injunction against the sale of the book, concluding that Godzilla was a famous mark and that others weren't entitled to use it. *Toho, Inc. v. William Morrow & Co.,* 46 U.S.P.Q.2d 1801 (C.D. Cal. 1998). This decision seems wrong. [The result is all the more remarkable because in the case, the defendant's book had disclaimers on both the front and back cover]. Edgar was using the trademark in a classical nominative sense – to describe the product that was trademarked. On the court's rationale, it is hard to see why a movie reviewer could write about Godzilla: The Movie without permission.

The case also raises troubling questions about how trademark law fits with the First Amendment. The court granted a preliminary injunction against core political speech, without even a demonstration that the speech was false (it wasn't) or likely to confuse readers. If (as the *Mattel* case that follows suggests) the First Amendment imposes any constraints at all on the reach of trademark law, this seems a good case for them.

The question of competition raises another interesting point of common confusion about trademark law. It should not matter that someone else has written an authorized history of Godzilla, or that Edgar's book cuts into the sales of that authorized book. This is indeed an economic loss to the trademark owner, but it's not one caused by consumer confusion or the appropriation of its mark.

PROBLEM 5-14

Anheuser-Busch sells beer under a variety of brand names, including Michelob. As part of a general trend of brand proliferation in the beer industry, Busch has recently produced sub-brands of Michelob, including Michelob Dry, Michelob Lite, and Michelob Ice.

After the waters near a Busch plant are polluted in an oil spill, Balducci runs the accompanying advertisement for "Michelob Oily" on the back of a humor magazine.

[see Figure 5-4 in text]

The ad identifies itself as a parody in micro-print along the side. The pictures in the ad are takeoffs from those in real Michelob commercials.

Anheuser-Busch sues Balducci for trademark infringement. At trial, Busch can show only a tiny percentage of consumers who thought Michelob Oily was a real product, but it proves that half the people surveyed believed Balducci had to get permission from Busch to run the ad. Who should prevail?

PROBLEM 5-15

The Coca-Cola Co. maintains an extremely strong and well-recognized trademark in the word "Coke" for its soft drink, and in the phrase "Enjoy Coke," particularly when used in connection with its red and white patterned logo. Gemini Rising, Inc., which distributes commercial posters, designs a poster with a logo identical to Coca-Cola's which reads "Enjoy Cocaine." After passersby who saw the poster complained to the local press, Coca-Cola brings suit against Gemini Rising. At trial, Coca-Cola offers evidence from a few members of the public who apparently believed that Coca-Cola had sponsored the posters, including one woman who threatened to organize a boycott of Coca-Cola products. What result?

Does your result change if Gemini Rising is a nonprofit political organization devoted to drug legalization? If it agrees to include a statement in medium-sized print at the bottom of the poster disclaiming any affiliation with the Coca-Cola Co.?

Analysis

Problem 5-14: This problem is based on *Anheuser-Busch v. Balducci,* 28 F.3d 769 (8th Cir. 1994). That case held that Balducci's parody was a trademark infringement, focusing on factual evidence suggesting that even though very few people thought "Michelob Oily" was a new brand of beer, nearly half of those surveyed thought that Balducci needed permission to run the ad. The court presumably saw this as evidence of confusion as to affiliation, but the rationale is troubling because it suggests that legal rules in trademark law will be determined by what the public thinks the rules are, rather than what they in fact are.

Should parody be protected by First Amendment? It is helpful to distinguish two situations: (1) the parody confuses consumers (presumably as to source or sponsorship only); and (2) parody does not confuse consumers, but they are aware of the connection to plaintiff's mark. Where parody is unsuccessful -- that is, where consumers think it is sponsored by the trademark owner -- the courts are relatively clear that the parody is not protected by the First Amendment. Thus, one rule of the trademark parody cases is that bad parodists may run afoul of trademark law. Where the parodist succeeds in conjuring up the trademark, but do not actually confuse consumers, the Lanham Act should not prevent the parody.

Dilution presents a more troubling issue. Parodists must necessarily rely on an association in consumers' minds between the parody and the famous mark. The parody will arguably cause "tarnishment" of the marks even if consumers aren't confused. Nonetheless, the court in *Cardtoons* (cited in the text) holds that there is a First Amendment defense to dilution that protects parodies.

The commercial nature of a parody may also be relevant. Where a parody is commercial in nature, courts may disfavor it even absent consumer confusion, because it cuts into sales.

Problem 5-15: This problem puts some of the principles stated above to the test. In the case, the court held that the trademark owner had been harmed by the inappropriate use of the "Enjoy Coke" slogan. *Coca-Cola Co. v. Gemini Rising, Inc.,* 346 F. Supp. 1183 (E.D.N.Y. 1972). The court relied in part on the commercial nature of the defendant's use (it sold posters), but it is not clear that that should matter where the defendant's sales are not in competition and are not the source of the plaintiff's injury.

F. International Issues in Trademark

G. Remedies

1. Injunctions

2. Damages

a. Infringer's Gain and Mark Owner's Loss

Lindy Pen, page 727, illustrates the statutory framework for computing damages under trademark law as well as the court's wide discretion in setting an amount. It may be useful to contrast trademark law's remedial framework with those in the copyright and patent fields. Trademark cases rarely produce the level of monetary award as their copyright and patent counterparts. For example, unlike patent law, trademark law does not provide for the award of a reasonable royalty, presumably because trademarks cannot be licensed without supervision or a transfer of goodwill.

PROBLEM 5-16

A small Vermont company named STW (and its predecessors) has used the mark "Thirst-Aid" for soft drinks since 1921. STW has never sold its products widely, however, and in fact its sales are declining. In 1983, Quaker Oats adopted the slogan "Gatorade is Thirst Aid" for its popular Gatorade beverage. STW sued for trademark infringement. At trial, STW proves that Quaker Oats knew of STW's trademark, but its lawyers advised it that the Gatorade slogan made "fair use" of STW's "descriptive" mark. The trial court disagreed, finding that Quaker Oats had infringed STW's mark in bad faith.

During the period that the "Thirst-Aid" campaign ran, pretax profits on the sale of Gatorade came to $247 million on sales of $2.6 billion. Quaker Oats proves that Gatorade had approximately $475 million in sales before the ad campaign. It also demonstrates that STW had previously offered to license the "Thirst-Aid" mark to another company for 1/3 of 1% of sales, and that STW's total goodwill in 1984 was less than $100,000 and declining. What damages should be awarded in this case?

Analysis

Problem 5-16: This problem is based on the case of *Sands, Taylor & Wood v. Quaker Oats*, which has a long and tortured history in the courts. The district court initially awarded $24.7 million in damages plus attorney fees to STW, a rate set at 10% of Quaker's total profits from Gatorade. The Seventh Circuit reversed the award of damages in a fractured opinion. One judge would have affirmed; the majority split on their analysis of Quaker's alleged "bad faith" and its consequences. Both agreed, however, that such a high rate would be a windfall in a reverse confusion case of this sort, since STW had certainly not suffered $24.7 million in lost goodwill. But the concurring judge would have permitted an award based on a deterrence rationale. On remand, the district court set a hypothetical royalty rate of 1% of sales for the first year and 0.5% of sales for subsequent years, with some adjustments. This produced a damages award of $10.3 million, which the district court doubled in order to deter conduct such as Quaker's. It also added an award of attorney fees and prejudgment interest. The Seventh Circuit affirmed the royalty calculation, but reversed the doubling for more explicit findings on the part of the district court. *Sands, Taylor & Wood v. Quaker Oats Co.*, 34 F.3d 1340 (7th Cir. 1994). The author of the original majority opinion dissented.

The problem brings out some of the complexities of trying to calculate damages in trademark cases. There is a general rule (discussed in detail the 1994 opinion) against using damages to punish defendants, at least outside of counterfeiting cases. At the same time, reverse confusion is troubling because bad faith acts by defendants may cause little or no remediable "damage," and yet still constitute undesirable conduct.

It is presumably irrelevant what the parties should have been willing to settle for, thought as Judge Cudahy notes in dissent, even $10 million is "beyond the wildest dreams" of STW. But arguably courts should take great care in awarding damages based on a defendant's profits to make sure that any profits awarded actually stem from the use of the mark, and not from other aspects of the defendants' business. Such a finding seems unlikely here.

b. Corrective Advertising

Big O Tire Dealers v. Goodyear Tire & Rubber Co., page 732, is an example of what might happen if there was no deterrence policy in trademark damages. An injunction alone would have been useless—the Goodyear executive told Big O that they would run over Big O by the time they were done litigating. The court ordered Goodyear to pay for corrective advertising in an amount proportionate to what it spent advertising its tires. Goodyear tried to argue that it would cost more to break the association with the mark than what Big O would actually have made from tire sales. Note the similarity between this argument and the notion of "waste" in contract law, which operates to prevent an award of damages that would exceed the market value of actual contract performance. (A classic example involves mining contracts with a "property restoration" clause; absent very particular stipulations, where the cost of restoring the land would far exceed the increase in market value such restoration would yield, courts are loathe to require full restoration. Why didn't the court follow this logic in *Big O*? Is there a punitive or deterrent element here that is not considered appropriate in the contract context? If the corrective advertising would truly be wasted, wouldn't we expect the parties to bargain for a cash settlement after the court awarded the "remedial advertising" damages – thus converting the award directly into a (punitive) damages provision?

Chapter 6: State Intellectual Property Law and Federal Preemption

A. State Intellectual Property Law

1. The Tort of Misappropriation

International News Service v. Associated Press, page 740, presents a good opportunity to revisit the underpinnings of IP protection; after three intensive chapters emphasizing the detailed statutory forms of protection, the students may welcome a return to a simple "common law" case. The holding, that INS engaged in unfair competition by misappropriating and selling as its own material stories taken from public bulletin boards and early editions, is only the starting point. One might begin by distinguishing the facts here from the trademark cases in Chapter 5. Here INS put its own label on AP's news stories, rather than putting the "AP" label on stories in fact written by INS. The *product* is stolen, rather than the *label.* To give AP some protection, the court created a quasi-property right. Holmes did not support the creation of a new property right. He saw the case as more of a misrepresentation case in which INS was representing AP's product as its own. Brandeis argued in his dissent that if a right is not covered by federal IP law, this should give the Court pause. If it was not intended to be covered by federal law then perhaps it was meant to be free to everyone. You might point out that this case is still relevant today, in the era of ubiquitous new technologies for distributing information. Courts often fall back on common law principles. For example, the NBA protested the broadcasting of sports scores to pages under a misrepresentation claim. Ebay is trying to go after meta-auction sites that take "newsworthy" facts from Ebay's online auctions. Misappropriation lives – at least until Congress gets around to legislating . . .

2. Protection by Contract

Contract operates as an alternative to intellectual "property" protection. As we saw in Chapter 2, parties can protect information against disclosure through trade secrecy agreements. A principal advantage of property over contract is that the state will enforce the "owner's" rights against others regardless of whether they are in a contractual relationship. In theory, a creator could seek to bind the "world" against unauthorized use or disclosure of his or her intellectual creativity through contract, but the transaction costs of doing so would obviously be prohibitive. But state-created intellectual property rights come at a cost. Federal and state intellectual property regimes limit the term and conditions of protection. Patents typically last for only 20 years from the date of application and copyright protection does not extend to data that is organized in an objective manner (such as phone directories (see *Feist*, page 329)). Trade secrets, as a hybrid of contract and property, can potentially extend much longer and apply to databases such as phone directories, but can typically only be asserted against those within the confidential relationship circle.

The advent of new products (such as mass marketed software) and distribution technologies (such as digital networks) has fueled a rise in the use of contract to protect intellectual creativity. Beginning in the 1980s, software vendors have sought to protect their products against misappropriation through shrink-wrap contracts. These modern forms of contracting have raised two sets of issues: (1) their enforceability as a matter of contract law; and (2) whether terms in such agreements that conflict or diverge from the provisions or limitations of federal intellectual laws can be enforced. We address the former set of issues in this section and the latter in section B(2) dealing with copyright preemption.

We illustrate the controversy over the enforcement of shrinkwrap and clickwrap agreements as a matter of contract through the juxtaposition of two prominent cases coming to different conclusions (on different facts). In *ProCD, Inc v. Zeidenberg*, page 752, Judge Easterbrook offers a pro-contract perspective in upholding and enforcing a software shrinkwrap agreement. In this case, Zeidenberg purchased an electronic nationwide telephone directory database, compiled at substantial cost, comprising more than 3,000 telephone directories. The outside of the box contained a notice indicating that additional licensing terms were inside the box. (In addition, notice and terms of the transaction were displayed on-screen every time the software was used. The licensing agreement further provided that if the purchaser did not agree to the terms upon reading them, the product could be returned for a full refund at the seller's expense.) One of those terms was that the purchaser could not disseminate the data contained in the directory.

Students who have taken contracts should spot the issue in *ProCD* pretty easily: can a valid and enforceable contract be formed where a buyer has not read or agreed to the shrinkwrap license? Relying on black letter law, they may be quick to answer no since the elements of offer and acceptance seem to be lacking. Likewise, when looked at under UCC Section 2-207 (on "fighting forms") or 2-209 (modifications), shrinkwrap licenses may appear seem faulty since the contract could be considered completed at purchase, and hence unmodifiable.

ProCD is a landmark case precisely because it rejects this analysis (performed both by the lower court in this case and in previous cases such as *Step-Saver Data Systems, Inc. v. Wyse Technology*, 939 F.2d 91 (3d Cir. 1991)). Instead, Judge Easterbrook looks to industry practice, the efficiency of shrinkwrap licenses, the use of similar "money-first" schemes in other industries, and the need to price discriminate to uphold the license as a valid contract. In particular, he relies on UCC section 2-204, arguing that by using the software, Zeidenberg agreed to the terms and formed a contract.

We return to this case in section B(2) to see how Judge Easterbrook grapples with Zeidenberg's argument that a contractual term barring dissemination of uncopyrightable telephone directory data is preempted by the Copyright Act. Note also that Judge Easterbrook leaves open the possibility that shrinkwrap agreements might be invalid under the unconscionability doctrine, although no such argument was put forward in this case.

In *Specht v. Netscape Communications Corp.*, page 759, Judge Sotomayor refused to enforce a mandatory arbitration clause contained in a clickwrap agreement for downloadable software on the ground that a reasonably prudent offeree would not know to look for notice of the additional term somewhere other than immediately before or near the download option. In this case, notice of additional terms was placed far enough down the page that users would have had to scroll further to see it. Because the court believed users were not on "inquiry notice" to search out additional terms, they could not be held to those terms. It would not be reasonable, in the court's view, to say that the defendant assented to the additional terms.

Given most students' experience in purchasing software and other technology products both online and through retail stores, it is worthwhile to explore their knowledge of contractual provisions and their sensibilities as to enforceability. What advice would they offer software vendors seeking to use these types of instruments? How do they evaluate the tradeoffs of numerous click through screens and quick online check-out/purchase? Which approach – freedom of contract (with onus on the consumer to be aware of fine print) or consumer protection – will best serve online commerce?

3. Idea Submissions

Nadel v. Play-by-Play Toys, page 768, explores the contours of New York's various common law doctrines relating to idea submissions. Nadel demonstrated a prototype of a plush toy with an "eccentric mechanism" to a Play-by-Play Toys executive with the informal (i.e., no written non-disclosure agreement) understanding that the company would keep the idea confidential and compensate him if Play-by-Play used the idea. When Play-by-Play later introduced Tornado Taz, featuring an "eccentric mechanism like that disclosed, Nadel sued for compensation under New York's law of idea submission/misappropriation/unfair competition (a property-based theory) and contract/quasi-contract. Play-by-Play defended on the ground that they had independently come upon this idea prior to Nadel's disclosure and that in any case it was commercially available prior to the date of Nadel's disclosure.

The case elucidates New York law with regard to whether novelty to the buyer or general novelty must be demonstrated to prevail in either of these branches of common law. A defendant can defeat a misappropriation cause action (i.e., without any allegation to a prior contractual agreement) by showing that the idea was generally known prior to the submission. By contrast, an idea submitter can prevail in a contact-based cause of action (i.e., where there is a showing of an agreement or understanding prior to the idea submission) if the idea is generally known so long as it was not known to the particular idea recipient. The lack of knowledge by the particular buyer serves as adequate consideration to validate an agreement not to disclose and a promise to pay for subsequent use by that buyer (cf. the Listerene Clause case, page 92).

The court's discussion of novelty (and its application to the facts of this case and other cases noted in the court's discussion) provides a fertile source of circumstances for explicating what is meant by the term "novelty." Some of the examples given – such as the proposal to use the name "Mr. Wiggle" to market Jell-O in the *Downey* case (discussed on page 771) and the proposal to develop a television sitcom about "Black American family life" in the *Murray* case (discussed on page 774) as well as the use of an eccentric mechanism in a plush toy – seem more to be about what we refer to as nonobviousness in the patent chapter. Apart from these semantic issues, do these standards conflict with the general principle of our free market economy that "ideas are free as the air" unless protect by a patent? Note that these common law doctrines in no way restrain non-parties from independently developing or reverse engineering products or script ideas.

Desny v. Wilder, page 779, explores the distinct realm of idea submissions in the entertainment industry. In this case, the California Supreme Court allowed an idea submission case to go forward against Billy Wilder on the basis of a relatively informal pitch transmitted over the phone to Wilder's secretary. The pitch was simply the idea for a motion picture centered around the life of Floyd Collins, who was trapped in an underground cave two decades earlier and was the subject of a widely reported (and ultimately unsuccessful) rescue attempt. In 1951, Paramount Pictures released Ace in the Hole, directed by Wilder and starring Kirk Douglas as headline hungry journalist who deliberately delays an attempt to rescue a man trapped in a cave, which was based loosely on the Floyd Collins' tragedy from 1925. The film plot closely paralleled the synopsis and historical material that Desny dictated to Wilder's secretary over the telephone. A critical fact in the case was Wilder's secretary's comment to Desny that Paramount would pay Desny if Wilder uses the story.

An idea is protected under California law if the idea recipient expressly promises to compensate the purveyor for use of the idea prior to the disclosure or if the circumstances preceding and attending disclosure, together with the conduct of the offeree acting with knowledge of the circumstances, show a promise of the type usually referred to as "implied" or "implied-in-fact." (page 781) The court found that Desny's initial blurting out of the idea to Wilder's secretary did not constitute a protected disclosure, but subsequent interaction – the secretary's statement that payment would be available if the plot sketch were used and Desny's preparation of a detailed story which he communicated – brought the transaction within the protection of California law.

As a result of the *Desny* doctrine, major film and television production studios are reluctant to consider unsolicited scripts and pitches in order to avoid being hit with a lawsuit after a successful release claiming that the idea was stolen. On pages 786-88, we discuss some of the institutions that have evolved in Hollywood to address this problem.

PROBLEM 6-1

In Buchwald v. Paramount Pictures Corp. (Cal. Super. 1990) (unpub.), the Washington humorist and columnist Art Buchwald submitted an eight-page summary of a film idea entitled "It's a Crude, Crude World" to executives at Paramount. The summary described in some detail the storyline, which involved a third-world prince who came to America for "a state visit." Buchwald gave a two-page overview of the plot to Paramount Pictures. Paramount subsequently entered into a contract with Buchwald whereby Paramount bought the rights to Buchwald's story and concept, with the aim of making a movie, starring Eddie Murphy, to be called "King for a Day." Another person would write the actual script, but "King for a Day" was to be based on "It's a Crude, Crude World." Because of various production difficulties, Paramount abandoned the project in March 1985. In May 1986, Buchwald gave an option on his film idea to the Warner Brothers Studio. In the summer of 1987, Paramount began development of a similar script by Eddie Murphy. In this movie -- which became the successful film *Coming to America* -- Murphy portrayed an African prince who comes to America in search of a suitable woman to marry.

The court described the plots of the two scripts as follows:

> In Buchwald's treatment, a rich, educated, arrogant, extravagant, despotic African potentate comes to America for a state visit. After being taken on a grand tour of the United States, the potentate arrives at the White House. A gaff[e] in remarks made by the President infuriates the African leader. His sexual desires are rebuffed by a black woman State Department officer assigned to him. She is requested by the President to continue to serve as the potentate's United States escort. While in the United States, the potentate is deposed, deserted by his entourage and left destitute. He ends up in the Washington ghetto, is stripped of his clothes, and befriended by a black lady. The potentate experiences a number of incidents in the ghetto, and obtains employment as a waiter. In order to avoid extradition, he marries the black lady who befriended him, becomes the emperor of the ghetto and lives happily ever after.
>
> In "Coming to America" the pampered prince of a mythical African Kingdom (Zamunda) wakes up on his 21st birthday to find that the day for his prearranged marriage has arrived. Discovering his bride to be very subservient and being unhappy about that fact, he convinces his father to permit him to go to America for the ostensible purpose of sewing [sic] his "royal oats." In fact, the prince intends to go to America to find an independent woman to marry. The prince and his friend go to Queens, New York, where their property is stolen and they begin living in a slum area. The prince discovers his true love, Lisa, whose father - McDowell - operates a fast-food restaurant for whom the prince and his friend begin to work. The prince and Lisa fall in love, but when the King and Queen come to New York and it is disclosed who the prince is, Lisa rejects the prince's marriage invitation. The film ends with Lisa appearing in Zamunda, marrying the prince and apparently living happily ever after.

Because of *Coming to America*, Warner Brothers decided not to pursue Buchwald's story. Buchwald then sued Paramount. The case turned on the contract between Buchwald and Paramount, which provided in pertinent part:

> "Work" means the aforementioned Material and includes all prior, present and future versions, adaptations and translations thereof (whether written by Author or by others), its theme, story, plot, characters and their names, its title or titles and subtitles, if any, ..., and each and every part of all thereof. "Work" does not include the material referred to in paragraph 2(f) above, written or prepared by Purchaser or under Purchaser's Authority * * * .
>
> ["Contingent consideration":]
>
> For the first theatrical motion picture (the "Picture"): If, but only if, a feature length theatrical motion picture shall be produced *based upon Author's Work.*

(Emphasis added.) How should the court rule?

Analysis

Problem 6-1: The court found for Buchwald on an idea submission rationale. [The decision was heavily reported in the popular and trade press, in part for its determination that the movie *Coming to America*, which grossed over $200 million, did not show a profit]. The facts of the problem present a common situation in idea submission law: the plots are similar, but certainly not identical. Whether Buchwald deserves protection depends on the level at which his "idea" can be protected. Certainly if the "idea" need only be "an African prince comes to the US and has to survive in the ghetto," Buchwald has a case. But the more general the idea, the more expansive the protection given to concepts which may not deserve it, and the greater the risk of frivolous idea submission suits.

> **PROBLEM 6-2**
>
> Lohr, an eccentric engineer, mails an idea she has had for a new invention to several engineering companies. The idea is mailed in a "double envelope." The outer envelope contains a confidentiality agreement, indicating that the contents of a second, sealed envelope are the property of Lohr and may not be used unless the user pays Lohr 10% of any profit that results. If the recipient does not agree to these terms, he is instructed to mail back the sealed, stamped, self-addressed envelope containing the idea. The "agreement" clearly provides that by opening the envelope, the recipient agrees to the terms.
>
> Dupco receives the agreement and opens the inner envelope. The next day, Dupco discovers that Lohr has posted the complete text of her idea on the Internet with no confidentiality restriction. Can Dupco use Lohr's idea without compensating her? Does it matter how novel or original the idea was on the day Dupco opened the envelope?

Analysis

Problem 6-2: We raised a similar issue in Problem 2-7 during our discussion of trade secrets and confidential relationships. *Smith v. Snap-On Tools*, 833 F.2d 578 (5th Cir. 1987) stood for the proposition that unsolicited unilateral disclosure of an idea does not create a confidential relationship giving rise to trade secret protection. However, it is possible that Lohr established the circumstances for a confidential relationship by attaching to an envelope containing the idea a confidentiality statement and demanding that the envelope not be opened and the idea not be used or disclosed unless the recipient agrees to the terms of the statement. In this case, Dupco has both notice of confidentiality and an opportunity to reject the information. In practice, large companies routinely reject unsolicited ideas without reviewing them unless the person submitting the idea signs a form waiving all rights to it.

Even if Lohr has not successfully created a confidential relationship, she might argue that she deserves to be compensated for the use of her idea. Solicitation of ideas and a policy of paying for them will not alone obligate a recipient to pay for a valuable idea, but both may be evidence from which a court might imply a confidential relationship. In *Joyce v. Halsey*, 551 N.E.2d 172 (Ohio 1990), the Supreme Court of Ohio held that a company policy of compensating employees for valuable suggestions did not create a property or contractual right to such compensation. Justice Holmes filed a vigorous dissent, citing a number of cases in which employee suggestion plans were held to create binding relationships.

In trade secrets law, Lohr's public disclosure of her idea (by posting it on the Internet) would destroy any claim to secrecy. But it does not necessarily destroy an idea-submission claim, since the gravamen of the claim seems to be that the defendant received an idea from the plaintiff and used it knowing that use obligated payment. Whether Lohr should be able to control material which is clearly in the public domain is a more troubling policy question, and relates to the similar efforts to keep control over unprotectable information through contracts.

4. The Right to Publicity

Midler and White are leading edge "right of publicity" cases. After the basic facts are on the table, some similarities with the misappropriation cases may be developed. What is "taken"? How much investment was required to produce it? What arguments can be made on behalf of the imitator/borrower? In addition to these issues, the presence of Lanham Act § 43(a) causes of action in these cases permits a review of "passing off" principles as well. Just because a voice may serve as an "indication of origin," dos this necessarily imply that a third party use of "the voice," i.e., an imitation, will confuse consumers? What about disclaimers?

Comedy III Productions, Inc. v. *Gary Saderup, Inc.*, page 804, provides an opportunity to discuss the tension between the right of publicity and freedom of expression. Celebrities, after all, are celebrities because society depicts and discusses them. When does a celebrity's interest in protecting the value of their image outweigh the public's right to freedom of expression? Drawing upon the copyright defense of fair use, the California Supreme Court read an analogous doctrine into the right of publicity in order to avoid a conflict with the First Amendment. The Court's analysis emphasizes the importance of allowing transformative uses to go forward. In a more recent case, *Winter v. DC Comics*, 134 Cal.Rptr.2d 634 (Cal. S. Ct. 2003), the California Supreme Court further explicated the nature of this inquiry in holding that a comic book series depicting characters loosely resembling well-known rock and roll performers and recording musicians Johnny and Edgar Winters as the Autumn Brothers, villainous half-worm, half-human offspring born from the rape of their mother by a supernatural worm creature that had escaped from a hole in the ground, as sufficiently transformative to defeat a right of publicity claim.

PROBLEM 6-3

In the late 1980s, the "New Kids on the Block" were an enormously successful pop music group, especially among the younger teen market. Capitalizing on this success, the New Kids sold over 500 products or services bearing their trademarked name. Among those services were "900 numbers" that fans could call to learn more about the New Kids, or to talk to the New Kids themselves.

During the height of the New Kids craze, the newspaper *USA Today* conducted a telephone poll that allowed readers to "vote" for their favorite New Kid (or for "none of the above" if they did not like the band at all) by calling a *USA Today* 900 number. As a part of the poll, the paper included captioned pictures of each of the band members. Suppose that the New Kids on the Block sued USA Today for infringement of their right of publicity. Do they have a claim under California law?

Analysis

Problem 6-3: The *New Kids* case is discussed in Chapter 5, because their primary claim was trademark infringement. The New Kids also brought a claim under state law misappropriation doctrine, but the Ninth Circuit held that it was a complete defense to a misappropriation claim that the name was used "in connection with any news, public affairs, or sports broadcast or account" which is truthful. The New Kids apparently did not object on publicity grounds to the use of their name and likeness. We have changed the facts to suppose that they had instead brought suit in California for violation of their "right of publicity." Can they prevent USA Today's conduct on this ground?

Under *Midler*, the right of publicity is quite broad. The elements of the tort are simple: (1) appropriation of "name or likeness" -- now extended by *Midler* and *White* to encompass the sound of your voice, the automobile you drive, and other distinctive attributes -- indeed, anything that reminds the public of you; and (2) the use must be for commercial advantage. Both of those elements appear to be satisfied here. While USA Today will no doubt assert a "news reporting" defense, as in the *Montana v. San Jose Mercury*

News case cited in the text, the claim is relatively weak because the use of 900 numbers appears to be for money-making rather than news-gathering purposes.

The problem points up some of the disturbing aspects of the right of publicity alluded to by Judge Kozinski in his dissent in *White*. The New Kids lost their trademark claim, arguably for good reason. The right of publicity threatens to run roughshod over the limitations that exist in copyright and trademark law, and indeed to run into serious First Amendment problems, because it gives individuals control over factual uses of their names even when the use relates to speech on a matter of public concern. Efforts to cabin the right of publicity have taken the form of news reporting exceptions, parody defenses, and the application of the First Amendment to publicity claims.

5. State Moral Rights

6. Trespass to Chattels

The inherent characteristic of the Internet to allow computer users to query webpages and use memory storage and processing capacity of computers owned by others has spawned a modern revival if not reincarnation of the trespass to chattels doctrine. *eBay, Inc. v. Bidder's Edge, Inc.*, page 820, is one of many new cases where plaintiffs have sought protection against unauthorized or "unreasonable" use of a servers' capacity. The *eBay* provides a detailed discussion of this emerging body of law.

Note also that the prevalence of various "'bots, robots, spiders, or webcrawlers" has been subject to various technical solutions that may have legal ramifications. Certainly an owner of property is entitled to protect his or her property; eBay and other online businesses install gatekeeper software which automatically refuses automated requests, such as the robots employed by Bidder's Edge. Self-help in the ejectment of trespassers is generally legal within reasonable bounds, but how does this doctrine fare in a website that holds itself open to the general public to do business? Can businesses charge a fee for a license to access its website in a discriminatory manner? Could it abuse the doctrine of trespass to chattels to engage in discriminatory or anticompetitive denials of access? Does this create new issues involving contract law or licensing, when small businesses attempt to access site?

PROBLEM 6-4

Infoplex is a search engine. In order to run a comprehensive search engine, Infoplex must collect and index data from over 1 billion Web sites. In order to keep its search engine up-to-date, Infoplex must revisit those pages at least once a week, and often more frequently. To do this, Infoplex uses automated software robots called "spiders." These spiders crawl the Web, automatically downloading all of the information on all of the Web sites it can find. Because of the practical impossibility of entering into contracts with the owners of all these Web sites – among other things, millions of new pages are added each year – Infoplex has configured its spiders to collect any data it can from any site that is open to the public.

Do any of the following plaintiffs have a claim against Infoplex for trespass to chattels based on its indexing of their sites?

a) Site A, which has a written "terms of use" statement precluding any collection of all or substantially all of its data by any for-profit company.

b) Site B, which uses a Robot Exclusion Header in the source code of its Web page. Such a header signals to robots that they are not welcome on the site. Not all robots recognize or respect such a header, though, and Infoplex has configured its robots to ignore such headers.

c) Site C, an Internet service provider which has sent a letter to the general counsel of Infoplex demanding that Infoplex pay it $1,000 per month for the right to index any of its customers' pages.

Analysis

Problem 6-4: This problem raises one of the most significant policy concerns with the application of the trespass to chattels doctrine. Internet search engines depend on the ability to search billions of Web pages every week, and Internet users in turn depend on search engines to help them find what they want. If search engines are subject to potential liability to every person with a Web page, they cannot function.

Under *eBay*, a trespass to Web server occurs when there is an unwanted electronic contact with the server, regardless of whether the server has been damaged as a result. The question then becomes what the owner of the Web server must do to communicate to Infoplex that it is not welcome. While in real property the onus might be on Infoplex to get permission in advance, such a rule obviously isn't workable on the Internet. Similarly, Site A's terms of service won't give Infoplex notice that their intrusion is unwanted, because the collection of information from the site is automatic. By contrast, site C directly contacted Infoplex and told them not to index the site without permission. This seems akin to what eBay did in its dispute with Bidder's Edge. Site B uses an automated means of communicating with search engines like Infoplex. Unlike a password protection, though, it doesn't physically compel compliance with the no-trespassing rule. No cases have determined whether a robots.txt file constitutes an enforceable notice preventing entry, but it seems plausible that they might.

The traditional doctrine of trespass to chattels requires proof of injury to the chattel, or at least dispossession of the chattel owner. The potential harm done by Infoplex is far less than even the dubious assertions of harm made in the *eBay* case. Search engines catalog a Web site no more than once a week, and do not normally interfere with its operation. Indeed, the fact that dozens of search engines have crawled most every site on the Web without untoward consequence suggests that plaintiffs in such a case will not be able to prove harm. But in the majority of cases since *eBay*, this may be irrelevant, as courts seem to be presuming harm from the mere fact of unauthorized access.

B. Federal Preemption

1. Patent Protection

Kewanee Oil, page 831, explains and clarifies the Supreme Court's framework for analyzing whether a state intellectual property law is preempted by the Intellectual Property Clause or the Supremacy Clause of the U.S. Constitution. The Court holds that the federal patent law does not generally preempt state trade secret protection.

Bonito Boats, page 835, involves a Florida statute prohibiting use of the direct molding process to duplicate a vessel hull. There were several problems inherent in the statute: no time limitations were imposed; the statute was retroactive; and the statute did not say where the boat had to be manufactured to infringe the right. It might be relevant to raise federalism issues here. You might point out that a special amendment to the Digital Millennium Copyright Act included special protection for boat hulls.

Copyright Preemption

In addition to validating the enforceability of the shrinkwrap contract at issue in *ProCD v. Zeidenberg* as a matter of contract law, Judge Easterbrook holds that the enforcement of a contractual restriction, imposed in a mass marketed software product, on the dissemination of an uncopyrightable database does not conflict with federal copyright law. Some scholars have asserted that federal copyright envisions not just the unprotectibility of data under federal copyright law but also an implied freedom to use and disseminate unprotected information – a sort of dormant Commerce Clause precluding states (and hence state contract law) from inhibiting the use of unprotected material, at least of publicly distributed (as opposed to trade secrecy) content. Judge Easterbrook reads federal copyright preemption much more narrowly. A recent Federal Circuit decision upholding a contractual restriction on reverse engineering of software follows Judge Easterbrook's freedom of contract analysis. See *Bowers v. Baystate Technologies, Inc.*, 320 F.3d 1317 (Fed. Cir. 2003).

PROBLEM 6-5

Presco is in the business of printing and selling academic journals to university libraries. When Presco receives a subscription request, it sends a form contract to the requestor. The requesting library is required to sign the contract before Presco will start the subscription. Presco's form contract provides in part that "Independent of and in addition to any provisions of state or federal law, the parties agree that Subscriber will not make, cause to be made, or allow to be made any copies of any Presco journals without the prior express written consent of Presco."

Is the contract provision preempted? Does it matter whether the subscriber's copying would constitute fair use under the copyright laws?

Analysis

Problem 6-5: The federal preemption of contract law is one of the most troubling issues in intellectual property. Clearly contract law is not preempted by intellectual property law in its entirety. Some have made the opposite claim -- that judicial enforcement of contractual provisions are *never* preempted, because contract law is somehow different from normal state statutes. Judge Easterbrook's opinion in *ProCD v. Zeidenberg* comes close to asserting this. The Presco problem presents the "hard case" for opponents of federal preemption. Arguably there are some aspects of the intellectual property laws which cannot be contracted around; the term of patents and copyrights clearly appears to be one, and perhaps fair use is another. On the other hand, there are unquestionably provisions of the Copyright Act which exist only as default rules, and which the parties can vary by contract. The problem is figuring out which are which. For more detail on these issues, see Mark A. Lemley, *Intellectual Property and Shrinkwrap Licenses*, 68 **S. Cal. L. Rev.** 1239 (1995); David A. Rice, *Public Goods, Private Contract, and Public Policy: Federal Preemption of Software License Prohibitions Against Reverse Engineering*, 53 **U. Pitt. L. Rev.** 543 (1992).

The problem also requires students to distinguish between section 301 preemption and Supremacy Clause conflict preemption. Under the judicial interpretation of section 301, the copyright laws do not preempt a state law if it requires an "extra element" not present in the Copyright Act. Most courts, including *National Car Rental*, have held that the agreement required in a contract case constitutes that extra element. However, it does not follow that there is never a preemption problem in contract cases, as the discussion above indicates.

3. Trademark Preemption

Chapter 7 Protection of Computer Software

This Chapter represents a distinctive feature of this casebook. We have found it helpful to segregate out, for emphasis, these materials on computer protection. The introductory material is an important component in the chapter. It is the special nature of software, in fact, that justifies a separate chapter in the first place. The goal here is to see how the various components of IP protection overlap and interact to form a comprehensive "appropriability environment" for this industry. Beginning with trade secret protection, and progressing through the various statutory forms of protection, we recapitulate the earlier chapters, applying their lessons in sequence to the unique problems of the industry.

A. The Economics of Computer Markets

B. Trade Secret Protection

PROBLEM 7-1

Microsoft Corp.'s Disk Operating System (MS-DOS) became the industry standard for personal computer operating systems. Microsoft sold several million copies of MS-DOS each year; there are estimated to be upwards of 25 million copies in circulation worldwide. Further, MS-DOS was normally "pre-installed" on most new personal computers, so that PC purchasers automatically purchase the operating system as well. Assuming that Microsoft has taken reasonable efforts to require both hardware manufacturers and end users to keep the program confidential, is Microsoft entitled to protect MS-DOS as a trade secret? What efforts would be "reasonable" under these circumstances?

Assume for the moment that Microsoft has succeeded in maintaining the secrecy of its computer operating system and has taken reasonable efforts to protect that secrecy. Are competing application programmers entitled to decompile the operating system to prepare application programs that will run on Microsoft's OS? Is there anything Microsoft can do that will prevent its competitors from legally reverse engineering its product?

PROBLEM 7-2

Software Incorporated (SI), the developer of application software, possesses a valid trade secret on the proprietary computer code in its Calcutec program and has taken reasonable steps to protect its secrecy. Q, A disgruntled employee of User Inc., a licensee of the Calcutec program, wrongfully makes the proprietary code widely available by posting it on BBS, an electronic bulletin board service, from which it can be easily copied. SI learns of this unauthorized disclosure within a few weeks and notifies BBS. BBS promptly removes Calcutec from the bulletin board and posts a notice there of its unauthorized disclosure of Calcutec, but not before Software Distributors, Inc., among other companies, downloads the program and distributes it. Software Distributors sells Calcutec, without designation of source or copyright, to Tech Corp.

- What actions does SI have against Q, User, BBS, Software Distributors, and Tech?
- What difficulties might SI encounter in maintaining such an action?
- Does "wrongful publication" of the Calcutec code on BBS negate its status as a secret, thereby placing it in the public domain?
- What does this problem suggest about the viability of trade secret as a means for protecting widely distributed software products?

PROBLEM 7-3

Bartles and Vine are graduate students in computer science who regularly log onto a Xanton Corporation computer using a remote, dedicated terminal provided by Xanton to the university. The Xanton computer is not open to the general public, but the students have permission to use it for certain limited purposes in connection with their research. Xanton gives similar permission to other students around the world.

Bartles and Vine are frustrated by the fact that they have to rely on the dedicated Xanton terminal; it is the only one in the computer lab, and it is frequently in use by other students. To solve this problem, they decide to write a program that will allow a PC with a modem to emulate a Xanton terminal so they can access the Xanton computer from home at any time. To accomplish this, the students log onto the computer using the remote terminal and engage in "black box" analysis of the terminal interface -- sending particular commands to see how the main computer responds.

Using the information they have thus acquired, Bartles and Vine write an emulation interface program for their PC. They call Xanton Corporation's public relations department, and a receptionist there gives them a telephone modem number. Bartles and Vine then use their PC to log into the Xanton computer.

Have Bartles and Vine misappropriated trade secrets allegedly contained in the Xanton interface? Does the result change if Bartles and Vine decide to market their emulation interface?

Analysis

Problem 7-1: In some ways this is the *reductio ad absurdium* of the contract law argument. If Microsoft characterizes each of its millions of sales as a "license," is it entitled to impose confidentiality restrictions on its licensees? Common sense would seem to say no. Rationales for this may differ. One might argue that there is a point beyond which the program is "generally known to or readily ascertainable by" everyone who wants it, or alternatively that there has been an affirmative act of disclosure. Nonetheless, *Data General* suggests that the public disclosure line will be hard to draw. *Data General* says disclosure through sale to certain individuals can still keep a secret, even though there were 500 copies sold. Further, note that in *Stac v. Microsoft*, [a patent case discussed in the section on software patents, *infra*] the jury found that *beta* versions of MS-DOS 6.0 distributed to several thousand customers contained protectable trade secrets. A reasonable argument would seem to be that if anyone can buy the software without restriction for a reasonable price, it is not a secret anymore.

There may be a legitimate difference between object code, which is evident to any purchaser, and hidden aspects of programs contained in source code. Here, the question may be how easy it is to reverse engineer a program to discover those secrets. If it is easy, then arguably the source code secrets are "readily ascertainable" by anyone who has the object code version. Even if reverse engineering is difficult, once it has been done successfully the reverse engineer can disclose the secret to the world without restriction.

Further, it is worth noting that there is some dispute about what constitutes an enforceable contract. There may be some justification for treating signed confidentiality agreements between business entities with more deference than shrinkwrap license provisions.

Problem 7-2: Once a secret is gone, it is gone forever -- there is no way to reprotect it. Thus, those who get it from public sources are free to use it. This is true even if the public disclosure occurs without the knowledge or approval of the trade secret owner. The trade secret owner's remedy in this situation is in theory to sue the one who disclosed it for the full value of the secret.

Thus, SI's actions vs.

Q -- he posted the program, which was secret, so he is liable not just for his own profits, but for any subsequent loss to SI from further disclosures. Of course, Q may not be able to pay.

User -- because it was their employee who posted the material, agency principles will determine their liability. User may be held liable if it encouraged Q, or if they negligently supervised him, but not otherwise.

BBS -- the bulletin board took the software and redistributed it. It was this act that presumably made the information public, and destroyed the secrecy. Under trade secrets principles, BBS's liability depends on whether they knew or should have known that the information was stolen. If so, they too are liable for the full value of the secret. If not, however, transmission of information they did not know was secret will not inculpate them.

SoftDist -- because their only act was to download the information after it became public, they are not liable -- there was no longer a "secret" to misappropriate.

TECH -- similarly, because they purchased the information after it became public, they are not liable.

This problem points up the delicacy of trade secrets embodied in publicly disclosed products. The problem with trying to use trade secret law to protect widely distributed products is that one publication destroys all your efforts at secrecy, except *maybe* those with whom you have a contract. You may have a cause of action against the individual who disclosed the secret, but that may prove small consolation if the individual cannot be found or is impecunious.

Problem 7-3: This problem is very loosely based on *Technicon Data Systems v. Curtis 1000 Inc.*, 224 U.S.P.Q. 286 (Del. Ct. Chanc. 1984). That case involved employees of a hospital using computer access purchased for the hospital to write their own programs. The court held that while reverse engineering is legal, the access to the reverse-engineered product must be lawful. It clearly was not in that case. We have modified the problem somewhat to present the issue more starkly. Bartles and Vine have lawful access to the Xanton computer, but their right to access the computer may be limited in scope or purpose. If a valid contract prevented access for such a purpose, it would be enforceable against Bartles and Vine. On the other hand, if there were no enforceable restriction on the use to which the access could be put, the fact that Bartles and Vine used their lawful access for a purpose Xanton did not foresee will not make their reverse engineering unlawful. For a controversial extension of this reasoning, see *Vault Corp. v. Quaid Software Ltd.*, 847 F.2d 255 (5th Cir. 1988).

C. Copyright Law

PROBLEM 7-4

Letni Corp. produces microprocessors, the central component of microcomputer systems. These "computers on a chip" are integrated circuits capable of performing arithmetic functions, manipulation of data, and other operations in response to object code instructions. Letni's 684 microprocessor currently commands a 70 percent market share of the microcomputer market. Letni's 684 chip utilizes a single "bus" or path for transferring data. It features 512 lines of microcode, each 21 bits long, which enables the microprocessor to interpret 133 assembly instructions.

CEN Corp., a competing microprocessor manufacturer, seeks to sell semiconductor chips capable of running the same software as Letni's 684 microprocessor. A prior patent cross-licensing agreement entitles CEN to duplicate Letni's 684 microarchitecture and hardware to the extent comprehended by the Letni's patent. To increase processing speed and capability relative to Letni's 684 chip, CEN designed its U2 microprocessor with a dual bus system and a larger micro instruction word size (29 bits). The 1024 lines of microcode enable the microprocessor to interpret 156 assembly instructions; 552 of these lines carry out the instruction set of the Letni 684 microprocessor. The remaining lines perform other functions not carried out by the 684 chip. Because of the dual bus architecture and larger word size, CEN was able to write shorter and more efficient microcode.

Nonetheless, there were a number of similarities in the microcodes of the two microprocessors. Letni brought suit, alleging: (1) microprograms are computer programs and hence protected by the Copyright Act; and (2) CEN's U2 microcode infringed the copyright of Letni's 684 chip.

How should this case be resolved? Should microcode be copyrightable? If so, what should be the scope of protection? Can a hardware manufacturer obtain copyright protection for the configuration of the hardwiring of its computer? If so, under what theory? If your answer is different from that for microcode, what explains the distinction?

Analysis

Problem 7-4: There is no question under the statutory language that both source code and object code gets protection. First, the definition of literary works is very broad -- any symbols qualify, and the legislative history indicates that computer programs are included in that list. Second, the definition of fixation expressly contemplates that perception only through machines is OK. Finally, CONTU report clearly contemplates inclusion of computer code. Microcode presents essentially the same issue -- if a program in object code is protectable, so should be its implementation on a chip. On the other hand, a potential problem with the expansive statutory language is that it also implies copyright protection for hardware implementations of computer instructions (in this case presumably as a sculptural rather than a literary work).

There are policy arguments that can be made against including source and/or object code within the scope of copyright protection, and many would apply equally well to microcode. They include

(1) communicative function. Based on *White-Smith (see page 336)*, one might argue that the literary basis of copyright is disserved by protecting combinations of symbols which can't be understood or even perceived directly by humans. This argument also disables most music copyright. [Note that there may be a distinction between projective devices and interpretive devices, and computers arguably perform the latter function].

(2) no "authorship" of object code (as distinguished from source code). Even if programmers write source code, and write converter programs, you cannot be said to "write" circuit switches. Note that in the early days, no one argued that hardwiring configurations were copyrightable as "literary works." If anything, they would have been sculpture, to which different rules apply. Should abstractability result in broader protection? CONTU argues that difference between hard-wired computer inventions and software code is that cost of reproduction has gone down, justifying more intellectual property protection. *Id.* at 18-19. Does this argument always justify increased copyright protection? Is it relevant to the subject matter issue? Note that this suggests object code should get more protection on a disk than it does in printed form, since it is easier to replicate in that form. Does that make sense?

(3) really the role of patent law to protect ideas, processes, systems, and methods of operation. Source code is really a means of operating the computer to achieve a particular result -- the result could be written in plain English, and what gets protected is the method of operating the computer to achieve that result. Certainly this is true of object code, and arguably is true of source code as well. [One problem with this is practical -- patent law at this time arbitrarily denied protection to computer programs, and copyright was a gap-filler].

Even once it has been established that microcode is copyrightable, the copyright protection will be limited by the extent to which microcode design is constrained by functional considerations. This problem therefore foreshadows the *Whelan-Altai* debate. One might go so far as to conclude that there are sufficiently few possible choices, and the choices are so heavily driven by a desire for efficiency, that the merger doctrine prevents any copyright protection for microcode. Alternatively, one might impose a higher standard on microcode copyright infringement suits, finding infringement only where the two chips were programmed in a virtually identical manner.

In the case (*NEC v. Intel*, 10 U.S.P.Q.2d 1177 (N.D. Cal. 1989)), the court concludes in a thoughtful discussion that Intel's microcode is copyrightable subject matter, but that NEC's chips were not sufficiently similar to infringe Intel's, and in any event that Intel had failed to comply with the then-extant copyright notice requirement.

PROBLEM 7-5

The Midwest Corn Cooperative Association (MCCA) is a nonprofit agricultural cooperative comprised of approximately 15,000 corn farmers in the midwestern states. MCCA's purpose is to assist its members in the growing and marketing of corn. During the mid-1970's, MCCA developed a computer software system called CornMart, that provided users with information regarding corn prices and availability, accounting services, and a means for electronically completing actual sales. The CornMart system was used by corn farmers and buyers through terminals connected by telephone lines to MCCA's large central computer.

CornMart was developed by a team of programmers that included George Cusher and Ben Fishman. In the early 1980s, after the program had been up and running for a number of years, Cusher and Fishman decided the system would have much greater usefulness if the CornMart program could be operated on personal computers, which were by then increasingly used by MCCA members. Cusher and Fishman took a complete source code version of CornMart and supporting program documentation when they departed MCCA.

In 1985 Cusher and Fishman formed Cornware, Inc., and began work on a personal computer version of CornMart. By early 1986 they succeeded in writing a personal computer version of CornMart that they marketed as Cornware. Soon after they began marketing their new software, MCCA sued alleging copyright infringement.

Expert testimony at trial established that Cornware and CornMart were very similar in terms of functional specification, overall structure, and documentation. The main difference between the systems was that CornMart is designed to run on a mainframe computer and Cornware on a personal computer. There was, however, no literal copying of code. Cusher and Fishman testified that they had not copied or modified the CornMart program but instead had "drawn on their knowledge of the corn industry and expertise in computer programming and design gained over many years." Expert testimony at trial indicated that it would take significant effort to modify a program as complex as CornMart to run on a personal computer, perhaps more effort than rewriting the program entirely. Nonetheless, there remained significant structural similarities between the programs, although two experts testified that residual similarity between the programs reflected features of the corn market and that different programmers knowledgeable about the corn industry could conceivably make similar judgments. For example, both programs were designed to present the same information as is contained on a corn recap sheet, a standard form used for corn transactions.

How would you argue the case for MCCA? for Cornware?

Analysis

Problem 7-5: This problem is based on *Plains Cotton v. Goodpasture*, 807 F.2d 1256 (5th Cir. 1987). In that case, the court held that the defendant's program did not infringe the plaintiff's. It based its factual decision largely on expert testimony presented at the preliminary injunction hearing, in which the defendant's expert testified that based on his comparison of the programs, there did not appear to be copying either of the literal code or of the "structure, sequence and organization" of the program. Instead, any similarities resulted from authorial style and from the specifics of the cotton industry. In dictum, the court rejected *Whelan*'s approach to nonliteral copying, instead endorsing the district court opinion in *Synercom* suggesting that nonliteral elements of computer programs should receive little or no protection. The court specifically noted that many of the similarities alleged to exist between the two programs resulted from external functional constraints, thus foreshadowing the *Altai* decision several years later.

The problem not only points out some of the vagueness of the *Whelan* test, but also the difficulty of taking seriously the Ninth Circuit's statement in *Sid & Marty Krofft* that infringement is to be tested by reference to the reactions of the ordinary observer, without expert testimony. Arguably a reasoned analysis in a case as complex as this one is simply impossible without reliance on the technical expertise of others.

PROBLEM 7-6

Demento Corporation ("Demento") produces Demento II, the leading home video game system. The Demento II consists of a console, which runs game cartridges and attaches to a monitor or standard television, and a control device, which enables the user to manipulate characters or other images of particular games on the screen. Demento licenses a limited number of games per year.

To prevent unauthorized game producers from manufacturing games to run on the Demento II console, Demento developed a "lock out" device that governs access to the console. The console includes a "master chip" or "lock" that will only run game cartridges that contain an appropriate "slave chip" or "key." When a user inserts an authorized game cartridge into the Demento II, the slave chip transmits an arbitrary data stream "key" that is received by the master chip and unlocks the console, allowing the game to be played. The unlocking device is a sophisticated software program encoded in the master and slave chips. There are a multitude of different programs capable of generating the data stream that unlocks the console, although it would be almost impossible to decipher the "key" by trial and error. It would be like trying to find a needle in a haystack.

The rapid growth of the home video game market eroded the revenue base of Mutant Corporation ("Mutant"), a leading maker of arcade video games. Mutant sought to license the right to produce game cartridges for the Demento II system, but it was put off by the limits on the number of new games that Demento would license per year and the high cost of each license. Mutant decided instead to develop its own slave chip that would unlock the Demento II game cartridge.

Mutant engineers first chemically peeled the layers of the Demento II chips to allow microsopic examination of the circuitry. Through this means, they were able to decipher the object code (series of "on" and "off" switches) and construct the series of pulsating signals that unlocked the master chip. Mutant discovered that only a relatively small portion of the coded message was necessary to unlock the Demento II console. From this information, Mutant software designers built a slave chip that successfully unlocked the Demento II console and enabled Mutant's game cartridges to run. It included the entire coded message for fear that Demento might later alter new versions of the Demento II system in such a way as to make Mutant's cartridges inoperable on newer units seeking the fuller coded message. To differentiate its product, the Mutant slave program was written in a different computer language and employed a different microprocessor than the Demento II system. Since the Mutant microprocessor operated at a faster speed than the Demento II chip, the Mutant program included numerous pauses.

Despite these differences, Demento promptly sued Mutant for copyright infringement after Mutant introduced its first game cartridge for the Demento II system. What is the unprotectable idea of the Demento II system? What is the protectable expression? Is the lockout code functional? How would this case be resolved.

Analysis

Problem 7-6: This problem is based on *Atari Games v. Nintendo of Am.*, 975 F.2d 832 (Fed. Cir. 1992). In that case, the court found that the code containing the Nintendo lockout device was copyrightable in part, since it was not driven exclusively by function. The court also decided, however, that Atari had a limited right to reverse engineer and copy that lockout code to the extent such copying was necessary to achieve compatibility between Atari's games and Nintendo's box. [Nonetheless, the court held that Atari had not lawfully reverse engineered the program, based on facts not presented in this problem]. On remand, the district court held that Atari could copy the specific lockout code used in a current version of the Nintendo box, but could not copy those portions of the coded message which were not currently used to control compatibility. The court reasoned that code which had no current function, but might have a function in the future, was copyrightable because it was not currently functional. Further, it held that there was no current right to reverse engineer such code, since the reverse engineering was not "necessary" to achieve compatibility at the present time. *Atari Games v. Nintendo*, 1993 U.S. Lexis 6786 (N.D. Cal. May 18, 1993). The result was to allow Nintendo to try to remain one step ahead of its competitors by changing its codes with some frequency. Since Nintendo games would include all the possible codes, but Atari's would not, only Nintendo's games would work with a wide variety of different box releases. Arguably this undermines the *Sega-Atari* appellate holdings of compatibility.

It is worth noting that Nintendo also patented its lockout code, a fact which raises the potential for patent-copyright overlap in cases like *Whelan*, which give broad copyright protection to the functional features of a computer program.

PROBLEM 7-7

Pueblo Graphics sells software that produces a variety of word processing fonts. (Fonts control the appearance of letters and numbers in typesetting). The software allows the fonts to appear on the screen in exactly the same way they will appear on the printed page. Pueblo's software contains a number of "classic" print fonts, such as Geneva, Helvetica, and Times Roman Bold. In addition, however, Pueblo has designed several new fonts that look significantly different than any fonts previously produced.

Pueblo would like to assert a copyright infringement suit against a competitor who has copied its fonts. The competitor wrote its own program to implement those fonts, so Pueblo wants to know if it can get copyright protection in the fonts themselves. How would you advise Pueblo? Is their claim appropriately characterized as one for a "user interface"? Why or why not?

Analysis

Problem 7-7: Protecting computer fonts is an interesting case in the limits of expression. There is no question that the *software* that generates those fonts can be protected. The real question is whether there is sufficient expression in the new shape of individual letters to justify copyright protection. Traditionally, courts and commentators have taken the view that fonts are not protectable under copyright, in the same way that short phrases can't be copyrighted. *Leonard Storch Ents. v. Mergenthaler Linotype,* 202 U.S.P.Q. 623 (E.D.N.Y. 1979); *Cf. Apple Computer v. Microsoft Corp.*, 799 F. Supp. 1006 (N.D. Cal. 1992) (spacing of fonts not protectable). But in one recent decision, a court held that Adobe Systems was entitled to protect not the fonts themselves, but the computer reference points that were used to create those fonts on screen and in a printed document. *Adobe Systems v. Southern Software*, No. C 95-20710 RMW (NDCA, San Jose Div., Jan. 30, 1998).

The difficulty with the issue has to do with the intermixing of creative and functional elements. Fonts are heavily constrained by readability and other use-related factors. Once a font is designed, in turn, deciding how to place reference points in order to generate the font on screen seems similarly dictated by function.

PROBLEM 7-8

Apple's Macintosh graphical user interface has three main components which are copied by Kiwi Computer in its competing operating system. The three components are "pull-down menus," in which the major classes of user commands are written in a bar at the top of the screen that can be "opened" by clicking on the relevant class of commands with a mouse and dragging the mouse downwards; a series of icons on the right-hand side of the screen to perform other common commands or to open particular folders; and "overlapping windows," which show the most recently used document or program "on top of" other open applications.

Apple contends that none of these three components is functional and points to other ways in which Kiwi could have implemented a graphical user interface. For example, Apple argues that Kiwi could have used "pull-up" or "pull-across" menus, or an expandable list of commands controlled by the keyboard or by voice rather than by the mouse. Kiwi responds that it is easier and more logical for most computer users to drag the mouse downward than to push it up or across. Apple points to alternatives to its overlapping windows such as "tiled windows" that appear side by side; Kiwi responds that tiled windows are inefficient because they limit both the number of windows that can be open and the size of each open window.

Are Apple's design features functional? Does you answer depend on the legal standard you apply?

PROBLEM 7-9

Intel manufactures generations of microprocessor chips with identifying number sequences. For reference, these number sequences are shortened to the last three digits and are commonly referred to by computer users in this way (e.g., the 286, 287, 386, 387, 486). Advanced Micro Devices, a competing microprocessor manufacturer, refers to its comparable chips by the same number sequences. Has AMD infringed an Intel trademark?

Intel refers to its latest generation of chip as the "Pentium." From a trademark perspective, what are the advantages and disadvantages of this change in naming convention?

PROBLEM 7-10

Sun Microsystems is a leading manufacturer of computer workstation systems. A recent entrant in the computer workstation software market is thinking about using the name SunRiver. Would Sun Microsystems be likely to enjoin the use of the this name? What information would you need to know to answer this question properly?

Analysis

Problem 7-8: We will consider the trademark issues in this problem in parts:

1. Distinctiveness: It is true that the Apple design as a whole appears to be distinctive, at least through secondary meaning -- people recognize it. This is particularly true because of the appearance of certain icons (the trash can), and the location of everything on the screen. Note that unlike copyright law, we don't care in this context whether Apple *wrote* the GUI or not -- the only question for trademark purposes is who uses it as a business identifier. This may get Apple around one of the big problems with its copyright case.

Note that the network externalities that favor standardization discourage the development of distinctive user interfaces -- you want yours to be as familiar as possible. On the other hand, from a trademark perspective, if it isn't distinctive, it isn't protectable.

2. Genericness: The question here is whether the components of the Apple GUI are so central to an industry that they are the natural way to "refer to" (and in this case, operate) a GUI. For example, the QWERTY keyboard is generic, even though when it started it was arbitrary as a means of arranging letters. Things can *become* generic over time, and once generic, they are unprotectable. Arguably, the pull-down menus are generic because they are prevalent in most operating systems today. [Note that success spells doom from a trademark perspective]. But the trash can icon probably isn't, because there are other ways of expressing the concept of a place to discard files.

3. Functionality: Trademark protection will not extend to any attribute of a design or name which is "functional." Courts debate definition of functionality, but it clearly applies if the design is necessary to the product, and probably even if the design gives a *cost or value advantage* to the product apart from its identification function. Some courts have gone so far as to find functionality in pleasing aesthetics, or in any design attribute which does anything other than identify the product. *Digital Equipment Corp. v. C. Itoh & Co*, 229 U.S.P.Q. 598 (D.N.J. 1985) is a good example. The court in *Itoh* suggests that standards are inherently functional, because of the need for compatibility in the computer industry.

Apple is in serious trouble on functionality grounds -- not only does each of its elements (pull-down menus, icons, and overlapping windows) exist to perform a function, but *the purpose of the whole interface design is to make the computer as simple and intuitive to use as possible*, not to identify Apple as the maker of the operating system. Logos are of course protectable, but that won't help Apple unless someone copied the logo itself.

4. Likelihood of confusion: This actually turns out to be a difficult factor. People spend a lot of money on computers, and they see the thing in a box which is well-labeled as belonging to the manufacturing company. So initial purchasers are not likely to be the victim of any confusion resulting from similar software formats. Where confusion may result is in Kellner's hypothetical -- people see a clone GUI (say, Hewlett-Packard's New Wave) and think it belongs to Apple. This is referred to as post-sale confusion. From a trademark law perspective, though, the confusion of observers is irrelevant unless it is likely to influence their purchasing decisions. This might be the case, if the confused observers wrongly "know" that all their compatriots have Apples, and they buy one because they want to be like everyone else. But if this happens, those who saw the New Wave interface will go buy an Apple computer by mistake. Apple is *helped* by this, not hurt.

Actionable consumer confusion is likely to occur only in the relatively rare "reverse-confusion" situation, where the big company using the mark or design is *not* the owner of the trademark. In that case, post-sale confusion may hurt the trademark owner. This might actually be true in the Apple-Microsoft case: Apple owns the trademark, but Microsoft Windows is so big that people who see an Apple GUI might actually think it is Microsoft's, and go out and buy Windows. If true, this would be actionable.

Alternatively, there might be a *dilution* claim -- even if people aren't confused, Microsoft is diluting the value of Apple's mark by repeated use.

Problem 7-9: This problem is based on *Intel v. Advanced Micro Devices*, 756 F. Supp. 1292 (N.D. Cal. 1991). The court there held that the x86 designation was generic. Central to this conclusion was the court's finding that the relevant consumer of microprocessors was a company serving as original equipment manufacturer (OEM), who would integrate the microprocessor into a computer system for sale to the public. Because those in the computer industry regularly used the x86 designation to refer to microprocessors build around Intel's design standards, Intel could not prevent its competitor AMD from using the designation.

Intel then made the marketing decision to move away from the x86 designation it had created. Its next chip after the 486 was the "Pentium" (maintaining a connection, since penta- means "five"); the generation after that, it introduced the "Pentium Pro," which departed from the designation entirely. It is a testament to Intel's market power in the microprocessor industry that the x86 designation was quickly abandoned by everyone else, with the likely result that it is no longer generic.

Problem 7-10: This problem is based on a series of disputes between Sun Microsystems and SunRiver Corp., discussed in *Sun Microsystems v. SunRiver Corp.*, 36 U.S.P.Q.2d 1266 (N.D. Cal. 1995). Sun Microsystems owns a large "family" of computer-related marks bearing versions of "Sun" (or analogous marks like "Solaris"). While both Sun and SunRiver operate in the computer industry, their goods were originally sufficiently different that Sun decided there was no likelihood of confusion. In the 1990s, however, SunRiver acquired two companies that compete directly with Sun. The district court enjoined the use of the SunRiver name on those two companies, finding that consumers would be likely to be confused because of Sun's large family of heliocentric marks. As discussed in detail in Chapter 5, likelihood of confusion is a highly fact-specific inquiry, and generalization in this area is quite difficult.

PROBLEM 7-11

Microsoft, one of the largest sellers of computer operating systems and application software, seeks to trademark its term "Windows" for its operating system interface. Should Microsoft be entitled to a trademark? How would you classify the mark? Against whom could Microsoft enforce the mark? How could manufacturers of application programs that make use of the "Windows" interface advertise compatibility with that interface?

Analysis

Problem 7-11: This problem presents two separate issues. First, Microsoft has undoubtedly built up secondary meaning in the term "Windows," so it is entitled to trademark the term unless it is determined to be generic for operating systems featuring a graphical user interface. Since these are often colloquially referred to as "windows-based" operating systems, there seems a reasonable argument for genericness. However, it may well be that Microsoft has effectively taken a once-generic mark and changed the public impression of that word, so that the public now identifies it only with Microsoft. If that is the case, Microsoft is entitled to trademark the word. The Trademark Office apparently thought so; it registered the mark in 1994.

A separate question is the extent to which Microsoft can prevent others from using the term "windows." At the very least, windows would appear to be a descriptive term, which means that competitors could use the term in good faith to describe features of their program under the "fair use" doctrine. Further, under the doctrine of non-trademark use, software companies should be able to accurately refer to Microsoft's operating system product by using the name Windows, for example in comparative advertising or (under *Princeton*) to truthfully advertise their compatibility with that operating system.

Chapter 8 Intellectual Property and Competition Policy

A. Principles of Antitrust Law

B. Monopolization

PROBLEM 8-1

Two companies that specialize in advanced metallurgy agree to cross-license future patents relating to the development of a new component for aircraft jet turbines. Innovation in the development of the component requires the capability to work with very high tensile strength materials for jet engines. Aspects of the licensing arrangement raise the possibility that competition in research and development of this and related components will be lessened. The Antitrust Division is considering whether to define an innovation market in which to evaluate the competitive effects of the arrangement. What factors should it take into account in making this decision?

Analysis

Problem 8-1: This problem is adapted from the Antitrust Division's Guidelines for the Licensing of Intellectual Property, where it is Example 3. What follows is the Antitrust Division's analysis of this problem:

> If the firms that have the capability and incentive to work with very high tensile strength materials for jet turbines can be reasonably identified, the Agency will consider defining a relevant innovation market for development of the new component. If the number of firms with the required capability and incentive to engage in research and development of very high tensile strength materials for aircraft jet turbines is small, the Agency may employ the concept of an innovation market to analyze the likely competitive effects of the arrangement in that market, or as an aid in analyzing competitive effects in technology or goods markets. The Agency would perform its analysis as described in parts 3-5 [of the Guidelines].
>
> If the number of firms with the required capability and incentive is large (either because there are a large number of such firms in the jet turbine industry, or because there are many firms in other industries with the required capability and incentive), then the Agency will conclude that the innovation market is competitive. Under these circumstances, it is unlikely that any single firm or plausible aggregation of firms could acquire a large enough share of the assets necessary for innovation to have an adverse impact on competition.
>
> If the Agency cannot reasonably identify the firms with the required capability and incentive, it will not attempt to define an innovation market.

The concept of an innovation market has been heavily criticized by a number of commentators, not least because it seems virtually impossible to measure "future capacity for innovation" in any meaningful way. The rather vague answer the Division gives to its own example seems to point up this problem. The Guidelines suggest that the Division will use caution in applying the innovation market concept, and indeed most applications to date have been in straightforward cases of potential competition (in the pharmaceutical industry, for example, where drugs must enter the FDA "pipeline" several years before they hit the market).

C. Agreements to Restrain Trade

PROBLEM 8-2

Advanced Micro Devices (AMD) and Intel both make microprocessor chips. Chip designs tend to travel in waves, or "generations," which reflect newer technology and which successively become the industry standard. The old generation of chips were known as 286 chips. They were replaced by the next generation, the 386. Intel has since developed three new generations of chips, the 486, the Pentium, and the Pentium Pro. In 1991, AMD filed suit against Intel, alleging that Intel was intimidating chip consumers into buying Intel's rather than AMD's 386 chips by threatening to withhold 486 chips from any firm that defects to AMD. The suit claims that this is an illegal tying arrangement.

How should such a "temporal tying arrangement" be treated under the antitrust laws? Is leveraging a problem here? Does it matter if Intel obtains a patent on the 486?

PROBLEM 8-3

Tastee Turkee (TT) is a national fast-food franchise that specializes in roast turkey meals. TT does not operate any of its own restaurants. However, it has a series of requirements that franchisees must meet in order to use the Tastee Turkee name. In addition to requirements regarding color scheme, logo, building, and products, TT requires that its franchisees purchase all of their packaging materials, food, and kitchen equipment from TT itself or from approved TT vendors.

Cantor is a franchisee who believes that he can obtain food and packaging material more cheaply from his own sources. When TT refuses to allow him to do so, he brings suit under the antitrust laws. Cantor's theory is that TT has tied the "Tastee Turkee" trademark and image to the purchase of various staple goods.

Is this a "tying arrangement"? If so, does it violate the antitrust laws?

Analysis

Problem 8-2: A tying claim requires (1) two products in two separate markets; (2) a forced purchase or tie; (3) market power in the tying product market; and (4) danger to competition in the tied product market. [Note that the precise standards used seem to vary from case to case].

The first issue in this case is whether the different generations of chips are competing in the same market. This is not easily answered. While they are not the same products, and indeed exist in different generations, there is certainly market overlap between the two -- at any given time, some people are buying 486 chips, while others are buying 386 chips. Nonetheless, because of the general trend to upgrade chips over time to take advantage of new programs, it is reasonable to expect that at least some subset of consumers will be in the market for a 386 chip at time A and a 486 chip at later time B. This is certainly true of the immediate consumers of the chips -- computer manufacturers.

Is Intel's alleged statement to consumers ("buy my old chips if you want access to my new ones") an example of "forcing"? The answer is probably yes -- while the consumer is not actually buying the tying product (the 486 chip) at the time the tie occurs, they are being forced to buy the tied product (the 386 chip) by the threat that the 486 will be withheld in the future. While such a threat would be hard to enforce against individual end users, it may be much easier to enforce against computer manufacturers. [Note that in the problem AMD has merely alleged, not proven, such a threat].

The tying product here is the new chip, in which Intel probably has market power, since it always comes out with a new generation of chips well before its competitors, and since its sales exceed those of its competitors even after they emulate the chip. If this threat was widely made and enforced, it seems likely to affect control over the 386.

The case was not litigated to judgment, although a preliminary motion on related issues is reported at *Advanced Micro Devices v. Intel*, 1991 U.S. Dist. LEXIS 21036 (N.D. Cal. Dec. 23, 1991).

Problem 8-3: Franchise agreements of this sort are quite common, and they are frequently challenged either by franchisees or by potential suppliers who would like to compete with the supplier chosen by the franchise. If one applies the standard tying analysis, the existence of two products seems reasonably clear (at least if "trademark goodwill" can be a product market), as does forcing. A more difficult issue is market power in the tying product (the trademark). If the trademark itself is the relevant product market, there is necessarily market power. A number of early cases in fact took this position. On the other hand, if the tying product market is "all trademarks," or "all franchises," no trademark owner will have market power. *See* Benjamin Klein & Lester F. Saft, *The Law and Economics of Franchise Tying Contracts*, 28 **J. L. & Econ.** 345 (1985).

The real issue in the franchise cases, though, seems to be one of efficiency. Even if a franchise tying agreement is a tying arrangement that would normally be condemned under the antitrust laws, there is a strong argument that it should not be illegal because it offers significant procompetitive benefits -- specifically, avoiding the problem of "free riders" who run shoddy restaurants in order to trade on the goodwill of the trademark owner, and reducing the search costs of consumers. *See generally* Alan J. Meese, *Antitrust Balancing in a (Near) Coasean World: The Case of Franchise Tying Contracts*, 95 **Mich. L. Rev.** 111 (1996).

For a few of the many franchise tying cases, see, e.g., Kentucky Fried Chicken Corp. v. Diversified Packaging Corp., 549 F.2d 368 (5th Cir. 1977); Siegel v. Chicken Delight, Inc., 448 F.2d 43 (9th Cir. 1971).

PROBLEM 8-4

Microsoft Corporation succeeds in registering a trademark in the name "Windows" to describe a graphical user interface on a computer operating system. Microsoft agrees to license the "Windows" trademark to certain companies who wish to indicate that their application programs are "Windows-compatible." However, Microsoft requires as a condition of the license that the companies sell only applications programs that run exclusively on Microsoft Windows operating systems. Has Microsoft violated the antitrust laws? What role should market power play in the analysis? Does the Windows trademark itself confer market power?

Analysis

Problem 8-4: Microsoft has in fact been charged with a variety of tying arrangements, as discussed in the text, but not with this one. There is at least a potential problem with any such action under trademark law, in addition to any antitrust problems. The "Windows-compatible" mark appears to be a certification mark, rather than a trademark attached to Microsoft's goods in the normal sense. Certification marks must be open to any company that meets the requirements for certification (ie. that is truly compatible with Microsoft Windows). Here, that does not appear to be the case.

From a tying perspective, the problem is not dissimilar from Problem 8-3 above. The significant difference is that Microsoft Windows does in fact have sufficient power in its market that use of the "Windows-compatible" logo may be necessary for effective competition. If that is so, denying that term to any company unless they refused to deal with competitors is effectively a tie between the two with a likely market effect. [Arrangements of this sort are sometimes called "tie-outs" rather than tie-ins, since the requirement is that one not deal with the defendant's competitors].

One might also approach this as an exclusive dealing arrangement, without regard for the tying aspects. Microsoft does have sufficient power in this market that a requirement that applications programmers write only for it would likely significantly reduce the number of programs written for Microsoft's competitors, and hence injure those competitors. Similar claims were in fact made against Nintendo in the 1980s and Sega in the early 1990s, when each were dominant in the video game market. For general background, see *Sega of America v. Accolade, Inc.*, 977 F.2d 1510 (9th Cir. 1992); *Atari Games Corp. v. Nintendo*, 975 F.2d 832 (Fed. Cir. 1992); Julie E. Cohen, *Reverse Engineering and the Rise of Electronic Vigilantism: Intellectual Property Implications of "Lock-Out" Programs*, 68 **S. Cal. L. Rev.** 1091 (1995) (discussing the antitrust claims).

PROBLEM 8-5

Discworld sues the two largest makers of compact discs, alleging that their patented processes infringe its pioneer patent on compact disc technology. After years of discovery, the parties settle the suit by agreeing that each company will license all its patents to the other two, forming a "pool." The settlement agreement contains a "grantback" clause, under which each party agrees to license to pool members any improvements in its technology. The parties to the pool also agree that they will license the collective patents to outside companies, but only if those outside companies agree to use only the technology developed and patented by members of the pool.

NextDisc, Inc., a new entrant into the compact disc market, is approached by the pool and asked to take a license. NextDisc considers the requested royalty to be outrageously high. Rather than taking a license, NextDisc sues the pool members for violating the antitrust laws. What result?

Analysis

Problem 8-5: The pooling of patents has long been a subject of antitrust scrutiny because horizontal agreement between competitors often signals a cartel. While cases in the 1940s and 1950s were generally hostile to patent pools, more recent cases have acknowledged that the cross-licensing of disputed patents can serve valuable procompetitive purposes. For example, in this problem Discworld is entitled to prevent each of its potential competitors from making compact discs using the patented process. If the patent is valid, and if it is sufficiently pioneering, the result might be that *only* Discworld could effectively participate in this market. If that is so, the effect of the pooling arrangement is to enhance rather than restrict competition. As a result, cross-licensing agreements used to settle legitimate, good faith claims of patent infringement are now given substantial deference by the Antitrust Division and the courts. On the other hand, the mere assertion of a patent claim cannot always serve to shield inquiry into a potential cartel. Where the patent is obviously invalid, or there does not appear to be a reasonable claim of infringement, the parties to the pool cannot "hide behind" the patent. Thus, resolution of this case will require at least some inquiry into the legitimacy of Discworld's patent claim, both against the pooling parties and against NextDisc.

A separate issue is presented by the grantback clause. These clauses are quite common in patent licenses, and they serve some valid purposes -- namely, protecting the interest of the patent owner in not having its own technology used by a licensee as the basis for an improvement patent in a subsequent generation. The Antitrust Division looks favorably on nonexclusive grantback licenses, as the one here appears to be, but disfavors grantback *assignment* clauses, since they may perpetuate the market power of the original patentee.

Finally, the requirement that new pool members use *only* the patented technology may have effects similar to an exclusive grantback agreement, by discouraging pool members from innovating in directions which might allow them to escape the reach of the patent.

PROBLEM 8-6

In the summer of 1991, personal computer giants Apple and IBM announced plans to enter into a joint venture to produce a new type of disk operating system (OS) called Pink. Pink would be used in connection with a new generation of high-speed microprocessors developed by Motorola that use reduced-instruction-set computing, or RISC. Pink has the added virtue of being able to run on several different types of microprocessors. Apple and IBM would each produce (compatible) computers using the new OS and microprocessors.

At the time of the agreement, both the OS market and the microprocessor market were "slaves" to the personal computer market, since every personal computer had to incorporate an OS and a microprocessor compatible not only with the computer but with each other. IBM-compatible machines (though not IBM's own machines) dominated the personal computer market, with Apple the most significant maker of noncompatible computers. Microsoft (which makes MS-DOS for use with IBM computers) dominated the OS market, and Intel dominated the microprocessor market. Apple also participates in the OS market, making Apple-compatible OS, and Motorola does the same in the microprocessor market. However, because the computer "sets" must be integrated, there was at that time little or no direct competition between Apple and Microsoft in the OS market, or between Intel and Motorola in the microprocessor market. The Apple-IBM joint venture would enter the OS market in force, and analysts speculated that it might well dominate that market. The venture would boost Motorola's position in the microprocessor market, but Pink's ability to run with different microprocessors would also allow genuine competition in that market. Finally, the joint venture would have a significant presence in the personal computer market, where it would greatly enhance compatibility among computers, which is universally regarded as desirable from an information-flow standpoint.

How should such a scheme be evaluated under the antitrust laws? Should it survive antitrust scrutiny? Do subsequent events in the computer industry shed any light on how to approach this issue?

Analysis

Problem 8-6: The antitrust concern about the IBM-Apple joint venture turned out in the end to be much ado about nothing. Not only did the joint venture never produce a marketable product, but both of the participants lost a significant amount of their apparent market power in this industry during the 1990s. This fact itself serves as an object lesson about the application of antitrust in technology industries. Common assumptions about companies that will dominate a market regularly turn out to be wrong, as things change in the industry with blinding speed. [There are other examples as well -- consider the antitrust concern over Microsoft's much-heralded introduction of the Microsoft Network in late 1995, which was supposed to dominate the online service provider market]. As a result, courts and antitrust regulators should approach high-technology markets with special caution.

If one looks at this case as it appeared at the time, without the benefit of hindsight, the net effect of the joint venture remains far from clear. While antitrust law is ordinarily and properly concerned about joint action between two of the largest competitors in a market, the peculiar dynamics of the computer market may make that concern misplaced. Specifically, in order to weigh the procompetitive and anticompetitive effects of this joint venture, one would have to evaluate any potential loss in head-to-head competition between the two companies, and compare that to the competitive benefits of having an operating system that would readily port to different computer/microprocessor systems.

D. Mergers and Acquisitions

PROBLEM 8-7

In the summer of 1991, Borland International announced its plan to buy Ashton-Tate Corp. Both companies are major players in the database software market for personal computers. Together, they would presumably become the dominant player in that market, reducing competition. However, the merged company also planned to enter the database software market for minicomputers, a market dominated at that time by Oracle Corp. Should antitrust law permit the expected increase in competition in that market to offset the damage to competition in the PC market?

The Antitrust Division expressed concern that the combined intellectual property libraries of Borland and Ashton-Tate will enable the combined company to prevent further entry into the database market. In particular, the division is concerned that large potential entrants like Lotus Corp. will be deterred by the threat of intellectual property litigation. How would you evaluate a proposal by the division, as a condition of permitting the merger, to require the new company to give up its right to sue new entrants for copyright infringement?

PROBLEM 8-8

Megaplex, Inc., is a major petrochemical manufacturer. Concerned that Newco is "gaining" on it in the market for new gasoline additives through greater research prowess, Megaplex approaches several solo inventors who hold patents in the field and "buys" the rights to the patents from the inventors. Armed with a patent portfolio that Newco will have difficulty "inventing around," Megaplex manages to maintain its market share in spite of Newco's research efforts. Has Megaplex violated the antitrust laws?

Analysis

Problem 8-7: When emerging software giant Borland International sought to acquire Ashton-Tate, its chief rival in the prepackaged database software market, the Justice Department imposed a novel condition on the merger. The text of the consent decree in this case indicates the competitive importance the Department attached to copyrights. The decree, to which Borland and Ashton-Tate stipulated, enjoined Borland from asserting any claim or counterclaim for copyright infringement of "the command names, menu items, menu command hierarchies, command languages, programming languages and file structures used in and recognized by Ashton-Tate's dBASE family of products, standing alone and apart from other aspects of those computer programs." At the same time, the final judgment states that it does not preclude Borland from asserting its right to use these items, or "from asserting copyright protection in and copyright infringement of the computer program code (including its structure, sequence and organization) and other aspects of the user interface of Ashton-Tate's DBASE family of products" (Patent, Trademark and Copyright Journal, 1991). The decree prompted Borland to drop a lawsuit brought by Ashton-Tate (which it inherited in the merger) against a smaller database producer, Fox Software. Microsoft -- one of the few software companies larger even than Borland -- subsequently acquired Fox, and thus immediately entered the market for Ashton-Tate-compatible database software.

Clearly the consent decree reflected the Justice Department's awareness of the impact of intellectual property rights on industry structure, especially entry. The dBASE family of software had acquired a huge and loyal following; these investments of time and money by these users mean that they faced very significant "switching costs" if they were required to learn a dBASE-competitive database program. By injecting the dBASE command structure into the public domain, the Department sought to lower these switching costs, and thereby make entry into the industry more likely. The desired effect was a reduction in the market power of the Borland/Ashton-Tate combine.

This episode illustrates the importance of intellectual property as a competitive weapon and a determinant of industry structure. The Department recognized that, as we saw in the case of Japan, the availability and extent of intellectual property protection can have an impact on software industry structure. Unlike Japan, however, the problem in the U.S. was not that rights were too weak to induce the prepackaged segment of the industry to take off, but rather that rights might be too *strong* to permit a healthy, competitive rate of entry. In this industry and others, policymakers are beginning to see that intellectual property influences much more than R&D spending. It is a key asset with very important ramifications for industry strategy and evolution. In terms of the Schumpeterian "perennial gale," intellectual property determines the degree of legal shelter an incumbent can count on. Strong protection, like a brick wall, protects such an incumbent from the winds stirred up by potential entrants, while weak protection is more like a tent -- it helps, but cannot be relied on when the winds get too strong. The Justice Department in effect made Borland give up its brick structure for a tent, in exchange for more market share. The idea was not so much to encourage entry for its own sake, but to permit the kind of cumulative advance (*across* firms) that can take place only in the presence of competition. In so doing, the U.S. government recognized the emergence of intellectual property in this industry as a key variable, at least as important as productive capacity or labor force advantages in a more traditional industry.

Of course, developments in a related market suggested that perhaps the Antitrust Division had picked the wrong target. In the market for spreadsheet applications, it was Lotus who sued Borland for copyright infringement, attempting to use its broad reading of its intellectual property rights to prevent effective competition by the next-generation Borland spreadsheet program. That effort eventually failed in 1996, as discussed in detail in Chapter 7. But the relative fortunes of Lotus (now a part of IBM) and Borland in both the spreadsheet and database markets since the decree suggest that the Antitrust Division may not have fully anticipated trends in this industry.

Problem 8-8: Acquisition of patents is treated under the merger provisions of the Clayton Act, § 7. However, as with the Antitrust Division's "innovation markets," evaluating the competitive impact of a patent assignment or exclusive license is a tricky matter. There is no good "market share" data that can be used in such a case; indeed in the innovation market context, the Division suggests that it may rely on R&D expenditures as a measure of "research market power," or even assume that all parties have equal power in the innovation market. Further complicating the issue is that each of the patents at issue can legitimately limit research and production (assuming that it is valid), so in evaluating anticompetitive effects one must be careful to distinguish between the market effect of each patent by itself and the market effect of their combination in the hands of Megaplex.

III. Additional Problems and Exam Questions

We have included some additional problems, somewhat broader in scope than many of the problems in the text. These problems can be copied and distributed to students as study aids, since they present a broader range of issues and require students to engage in "issue-spotting." Alternatively, they may be used as exam questions.

Question 1

Superseed ("S") is an Iowa company in the business of selling hybrid and genetically altered corn seeds. S maintains several farms throughout the Midwest where it blends different varieties of corn and tests the results. When S finds a new hybrid strain which has higher yield, disease resistance, or some other useful characteristic, S reproduces the seed and sells it to farmers.

On July 4, 1992, scientists at S's facility 40 miles outside of Omaha, Nebraska began working on a new strain of corn called "ultra-brite" or UB, for its spectacular color. It tested a number of different UB hybrids in its fields during the fall of 1992, including the "UB40" (the hybrid at issue in this case). During this fall crop, S's field scientists identified UB40 as a promising hybrid for possible sale. After analyzing the results in their Des Moines laboratory, S's laboratory scientists confirmed this conclusion in a written report on January 20, 1993. S began selling UB40 seeds to farmers on March 23, 1993. On January 19, 1994, S applied for a utility patent claiming "the hybrid corn seed strain designated UB40." The patent was granted on December 9, 1994.

Because seed corn is a highly competitive business, S takes a number of precautions to protect its new hybrids from discovery by competitors. S tests its corn hybrids in isolated fields far from major cities or roads, and does not widely disseminate information about what seeds are being tested in what location. However, S does not fence or otherwise prevent unauthorized access onto its fields. S also maintains its laboratory data under lock and key, and restricts access to its laboratories using a passcard system. Finally, all of S's employees are required to sign a confidentiality agreement stating that they will not publish or otherwise disclose any proprietary information belonging to S.

Holdup ("H"), a long-time competitor of S's, began selling a new corn seed it called "Brite-Line" in September 1994, which it continues to sell to this day. Suspicious that H had stolen their hybrid, S purchased samples of Brite-Line corn and subjected it to genetic analysis. Brite-Line was not identical to UB40, but it was sufficiently similar that the genetic engineer stated in her report that it was "pretty likely" Brite-Line was based on UB40. Based on this information, S filed suit on December 12 for misappropriation of trade secrets and patent infringement.

H denied ever obtaining UB40 from any source, and discovery was unable to provide any direct evidence that H had in fact taken UB40. However, discovery did disclose that a subsidiary of H owned a field next to S's Nebraska facility, and corn seed experts testified at trial that hybrid plant seeds will sometimes scatter to neighboring fields in high winds. At trial, S argues that because of the similarity between the two seeds, the court should presume that H had access to S's proprietary seed line, and argues that such access was improper.

How should the court rule on S's claims for patent infringement and misappropriation of trade secrets?

(End of question 1.)

Question 2

Positivland ("P") is a techno-ambient band based in New York City. P makes its music by what it calls "musical collage" -- that is, it takes a variety of pre-existing sounds from a variety of sources and mixes them together in interesting and sometimes meaningful ways. P is quite proud of the fact that none of the three CDs they have produced have ever contained any material they recorded themselves. Indeed, none of the members of P play any musical instruments.

P's recent "hit" single (a "hit" in the techno-ambient music business is likely to sell no more than 5,000 copies in the United States) is called "The South Goes North." The song is 4 minutes long. It contains 43 different sound samples, none greater than 15 seconds in length. The samples are from a variety of sources. Three are taken from public speeches of Virginia Senate candidate Oliver North; nine are from songs of different musical groups; four are from excerpts of television news broadcasts on the Virginia Senate race; and the remainder are ambient sounds recorded from a variety of sources. The ambient sound recordings are in the public domain; the authors of all the other recordings claim copyright protection.

Rap artist Nail, whose popular song "It Just Ain't So" is sampled repeatedly in the song, files suit against P for copyright infringement. The sample of Nail's song consists of the title phrase "it just ain't so," repeated three times during "South Goes North." On each occasion, the phrase appears immediately after an excerpt from an Oliver North speech. The total length of the sample is 4 seconds, meaning that a total of 12 seconds of Nail's music is used in P's song. Among P's defenses is that it is parodying North's speeches.

Demos Press, an alternative literary publishing company, decides to incorporate the "lyrics" from P's song in a book of modern poetry it is publishing. To accomplish this, a Demos employee transcribes the literal text of the song into print, and breaks it into "lines" of poetry. P sues Demos to enjoin publication of the book.

How should the two copyright suits be resolved?

(End of question 2.)

Question 3

The Supreme Court is currently considering whether color itself should be entitled to trademark or trade dress protection. Should a plaintiff be entitled to trademark or trade dress protection for color alone? Should any limits be placed on color trademarks? Explain your reasoning, with particular attention to the theories and policies of trademark law.

(End of question 3.)

Question 4

A, an anthropologist, has spent years studying a remote tribe in inland Papua New Guinea. Over the years, and from studying medical records of the tribe, A makes a startling discovery: while members of the tribe get cancer at about the same rate as people elsewhere, <u>no member of the tribe has ever died of cancer</u>. Intrigued, A persuades one of the tribal cancer patients to give up a sample of the cancer tissue and a blood sample, explaining that the samples "may help people everywhere."

A returns to the United States in June 1994, where he shares his discovery with his friend B, a molecular biologist. B takes the samples to the lab at the university where she works (the University of Northern California, or UNC), and begins work analyzing them. After 6 months of constant work, B and her team of graduate students isolate a gene sequence in December 1994 which they believe is responsible for inhibiting the malignant growth of the cancer cells. In the meantime, A has published an article on his discovery in the January 1995 issue of the Journal of Medical Anthropology. The article, which was actually mailed in mid-November 1994, discloses A's discovery, but does not discuss any of B's work on the cancer tissue.

G, one of the graduate students on B's team, completes his degree in May 1995 and goes to work for Pharmacom, a multinational pharmaceutical company. Pharmacom assigns G to work on developing an anti-cancer treatment based on the information disclosed in A's article. G discloses to Pharmacom his prior work with B's team, and tells Pharmacom that B has isolated a gene sequence, but does not tell them what the gene sequence is. When questioned about the procedures at UNC, G explains that the lab in which he worked was open to any member of the department, and that there were no special security precautions taken with respect to B's experiments. G did, however, sign an employment agreement with UNC agreeing to assign "all interest whatsoever in any intellectual property rights, whenever created, if directly related to any work you do while at UNC."

Without G's direct participation, and based on A's article, Pharmacom returns to Papua New Guinea and obtains blood samples from other members of the tribe. After analyzing those samples, Pharmacom discovers that there are in fact <u>three different</u> gene sequences which have the same cancer-inhibiting effect. After G identifies the gene sequence that B's team produced, Pharmacom abandons work on that sequence and begins work on a means of injecting the other two sequences into human tissues. All three sequences share about 80% of the same base pairs, and all three have very similar (though not identical) functional characteristics.

In December 1995, UNC receives a patent covering the human gene sequence B's team identified in the lab. In the patent specification, UNC discloses the location of the gene sequence, and describes it in detail according to its functional characteristics, but does not list the actual base pairs in the sequence. The claim is of the following form:

1. A human gene sequence located at region MM of chromosome N, with the following characteristics:

   a. . . .

   b. . . .

<u>Questions</u>

a) Is UNC's patent valid?

b) Is it relevant that the Papua New Guinea tribe objects vociferously to what they call "patenting our people and our heritage"? Should it be?

c) What causes of action could UNC assert against Pharmacom? Against G? Is UNC likely to prevail?

(End of Question 4)

Question 5

Funcorp, Inc, is the worlds largest producer of children's entertainment. Funcorp's diverse interests are based around dozens of enormously popular children's movies. Funcorp produces the movies, and sells them in video form as well as showing them in movie theatres. Funcorp also sells children's books, adult and children's clothing, stuffed animals, posters, coloring books and stencil sets, all based on the characters and scenes from its movies. Funcorp also runs several children's theme parks which include costumed characters from its movies, and those characters sometimes make public appearances in other locations as well.

The Working Parent Co. is a sole proprietorship run out of her home by Q, a mother of two small children. Working Parent is a day care facility whose only employee is Q. While Q created Working Parent in the hopes of developing a good-sized business, and has advertised the company's services, to date Working Parent has not been very successful. Q takes care of her own two children, three of her neighbor's children, and one child whose parents responded to the Working Parent ad.

All of the children are big fans of Funcorp's films. To keep them entertained, Q regularly buys videocassettes of Funcorp movies from her local video store and shows them to the children. Q also helps the children draw pictures of their favorite Funcorp characters, and hangs some of the better pictures on the walls of her home. For Halloween, Q dressed up as a Funcorp character in a costume she made herself, and painted a 6-foot image of another Funcorp character on the wall of the children's playroom.

Working Parent receives a letter from Funcorp's attorneys, detailing the activities described in the last paragraph and demanding that Working Parent "cease and desist immediately from these and other similar acts of copyright infringement" or face a lawsuit. Alternatively, the letter suggests that Working Parent could purchase a "day care use license" at a cost of $100 per child per year.

Have Q and Working Parent engaged in copyright infringement? Do they have any valid defenses to a claim of infringement?

(End of Question 5)

Question 6

ProTour, Inc., owns the ProTour golf course outside the Bergstrom airfield in Austin. The designers of ProTour decided to appeal to "low-budget but serious" golfers by creating an 18-hole "fantasy" golf course, in which each hole is a replica of a hole from a famous golf course elsewhere in the country. To accomplish this, ProTour visited 16 famous golf courses, including Pebble Beach, Augusta, and Pinehurst. They took video cameras and photographed the courses, rented helicopters and flew over the courses, and purchased original blueprints of the courses. They then copied the original holes almost exactly, even importing vegetation native to the copied golf holes. However, there are some inherent differences between the original holes and the ProTour holes. For example, the hole copied from Pebble Beach does not have an ocean nearby, and airplanes from Berstrom regularly fly over the course.

ProTour markets its golf course as "the cheapest way to tour with the masters," and places signs at each hole describing the location and significance of the original hole that is copied. However, ProTour also places disclaimer signs along the course, indicating that none of the original golf courses "endorse, sponsor, or are affiliated with ProTour in any way."

A group of golf courses whose holes have been copied by ProTour files a lawsuit claiming that ProTour has infringed their trade dress and diluted their distinctive marks. Are the plaintiffs likely to prevail? Explain how your answer comports with the underlying policy rationales of trademark law.

(End of Question 6)

Question 7

Four companies compete in the manufacture of specialized chemical solvents used to clean up certain types of spills which occur in semiconductor manufacturing. The companies are Acme Products, Basic Chemistry, Chemical Corp. of America, and Dox, Inc. In 1981, Acme develops a new chemical compound ("solvent X") which its private laboratory tests reveal to be significantly better at cleaning spills than the existing solvents used by all four companies in the past. However, because Acme is already a leader in the existing chemical industry, and because producing the new compound would require some expensive changes in machinery, Acme decides not to use this new product in its business. It does, however, file a patent application in 1982. The patent is delayed in prosecution, both because of the death of a patent Examiner and because Acme abandoned and refiled the application on several occasions. The patent finally issues in April 1994. The broadest claim reads simply "solvent X." The specification discloses that solvent X is part of a new class of chemical products, and suggests (but does not conclusively demonstrate) that variants on solvent X could be made by adding to or slightly altering the chemical structure of the solvent.

In 1988, research scientists at Basic independently develop a closely related compound ("solvent Y"). Solvent Y is functionally identical to solvent X, and differs chemically only in the addition of a short alcohol sequence extending from the middle of the carbon chain in the structure of the active chemical ingredient. Basic decides to use solvent Y in its business, but it is concerned about disclosing the solvent to its competitors. Basic therefore decides that rather than selling the new solvent to semiconductor companies, Basic will agree to perform any necessary clean-up work itself in return for a fee. Included in this contract is a nondisclosure agreement, which requires the semiconductor companies to keep secret any information they discover about solvent Y, and to return any samples of the material that Basic has inadvertently left behind.

In addition, Basic licenses Chemical to produce and use limited quantities of solvent Y in the state of Washington, where Basic does not operate. The agreement between Basic and Chemical is entitled "Agreement for the Disclosure and Use of Trade Secrets." It contains a provision disclosing the chemical structure of solvent Y (referred to in the contract as "the Secret Formula"), and further provides that "Chemical agrees to pay Basic a royalty of $100 for each liter of the Secret Formula produced, whether or not used."

In 1995, Acme sues Chemical for patent infringement, alleging that Chemical is "making" and "using" products covered by its patent in violation of 35 U.S.C. § 271. Chemical denies that it is liable to Acme, and brings a cross-claim against Basic seeking to terminate its obligation to pay royalties under the license on the grounds that there is no longer a trade secret after Acme's patent disclosure. What result?

(End of Question 7)

Question 8

ProCall is a company which has collected "white pages" telephone information from the entire United States, and made it available on one set of CD-ROMs. ProCall obtained the basic telephone data --

name, area code and phone number, and in some cases street address -- by purchasing the rights to it from local phone companies. In some cases, however, when local phone companies refused to sell the data, ProCall scanned the data into its computers using the paper phone directories. In addition to the data obtained from the phone companies, ProCall adds the name of the city and state from which the directory listing was taken. Sometimes this is apparent from the phone book itself, but in other cases ProCall actually checks the geographic records of the local phone exchange by computer to determine the city in which the listed individual lives. ProCall also designed a computer program to search and sort this massive collection of data; it claims that its search program is substantially faster than equivalent programs sold on the open market. ProCall estimates that it spent $4.5 million to compile this data and write the program. It sells 3-CD sets for $129.95 (though the cost of producing each CD set is just over $12).

Dwyer is a graduate student with access to the World Wide Web. She purchases a copy of the ProCall CD set. She copies the data (but not ProCall's search software) onto her computer network, writes her own search software, and makes the ProCall nationwide phone directory available for free on the World Wide Web. Dwyer gets no profit from this activity, other than what she calls "the satisfaction of helping people."

When ProCall learns of Dwyer's actions, they sue her for copyright infringement, seeking damages and an injunction preventing her from operating the Web site.

Questions

1. Is ProCall likely to prevail on their copyright claim? Why or why not?
2. What could ProCall have done differently to help protect its investment in the phone directory?
3. Assuming that ProCall loses its copyright suit, does that suggest a problem with the current rules governing intellectual property? In particular, should Congress pass a new law providing some form of protection for databases?

(End of Question 8)

Question 9

The Techno-Ambient Music Hall of Fame ("Hall") is located on the waterfront in Santa Teresa, California. Several years ago, the owners of the Hall hired world-famous architect Y.B. Poure to design a "distinctive" building to house the Hall and its exhibits. Poure worked for three years to design and then build the Hall, which is a giant glass and steel pyramid containing within it an inverted glass pyramid, which is suspended inside the building as a sculpture. Because of the coloring of the interior glass and the transparency of the exterior glass, the dual pyramid structure is visible from the beach outside. In designing the building, Poure was asked to "use his imagination" subject to the following constraints: the walls must be at least partially transparent, and the interior geometry should be acoustically designed to allow ambient music to be performed therein.

The Hall won several design awards, but was the subject of considerable controversy in the Santa Teresa beachfront neighborhood due to its size and its unusual design. Since the Hall opened last year, it has had approximately 50,000 visitors, including many from other countries. In part, this was due to the Hall's aggressive advertising in music industry trade publications. A gift shop inside the Hall sells postcards and posters featuring a photograph of the building taken at night. The postcards sell well (upwards of 3,000 have been sold), but the posters have been less successful (only a few hundred have been sold).

Lance, a self-employed photographer, took a photograph of the Santa Teresa skyline at night, as viewed from the beach. The skyline contains a number of buildings, but the Hall is the most prominent thing in the photograph, both because it is so brightly illuminated and because of its size and beachfront location. Lance used the Hall as the centerpiece of the photo, shooting from such an angle that it appears to be anchoring the skyline. Lance has been selling limited-edition reproductions of his photograph (which he calls "Music Hall of Fame and City Skyline") in local galleries for several hundred dollars each.

Hall filed suit in federal district court against Lance, claiming that he had engaged in trademark and trade dress infringement.

Questions

1. Is the Hall likely to prevail in its suit? Why or why not?
2. Why didn't the Hall bring a copyright infringement claim?

(End of Question 9)

Question 10

As a law clerk to the Supreme Court Justice who will cast the deciding vote in the Lotus v. Borland case, you have been asked to provide the Justice with a summary of how you would resolve the case. Because the case is before the Supreme Court, you are not strictly bound to follow the precedent of any court, including prior Supreme Court decisions. However, the Justice has indicated that it would be "nice" if you could explain whether and how your proposed resolution is consistent with existing caselaw. The Justice has also asked you to comment on the effect (if any) that the growing availability of software patents should have on this decision.

(End of Question 10)

Question 11

a. In August 1995, Microsoft introduced its new operating system, Windows 95, amid much fanfare. Windows 95 builds upon Microsoft's enormously successful prior operating systems, MS-DOS and Windows, which together have an "installed base" of 115 million customers nationwide (out of approximately 135 million total PC and workstation operating systems). In the first half of 1995, MS-DOS and Windows together had an 87% share of new sales of operating systems. Other competitors in this market included Apple, with 7%, IBM, with 3%, and Sun, with 2%. At the time of its introduction, Windows 95 was widely expected to capitalize on the success of prior Microsoft products, and come to dominate the market for next-generation operating systems.

Included on the user interface of the Windows 95 operating system is an icon labeled "MSN." "MSN" refers to Microsoft Network, an online service started by Microsoft at the same time Windows 95 was launched. Clicking on the MSN icon automatically puts the user into the Microsoft Network, where they can sign up for membership by giving a credit card number.

Microsoft Network will compete with other online service providers, each of whom offer a separate online "community" for their users. At the time of its introduction, Microsoft Network's main competitors were America Online, with 3 million subscribers, Compuserve, with 1.4 million, and Prodigy with 2 million.

[Because it had just been introduced, Microsoft Network had no subscribers at this time]. Other competitors include Apple's e-world, Genie, and Delphi, each of which have fewer than 300,000 subscribers. Each of the online services (including Microsoft Network) also offers access to the Internet. Approximately 1,400 other companies ("Internet Service Providers" or ISPs) provide "direct" commercial Internet access, and most universities and government organizations do so as well.

If you are a Windows 95 owner, getting to the Microsoft Network (and hence to the Internet) is easy -- you just click on the MSN icon. Joining a competing online service or an ISP is more difficult. To do so, you must obtain the connection software from the company, and install it on your computer, a process which can take 1-2 hours. If you were already a subscriber to a competing online service, you still must reinstall that service after you have loaded Windows 95 onto your computer, because Windows 95 automatically deletes those preinstalled programs. Further, there have been widespread complaints that competing online service software does not work well with Windows 95, and some have speculated that Microsoft has deliberately made connection more difficult.

Based on the information described above as of August 1995, is Microsoft violating the antitrust laws? Why or why not? Is there some specific characteristic of online services or the Internet that makes this market unique?

b. By December 1995, four months after the release of Windows 95, the Microsoft Network had 525,000 subscribers. This was significantly below the estimated 2 million subscribers many analysts had expected. Microsoft has concluded that its membership is small because it lacks good "content" for its online service. As a result, Microsoft (and Bill Gates personally) have begun purchasing the exclusive electronic rights to a significant number of works of art and literature, with the announced intention of making Microsoft Network "the place to go for information, entertainment and culture online."

Do these facts change your assessment of the antitrust question? How?

(End of Question 11)

Question 12

"Newtech" is a venture capital funded semiconductor start-up company which has been in existence for six months. They have just been sued by Company "A", a $1-billion major semiconductor company, and the former employer of the founders of Newtech. The complaint seeks a temporary restraining order, preliminary injunction, and damages for trade secret misappropriation, unfair competition, and breach of implied and express contract. The facts leading up to this point are as follows:

Approximately one year ago, Bob, the manager of a division of Company "A", which produces a special kind of semiconductor circuit, had lunch with his friend and colleague, Dave, the head of the circuit design group in their division. The conversation turned to their mutual frustration in developing and marketing new products. They both lamented the rapid growth of Company "A" and the increasingly large bureaucracy within it that made difficult the task of getting products to the customers. They reminisced about how much fun it was in the old days, and how much more satisfying their jobs were. Bob suggested that they should do something about this and form their own company. Dave responded that he would love to do that.

From that point forward, Bob gave increasing amount of thought to forming a new company, and talked to two other people within his group about the possibility. They were Vera, the manager of the division process engineering group, and Paul, the head of the finance group. All expressed interest, and the founding group was set. None was an officer of Company "A", but all were part of senior management. They were either friends or friendly acquaintances.

Over the course of the next six months. Bob took the lead in talking to venture capitalists about the possibility of funding a new semiconductor venture, and organized meetings at his home in the evenings and on weekends with the founding group to develop a business plan. Bob used a number of materials available to him as division manager in developing the business plan, including industry database services, general formulas concerning head count, and capital requirements which he had learned while at Company "A", and certain public information contained in the highly proprietary five-year business plans of Company "A". He also used the portable computer which had been given to him by Company "A" for use in his job.

The founding group had several meetings with venture capitalists and attorneys concerning the formation of their new venture. The company was initially financed with $5 million. The founding group all resigned together, and established headquarters for the new venture five miles away from Company "A". The business plan called for the development of specialty semiconductor products which competed directly with, and in most cases substituted for, most of the products which the specialty division of Company "A" produced. The new vice president of engineering, Dave, worked on these designs, which he had also worked on while at Company "A". The process was in most respects similar to the process used by the specialty division. Of Company "A" and, again, was something which the new vice president of process engineering, Vera, worked on while at Company "A". After about one month, Newtech identified and extended offers to an additional four employees of Company "A", consisting of a process engineer, two design engineers, and a lower level layout technician. At that point Company "A" filed its suit in state court. While the trade secret claims set forth a number of specific trade secrets relating to the design and process of the relevant specialty semiconductors, at the time suit was filed, Newtech had neither products nor a process for manufacturing them.

Consider the following questions:

(1) Based upon the existing legal doctrines, how would a court resolve the recently filed lawsuit?
(2)How would you advise the start-up about responding to the suit?
(3) What should the start-up have done at the outset of the venture to reduce the risk of a damaging law suit?

(End of Question 12)

Question 13

Demand Video (Nasdaq symbol "DeVo") makes "video on demand" systems for use in hotel rooms throughout the United States. DeVo has gone through a period of explosive growth in the past several years, as video on demand systems have replaced cable and pay-per-view in many high-end hotels. [A video on demand system allows the user to order a video from a menu, and receive it almost immediately. By contrast, prior hotel systems broadcast the videos from a central location in the hotel, and required users to tune in at a specific time]. DeVo is now the largest supplier of video on demand systems in the U.S., having 28,000 units in 450 hotel rooms around the country.

DeVo's success is due not only to its famous marketing campaign ("We are DeVo"), but to the advanced technology in its set-top boxes. This technology allows hotels to control access to films in a distributed manner, rather than from a central location. The boxes keep a record of what movies have been requested, allowing for automatic hotel billing and the computation of copyright license fees. DeVo has not patented its technology. However, it has a strict policy of never selling its boxes to hotels. Rather, it signs a complex lease agreement with those hotels that use its system. The lease requires a refundable deposit on the boxes themselves and periodic lease payments. DeVo demands that hotels return all of the boxes to it for repair, replacement, or if the lease terminates. It has refused to enter into a contract with at least one hotel that wanted to buy (rather than lease) the equipment, and it has sued another hotel chain during a contract dispute in order to recover the boxes. Further, the boxes themselves are padlocked. While DeVo gives hotels technical information necessary to operate the system, the lease agreement includes a confidentiality provision binding hotel employees covering both the boxes themselves and the technological information. However, it does not require the hotels to obtain similar assurances from their guests, and hotels do not do so.

Viewmaster, a small competitor of DeVo, has had trouble matching DeVo's box technology. Frustrated by DeVo's continuing dominance in the industry, and the high prices it charges, Viewmaster's president decides to take action. The president and a design engineer rent a hotel room that contains a DeVo box. The Viewmaster employees use running water, a loud radio, and a Do Not Disturb sign to make sure that no hotel employee can see or hear what they are doing. They take the box out of the TV cabinet, and using power tools bypass the padlock and open up the box. By observing the contents and running electronic tests on the circuitry in the box, they are able to gain an understanding of how it works sufficient to allow them to build similar boxes. Once the testing is complete, they put the box back together, and it continues to function properly.

When DeVo learns of Viewmaster's activities (from a disgruntled ex-Viewmaster employee), they sue for misappropriation of trade secrets. What result?

(End of Question 13)

Question 14

The "Java Jacket" is a cheap cup holder designed to insulate hot drinks contained in paper cups. It consists of a band of cardboard approximately two inches high and 1/16 inch wide which wraps around the middle of a paper cup, and which can be slid over the cup. The cardboard has a series of depressions in it which reduce the surface area touching both the cup and the hand of the person holding it, thus reducing the rate of heat transfer to the hand. The manufacturer of the Java Jacket obtains a patent whose broadest claim reads:

1. A holder for encircling a liquid-containing cup to reduce the rate of heat transfer between the liquid contained in the cup and a hand gripping the holder encircling the cup, comprising a band of material formed with an open top and an open bottom through which the cup can extend and an inner surface immediately adjacent the cup, the band including a plurality of discrete, spaced-apart, approximately semi-spherically shaped depressions distributed on substantially the entire inner surface of the band so that each depression defines a non-contacting region of the band creating an air gap between the band and the cup, thereby reducing the rate of heat transfer through the holder.

This patent was obtained over prior art which showed ring-shaped cup holders, and cup holders composed of thick (1/2 inch or more) foam rubber insulating material. Among the advantages of the Java Jacket over the prior art are the cheap materials and the ease of storage and use.

The patentee brings suit against the manufacturer of an insulating cup holder that consists of a thin band of styrofoam of exactly the same shape as the Java Jacket. The styrofoam is approximately 1/32 of an inch wide. It does have natural "depressions" on its surface and throughout the material that reduce the surface area in contact with the cup, though they are caused by air pockets produced automatically when the styrofoam is made, and are of all different shapes.

Does the styrofoam cup holder infringe the patent claim, either literally or under the doctrine of equivalents?

(End of Question 14)

Question 15

"Titanic" is one of the most popular movies in history. After an amazing theater run, the film was released on video in 1998. While its audience is widespread, it is particularly popular among pre-teens and teenagers.

Not everyone was pleased by the success of the movie, however. In particular, some parents objected that two scenes in the film were inappropriate for minors. One of these scenes depicts the heroine posing nude for a drawing, and the other shows the two lead characters steaming up the windows of an antique car during (off-screen) sex. Neither scene is particularly long, and while the drawing scene is important to the plot, the parents argued that it did not need to be shown in such detail.

In an effort to address these concerns, the Legion of Decency (a group of parents opposed to sex in the movies) approaches Titanic's director, and asks him to release a "family-friendly" version of the film. He refuses, claiming his film is "perfect just as it is."

Rebuffed, the Legion of Decency begins to purchase copies of the Titanic video in stores. Using a commercial videotape editing device, they remove the two offending scenes from the videos they have purchased. The movie is shortened by approximately 29 seconds (out of 3 1/2 hours) as a result, but is otherwise unchanged). The Legion then resells the individually altered videos through its newsletter to interested parents. They clearly label the video as "An Edited Version of the Original Titanic Video," and inform purchasers that the director has not approved the edits. After some debate among its board members, the Legion decides to sell the videos for the same price it purchased them from a video store, since otherwise parents might be tempted to buy the cheaper version in stores. Because the Legion bought each video and then altered it before reselling it, however, they actually lose money on each copy they alter.

The owners of "Titanic" sue the Legion for violation of the intellectual property laws. What result?

(End of Question 15)

Question 16

Should trade dress and product configurations ever be considered "inherently distinctive"? If so, under what circumstances? Please consider both how your answer comports with the statute and Supreme Court caselaw, and any relevant policy considerations.

(End of Question 16)